Japanese Gardens

Other Publications:

THE GOOD COOK

THE SEAFARERS

THE ENCYCLOPEDIA OF COLLECTIBLES

THE GREAT CITIES

WORLD WAR II

HOME REPAIR AND IMPROVEMENT

THE WORLD'S WILD PLACES

THE TIME-LIFE LIBRARY OF BOATING

HUMAN BEHAVIOR

THE ART OF SEWING

THE OLD WEST

THE EMERGENCE OF MAN

THE AMERICAN WILDERNESS

LIFE LIBRARY OF PHOTOGRAPHY

THIS FABULOUS CENTURY

FOODS OF THE WORLD

TIME-LIFE LIBRARY OF AMERICA

TIME-LIFE LIBRARY OF ART

GREAT AGES OF MAN

LIFE SCIENCE LIBRARY

THE LIFE HISTORY OF THE UNITED STATES

TIME READING PROGRAM

LIFE NATURE LIBRARY

LIFE WORLD LIBRARY

FAMILY LIBRARY:
    HOW THINGS WORK IN YOUR HOME
    THE TIME-LIFE BOOK OF THE FAMILY CAR
    THE TIME-LIFE FAMILY LEGAL GUIDE
    THE TIME-LIFE BOOK OF FAMILY FINANCE

Japanese Gardens

by
WENDY B. MURPHY
and
the Editors of TIME-LIFE BOOKS

TIME-LIFE BOOKS, ALEXANDRIA, VIRGINIA

THE AUTHOR: Wendy B. Murphy is a writer whose diverse interests range from gardening to architectural history. Formerly an editor with Time-Life Books, she contributed to The Art of Sewing, The TIME-LIFE Library of Boating and The Emergence of Man, and recently wrote *Gardening under Lights* for The TIME-LIFE Encyclopedia of Gardening. She divides her time between an island home in Maine and a 150-year-old farmhouse in Connecticut.

CONSULTANTS: The late James Underwood Crockett, author of 13 of the volumes in the Encyclopedia, co-author of two additional volumes and consultant on other books in the series, was a lover of the earth and its good things. He graduated from the Stockbridge School of Agriculture at the University of Massachusetts and worked all his life in horticulture. A perennial contributor to gardening magazines, he also wrote a monthly bulletin, "Flowery Talks," distributed through retail florists. His television program, *Crockett's Victory Garden,* shown all over the United States, won countless converts to his approach to growing things. Kaneji Domoto is a landscape architect who lives and works in New York. Jerry Hill, a nurseryman since 1938, is owner of a nursery specializing in camellias and other Japanese plants. Koichi Kawana teaches environmental design at the University of California, Los Angeles. He also designed the Japanese gardens at the Missouri Botanical Garden, the Denver Botanic Gardens and the Chicago Horticultural Society Botanic Garden. Conrad B. Link is a professor of horticulture at the University of Maryland, College Park. H. Carroll Parish, a former dean at the University of California, Los Angeles, is chairman of the Japan America Society of Southern California in Los Angeles. William Louis Stern is a professor of botany at the University of Maryland, College Park.

THE COVER: Waves of raked gravel eddy around islands of mossy rocks in an American courtyard garden that takes its inspiration from the traditional dry gardens of Japan. A Japanese black pine leans over the island in the foreground and a dwarf Keisk rhododendron softens the rocks' rugged contours.

Library of Congress Cataloging in Publication Data
Murphy, Wendy B.
  Japanese Gardens.
  (The Time-Life encyclopedia of gardening)
  Bibliography: p.
  Includes index.
  1. Gardens, Japanese. I. Time-Life Books. II. Title.
SB458.M87   635.9   79-15137
ISBN 0-8094-2631-5
ISBN 0-8094-2630-7 lib. bdg.

For information about any Time-Life book, please write: Reader Information, Time-Life Books, 541 North Fairbanks Court, Chicago, Illinois 60611.

CONTENTS

1 Landscapes of the imagination
7

Picture essay: MASTERWORKS OF JAPANESE GARDENING ART
18

2 Putting principles into practice
33

Picture essay: SUMMONING UP THE SIGHTS AND SOUNDS OF WATER
44

3 Plants with an Oriental heritage
53

Picture essay: FASCINATING IMMIGRANTS FROM THE FAR EAST
64

4 Delicate finishing touches
75

Picture essay: ARTISTIC ACCENTS WITH ANCIENT TRADITIONS
86

5 An encyclopedia of Japanese plants
97

APPENDIX

American parallels with Japanese climate   151

Characteristics of 98 Japanese plants   152

Acknowledgments   154

Picture credits   154

Bibliography   155

Index   156

Landscapes of the imagination 1

Four centuries ago the great Japanese tea master Sen Rikyu prepared his garden for autumn visitors by sweeping up the fallen leaves, then shaking a tree to deposit a few dead leaves on the ground. In the autumn, Rikyu said by way of explanation, a garden without fallen leaves was unnatural. Rikyu's insistence on such nuances of naturalness may seem extreme, but it tells much about the spirit that animates Japanese garden design, today as in Rikyu's time. It is a spirit that Westerners may not at first find easy to grasp. But when they do, it often comes as a revelation, a new way of looking at a garden and sometimes, through the garden, a new way of looking at the larger world beyond.

Perhaps the best way to understand what a Japanese garden is is to understand what it is not. It is not, for example, simply a picturesque collection of oddly shaped rocks and twisted trees set off by stone lanterns, arched bridges and fish ponds—though that, unhappily, is what some Occidental visitors perceive it to be and have imported to the West. Neither is it composed of flower beds and formal plantings with the familiar geometry and symmetry of classical French and Italian garden design, nor does it have the romantic imitations of nature conceived by English landscape artists. Japanese garden designers neither copy nature nor totally re-arrange it. Instead, they chart a subtler course that lies in-between. From the natural landscape they select and distill just those particular elements they want, placing them with infinite care to symbolize and suggest, to conceal and reveal. In effect, they paint a partial picture to which the observer makes his own contribution. Drawn into the picture, he discovers ideas and relationships in its colors, lines and forms and from them completes the scene in his mind's eye, to his own satisfaction and delight.

At the same time the garden's design may also incorporate ideas and concepts drawn from ancient myths and beliefs, for in

Although built partly as a monastic retreat for the Shogun Ashikaga Yoshimitsu, this 14th Century garden contained such extravagances as a Chinese-style pavilion, a boating pond and a pavilion for snow viewing.

Japan garden-making is not a purely ornamental art. It is central to the cultural life of the country, as esteemed as literature, music and painting and, like them, capable of expressing profound truths. Many of these ideas and concepts stem from the doctrines of Zen Buddhism. But it is not necessary to comprehend those doctrines in order to appreciate their influence on Japanese gardens. Indeed, many of the most popular tenets of contemporary Western design were worked out centuries ago by Japanese esthetes and landscape artists. Such ideas as the "back to nature," movement, the belief in "indoor-outdoor living" and the concept of the garden as a personal, private retreat were practiced and refined in Japan long before they became American catchwords.

TAKING CUES FROM NATURE

Living close to nature was, in fact, the essence of Japanese life, and to a great extent it still continues to be. It starts with the design of the traditional Japanese house, with flexible, airy interior spaces opening through sliding screens onto sheltered verandas and from verandas onto intimate gardens that are themselves outdoor rooms enclosed by fences and walls. Within this scheme of things, materials are lovingly studied and deployed with a view to bringing out their essential nature—the rich grain of unfinished wood, the smooth translucence of a rice-paper screen, the rugged strength of a rock, the lyricism of water, the linear grace of bamboo, the gnarled branching of juniper boughs and the velvety softness of moss. For the Japanese garden owner, the ultimate reward is the contemplation of the timeless beauty of these materials in various lights and weathers and seasons.

AMERICAN ADAPTATIONS

The same rewards are just as accessible to American gardeners, as are the materials that supply them—including most of the plants used in Japanese gardens, or close facsimiles (see Chapter 3). The Japanese approach to gardening is in fact peculiarly well-suited to modern life styles. It requires only a few essential elements instead of massed effects. It makes much of limited spaces and a modicum of sun—two qualities especially advantageous to city gardens and small suburban lots. And it makes very few demands on the gardener's time. Once established, a Japanese garden does not require as much maintenance and care as a conventional flower garden, needing only occasional raking, pruning and cleaning to keep it neat. Indeed, one Japanese landscape architect who practices in the United States claims that he can hardly keep up with the requests for Japanese rock-and-gravel gardens from Americans "too busy to care for lawns and flowers."

A Japanese garden also has other advantages. Because its underlying structure is simple, strong and permanent, it is a pleasure to behold, even in the dead of winter. And it places a high value on privacy and serenity, two commodities increasingly hard to come by in today's crowded world. To this end, the Japanese garden celebrates restraint over display; it aims at what the Japanese call *shibui*, a beauty that is quiet, refined and tasteful. Constancy—as expressed in the muted colors of rocks, sand and slow-growing evergreens—is more important than the bright transitory colors of flowers and autumn foliage, which are viewed only as seasonal counterpoints. Asymmetry and mystery are preferable to orderly balance. This preference can be seen in the off-center placement of plants, rocks and ornamental accents, in the partial concealment of a path or a waterfall that draws the observer onward, in the pruning of trees and shrubs to emphasize their natural form and hint at shapes the mind must complete.

Such mastery of the garden art is rooted in traditions that go back well over a thousand years. Probably no other people on earth have been more intimately or seriously involved with gardening for a longer period of time—or love their gardens more. And when one looks at the natural landscape of Japan, it is not difficult to see why. The country is a chain of volcanic islands, four large ones and a multitude of small ones. Its hills and valleys are cloaked in greenery from abundant rainfall and its mountainsides are laced with countless waterfalls and rushing streams. In such surroundings, where typhoons, floods and earthquakes emphasize the unpredictable powers of nature, the early Japanese came to regard their rocks, seas and forests as the abodes of good and evil spirits, and to look upon nature with awe.

Out of this primitive animism came Japan's oldest living religion, Shinto—one of whose shrines, at Ise, contains what is probably the forerunner of the Japanese garden. Ise, which is still meticulously maintained and is considered one of the holiest places in Japan, consists of five unpainted wooden buildings with a graveled court where priests conduct sacred ceremonies. The court is surrounded by groves of giant oaks and Japanese cedars that shelter it from the secular world, and it is called a *niwa*, the Japanese word for garden. The word derives from the ancient word *hanima*, meaning ground set aside for a special purpose.

Over the centuries, as Japan's troubled provinces were unified under an Emperor and life became more peaceful, the gardens became less austere. Traveling around the countryside with his courtiers from the inland capital at Nara, the Emperor was enchanted with the natural beauty of his native land, especially its seacoast. In time a part of the imperial garden's graveled court was trans-

A CASE OF POETIC INJUSTICE

For hundreds of years English translators have been calling the Japanese apricot a plum. Admired for its flowers and picturesque branches, the ume, or flowering apricot (technically, prunus mume) has been celebrated in countless poems, paintings and stories. In rendering the poems into English, translators substituted plum for apricot—perhaps because the shorter word better matched the quick cadences of Japanese verse. Though botanists looking at an ume can see immediately that the fruit is a Japanese apricot, the misnomer remains: to this day English translations of Japanese poems call apricots plums.

SEACOAST INSPIRATION

The elements of style

The evolution of Japanese gardening through the centuries has resulted in a variety of garden styles. There are hill gardens, rock-and-sand gardens, tea gardens and stroll gardens. Most are either wet gardens, containing water, or dry gardens, which only suggest water's presence with rocks, pebbles, fine gravel or some combination of these.

Gardens in Japan were first developed for large imperial or religious estates. Later their principles were applied to ever-smaller private properties, in which a sort of gardening shorthand was used to suggest the larger elements. How this worked is demonstrated below in one of the oldest styles, the *tsukiyama*, or hill garden.

HILL GARDENS OF ALL SIZES

1. *To create a hill garden with mounds of soil, first make a plan on paper to determine where you will construct the hills. The finished garden should evoke a natural scene. When a line is drawn through the center of the sketch (dashed line), the halves should not match, since the primary esthetic principle of Japanese garden planning is asymmetry. During excavation, put the dark, rich topsoil to one side (left in inset). Pile subsoil on the hill site (right in inset). Tamp the mound well, topping it with a layer of topsoil.*

   Next embed rocks or logs where erosion might occur. Arrange plants to look like natural growth. Do not overplant; empty space imparts an uncluttered feeling. The valley made by the excavation can become a path, a stream or a pond. Or fill it with gravel to simulate water. Finish the hills by planting a ground cover.

2. *To create a modest hill garden, even in one corner of your yard, build up a small mound of soil. Then use rounded plants such as azaleas or boxwood to suggest hills. Grow taller plants behind for contrast and height. To emphasize the design or to hold the soil of a mound in place, edge the bed with stones or with cut logs driven into the ground (inset).*

3. *To create a hill garden in a tiny space, use a single rock to suggest a hill. Add a few taller plants behind the rock and one or two shorter plants in front to soften the scene. Dress the ground with gravel, moss or a low ground cover.*

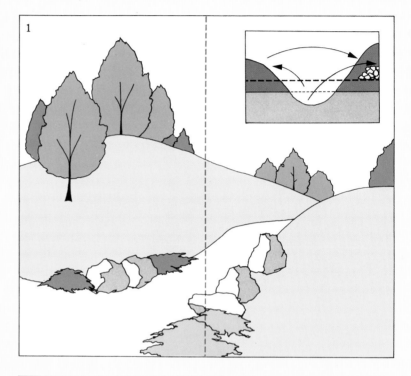

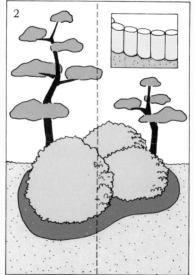

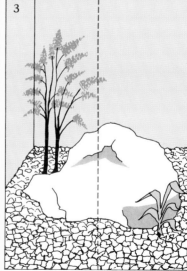

formed into a pond with a stone- and pebble-strewn shore, which represented the sea. Trees, rocks and flowers were also introduced into the scene. Soon some of the courtiers started to emulate the Emperor by building gardens of their own. When one of them created an island in his pond, he promptly became known as "The Garden-Island Minister."

A second influence on Japanese garden-making arrived from the Asian mainland, with Buddhism. In 538 A.D., a Korean King sent a gift to the Japanese Emperor, a golden statue of the Buddha and a collection of his sutras, or precepts, written in Chinese characters. The Japanese, who had no writing, and whose religious symbols were magical rocks, were dazzled by the religion. The Japanese court adopted Buddhism and began an exchange of students and artisans with the mainland, so that the Japanese could learn about the arts practiced there. Not long afterward, a ship-wrecked Korean artisan presented himself at the Japanese court, claiming that he had great skill in Chinese landscape gardening. He was promptly hired to redesign the palace garden of Suiko, the reigning Japanese Empress.

One of the Korean's additions that particularly delighted his royal client was a *shumisen,* a miniature version of the mountain regarded in Buddhist cosmology as the hub of the universe. Though his *shumisen* has long since disappeared, along with the rest of Empress Suiko's garden, it is believed to have been a single massive stone, perhaps as much as 10 feet tall. He also provided the Empress with what the records call a "bridge of Wu," which was probably nothing more than steppingstones leading from the shore of a pond to the *shima,* or island, within it—but which in later gardens was translated into the familiar high-arched span.

Empress Suiko's first essay into Chinese gardening quickly became a fad, spreading to the rest of the imperial court. Over the next two centuries the Nara region was dotted with noblemen's gardens, each with its own pond, mountain and islands. But in 784, the gardens at Nara had to be abandoned. Alarmed at the increasing power of the Buddhist clergy, which threatened even that of the imperial family, Emperor Kammu decided to move his capital to a new location, 25 miles away, leaving the troublesome clergy behind. At this new capital, called Heiankyo and later Kyoto, the gardens became among the loveliest ornaments of the elegant Heian society that flourished there.

At first the artisans at Heiankyo, as at Nara, relied on Chinese models. But as they became more knowledgeable, their own Japanese predilections for refinement and naturalness began to dominate

GIFTS FROM THE MAINLAND

ELEGANCE AT KYOTO

their work. Heian palaces and pavilions, composed of a succession of apartments, seemed to reach out and incorporate the garden into their designs. Arcades and roofed walkways linking the apartments were flanked by planted areas, and individual rooms looked out onto intimate garden courts. In the garden itself, pond, islands, plantings and paths were melded together to form a harmonious whole instead of being treated as separate elements. Flowering plants such as cherry, apricot, wisteria, iris and andromeda, as well as wildflowers such as mountain violets and bellflowers, were introduced into the scene in opulent quantities, reflecting the light-hearted life of the period. The weeping willow, which was inherited from Chinese gardens, trailed its branches in the waters of the pond. And the pond itself became large enough to accommodate a dragon-prowed boat in which Japanese lords and ladies could have musicians or dancers perform for them.

LANDSCAPING WITH WATER

Thanks to the natural springs that bubbled up all over Kyoto, Heian garden designers were able to incorporate myriad streams and waterfalls into their plans. And with the help of a small army of laborers they could cause these water displays to flow in any way they chose. Indeed, so sensitive did the designers become to the character of flowing water that they devised a dozen or more words to describe the various kinds of waterfalls. There was, for example, *ito-ochi,* water that fell in a threadlike pattern; *nuno-ochi,* water that fell in a broad sheet; and *tsutai-ochi,* a waterfall that trickled over rocks.

During this glorious Heian period, which lasted from the Eighth to the 12th Century, islands in the garden pool became even more popular and took on new symbolic forms. Perhaps due to rumblings of civil trouble in the provinces, it was rumored in court circles that the gods were about to desert Japan for legendary mystic isles. In the hope of averting such a catastrophe, many noblemen built replicas of the isles in their own gardens.

GARDENING AS FINE ART

Often the designers—the men who drew the sketches and supervised the critical gathering and arranging of stones—were members of the priest class. But just as often they were the noblemen themselves, for gardening was held in such high esteem as an artistic pursuit that it was on a par with painting and writing poetry. One treatise on garden design was written by an 11th Century nobleman, Tachibana Toshitsuna. Called the *Sakuteiki,* literally "notes on how to make gardens," it is filled with explicit instructions—and dire warnings about what would happen if the instructions were not followed to the letter.

Among the more explicit rules in the *Sakuteiki* is a passage on rocks. "Do not set upright a stone that was naturally flat, or vice versa; violations of this will surely bring evil fortunes. . . . The usual places to set rocks are where the stream emerges into the courtyard, where it curves around a hillock, where it empties into a pond, where it bends in passing a building. Other stones should be set out only after due consideration, lest they spoil the effect. Within the stream itself, the most suitable place for stones is at the bend, for two reasons: first, the esthetic effect; second, to prevent the point of land from being washed away." All of these recommendations, it should be observed, are still considered to make good practical and artistic sense.

An even more intimate picture of Heian garden design is revealed on the pages of *The Tale of Genji*, a fictitious account of the amorous adventures of Prince Genji, written by Lady Murasaki, a lady-in-waiting at the imperial court. At his palace in Kyoto, says Lady Murasaki, Prince Genji ordered individual gardens to be built outside the suites of his many loves. He took great pains to have slopes cut away, streams dammed and just the right kinds of plantings introduced, so that "each occupant of the various quarters might look out her windows upon such a prospect as pleased her best." For his favorite consort, a lady who was especially fond of springtime, a bank of earth was raised and planted with a profusion of early-flowering trees, while just underneath her windows, borders of cinquefoil, rock azalea and other plants were arranged to provide a glorious spring display.

Toward other ladies, Genji was hardly less attentive. Lady Akikonomu, whose favorite season of the year was autumn, had a "garden full of such trees as in autumn-time turn to the deepest hue." Another mistress, who was known as the Lady from the Village of the Falling Flowers, took special delight in summer and therefore had quarters that looked upon a cool spring and a grove of "tall-stemmed forest trees whose thick leaves roofed airy tunnels of shade." Nearby, to remind her of past pleasures, was a hedge of deutzia, "whose scent reawakens forgotten love." Finally, for Lady Akashi, a garden was fashioned that, according to her preference, looked its finest in winter. The garden included a "close-set wall of pine trees, planted there on purpose that she might have the pleasure of seeing them when their boughs were laden with snow; and for her delight in the earlier days of winter there was a great bed of chrysanthemums, which he pictured her enjoying on some morning when all the garden was white with frost."

Unfortunately, the opulent, enticing gardens of the Heian aristocracy, while mirroring its refinement, also signaled its decay.

PLANTS IN FAMILY CRESTS

As far back as the 10th Century, Japanese noblemen adopted the practice of marking ceremonial robes and carriages with a mon, or family crest, signifying social status. In time the mon was used to distinguish opposing armies. Samurai crests were often based on inanimate objects, but noble families preferred garden subjects like the chrysanthemum, wisteria, peony, bamboo, pine and iris shown above. The chrysanthemum mon is the symbol of the Imperial family; with 14 petals, as here, it identifies a prince. With two more petals it would be the mon of the Emperor. The wisteria mon, upper right, belongs to the Fujiwara family, one of whose members is credited with originating the mon idea.

Increasingly preoccupied with trivia, the Heian nobles were challenged by a new warrior class, the samurai, who seized political power in a prolonged civil war, reduced the Emperor to a figurehead, and moved the real seat of government to Kamakura, a small town near the mouth of Tokyo Bay.

THE SAMURAI VISION Many samurai were recent converts to the Buddhist "Pure Land" sect and their gardens reflected the sect's religious doctrines. In return for death in battle, Pure Land Buddhism promised its followings an afterlife in a paradise where the ground was spread with golden sand, the trees were hung with gems and a perpetual shower of petals fell from the sky. The samurai's garden was based on this vision. Although it contined some elements of Heian design, its purpose was to please Buddha rather than mortal man, and many of the Heian elements took on new religious significance. The far side of the pond, for instance, became a symbol of paradise, and its connection with the mainland was an arched bridge whose ascending and descending curves represented the difficult path to be trod in getting from this world to the hereafter.

Among other samurai contributions to the furtherance of garden design were the use of a growing number of garden specialists called *ishitate-so,* "priests who arrange stones." But these contributions pale beside those of one shogun family, the Ashikagas. Under their rule the seat of government was reestablished at Kyoto and the Ashikaga family became, like the Italian Medici, great patrons of many arts. The most discerning of them, Ashikaga Yoshimitsu, encouraged artists and artisans to develop the Japanese style of flower arranging called *ikebana* and the deliberate dwarfing of trees and shrubs known as bonsai. But his finest achievements are probably the lovely gardens, temples and palaces he ordered built, one of which, Kyoto's exquisite Golden Pavilion, is still admired by thousands of sightseers every year *(pages 22-23).*

AUSTERITY AND ZEN By the 13th Century, still another Buddhist sect from China, called Zen, became popular in Japan and imposed even more rigorous ideas on Japanese garden design. Zen gardens differed radically from the pleasure gardens and earthly visions of paradise created in former times. To reflect the austerity and self-discipline that was preached by Zen monks, their designers used few if any flowering plants, since they believed these to be gaudy, evanescent distractions from what should be the main purposes of men's minds: the contemplation of eternity. And for that purpose the unchanging, quiet hues of evergreens and mosses, of sand, gravel and stone, were thought to be the most appropriate.

Like Zen landscape painting—which reduces the particulars of a scene to a few stylized brush strokes representing, for example, tree, rock, sky and earth—the material objects in a Zen garden stand for something other and larger than themselves. They are supposed to suggest oceans, mountains, islands, waterfalls. In perceiving these representations of nature as large-in-small, the viewer is helped to perceive the presence of Buddha in all things, by much the same reasoning that led medieval Christians to see God in a blade of grass or in a grain of sand. The gardens are, as one writer has called them, "gardens of the mind."

Carried to its logical extreme, as it was at some later Zen temples, this approach eliminated one by one such recognizable elements as trees, shrubs, bridges, islands and even water itself. All that remained were rocks, raked sand and patches of moss that happened to grow in shaded places. Such compositions were called *kare sansui,* or "dry landscapes," a type of Japanese gardening that is still every popular. To Western eyes, some of these dry-landscape gardens are scarcely recognizable as landscapes at all; they seem more like abstract paintings or sculpture, which in a sense they are. The finest of them, created a full five centuries ago, look surprisingly modern. They also look exactly as they did when they were first built, right down to the patterns of carefully raked sand that evoke the ripple and flow of rivers and seas. To many Japanese the dry-landscape garden is the spiritual garden, the quintessential landscape that evokes endless imagination. Certainly, in its achievement of maximum effect with minimum materials, it is unique in the history of garden design.

The most famous dry-landscape garden is the one built at the Ryoanji, a temple in Kyoto, in the 15th Century *(page 24).* Flanked on two sides by walls and on the other two sides by temple buildings, the garden is about the size of a tennis court, and just as flat. It contains 15 moss-edged stones of various sizes set in a sea of fine gray pebbles—and nothing else. The stones are arranged in five groups of two, three or five stones each, and around the groups linear patterns of raked pebbles form concentric ripples. Since it is a viewing garden, no one is allowed to set foot in the garden except the lay brothers who keep it raked. But visitors come from all over Japan and all over the world to sit on the garden's dark, polished veranda; some stay for hours on end, speculating on the meaning of Ryoanji's sermon in stone and sand.

Some observers see the design simply as rocks in a river; others see it as legendary mystic isles. A few analyze the garden's design on purely esthetic grounds, and regard it as an exercise in grouping, balance, movement and rhythm of such extraordinary har-

A TEMPLE GARDEN

Visitors to Kyoto in the 18th Century frequently made a special pilgrimage to the Myoshinji temple to view its famous dry garden, an arrangement of rocks and low-pruned plants. The illustration of which this is a detail appeared in a guidebook, Views of Celebrated Gardens of Kyoto, published in 1799. The stones were generally said to represent the 16 disciples of Buddha recognized by the caretakers of the temple, the Nichiren sect.

mony that to move a single stone would destroy the entire effect.

While Buddhist priests in temples like Ryoanji were working out the pattern for one sort of garden design, Japanese tea masters were refining another. Tea, also introduced into Japan from the mainland, was originally drunk by Chinese priests in preparation for religious meditation, in order to induce wakefulness. In Japan, however, tea-drinking became more diversified. It was a secular as well as a religious activity, and was practiced not only in Buddhist temples but also in the households of cultured gentlemen. Tea-drinking followed a carefully defined ceremony, formalized in the 15th and 16th Centuries and still observed essentially unchanged today. In this ceremony, every detail—the small crawl-in door, the austere decoration of the room in which the guests gathered, the rustic appearance of the communal tea cup—was meant to instill a sense of humbleness and to contribute to an atmosphere of serenity.

By the late 16th Century, the tea ceremony had moved from the distractions of the house proper to a small shelter that was set into its own special garden. Unlike the Zen sand gardens, which were largely meant to be viewed, the tea garden was meant to be experienced at close range by walking through it on the *roji,* or "dewy path," leading to the teahouse. The rules for the design of the *roji,* most of which were formulated by the great tea master Sen Rikyu, said that it should remind one of following a trail through fields or along a shoreline to a sylvan retreat. In effect, the *roji* was supposed to provide a transition that allowed the participants in the tea ceremony to leave behind the anxieties and busyness of the world outside and prepare for the spiritual experience that awaited them within the teahouse.

A CLASSIC TEA GARDEN

To this end the classic Japanese tea garden was divided into two distinct parts, separated by a simple gate, usually of bamboo. Outside, in the first part, the mood was one of expectation, in preparation for the spiritual experience that was to follow. The path itself was paved with rudimentary steppingstones, arranged with studied casualness, to keep the guests' feet dry. One or more stone lanterns lighted the path at dusk, and along the way to the teahouse there was a stone water basin for rinsing the mouth and hands before the ceremony. Plants along the path were selected and arranged to create a mood that became progressively more restful; those in the inner garden were mostly mosses, ferns and the kinds of shrubs found in remote mountain woods. The sole flower was generally saved for the teahouse itself, where a single perfect blossom of the season was displayed in an otherwise austere interior.

PETALS FOR A TASTE OF FALL

Chrysanthemums grown in most parts of the world are bitter to the taste, but soil and temperature in northern Japan combine to produce flowers that have a flavor faintly reminiscent of spinach. Many Japanese regard these dainty petals as a delicacy, setting them afloat in clear hot soups or serving boiled petals seasoned with soy sauce, mayonnaise or vinegar. Along with flavor and color, chrysanthemums have a symbolic dimension. Their appearance on a plate or in a bowl is a subtle culinary reminder of the onset of autumn.

From the tea garden it was only a short step to the final triumph of Japanese garden design, the *kaiyushiki,* or "stroll garden." Combining the rustic nature of the tea garden with the visual delights of the paradisiacal gardens of earlier times, the stroll garden was meant solely for enjoyment. Stroll gardens, which first appeared in the 17th Century, contained virtually all the traditional design elements—ponds, mountains, islands, streams, bridges, lanterns and steppingstones—but they were used in a much freer way. The main feature of the garden was a pond with irregular banks, peninsulas and islands, artfully designed to look as if it had been created by nature. Around the pond ran a path; here and there its pattern of steppingstones was deliberately altered, or the path was interrupted by a turn in a bridge. The purpose of this was to arrest the strollers, force them to slow down, so they could view a choice pine specimen or grove of bamboo, for instance, or the lovely cascade of a waterfall.

Sometimes the strollers were deliberately beckoned onward by a partially screened view of, say, a lantern or shelter, which only further walking could reveal in full; this technique was called *mie-gakure,* "seen and hidden." At other times the designer made use of *shakkei,* "borrowed scenery," in which the garden's size was perceptually enlarged by the inclusion of a view beyond the garden. In the stroll garden of one imperial villa outside Kyoto, for instance, a row of trees is deliberately broken at one vantage point, calling the stroller's attention to a view of surrounding mountains. Many gardens in central Japan similarly "borrow" the great snow-capped cone of Mount Fuji.

Some of the most famous stroll gardens were laid out on a large scale; in Kyoto, the stroll gardens at Katsura and Shugakuin on opposite sides of the city occupy more than 10 acres each. Built with an opulence that not even their princely owners were able to maintain, a number of great gardens have passed into public hands. Today many are national treasures, intended for the enjoyment of all the people of Japan, and for tourists as well. But even as these gardens became historical artifacts, the principles they perfected were being incorporated into thousands of gardens of more modest size. Tucked behind farmers' cottages and the townhouses of Japanese merchants, arranged as welcoming courtyards in front of restaurants and banks, even set on the rooftops of Tokyo office buildings for young workers and executives to stroll through on their noon-hour break, are gardens that keep Japan's ancient traditions very much alive. And those traditions are just as applicable to gardens in San Francisco, Montreal and Philadelphia.

MANIPULATING THE VIEW

Masterworks of Japanese gardening art

Like artists who use more conventional materials—paint, stone, clay, wood—Japanese-garden artists have left a legacy of works so distinctive that many are officially classified in Japan as national treasures. Designers of the masterpiece gardens shown on the following pages all took nature as their subject as well as their medium, creating idealized or abstract versions of the natural landscape of Japan. Yet the gardens they produced are as different from one another as a Rembrandt painting is from a Picasso. Each garden is shaped by the esthetic canons of a particular age, which in turn are reflections of the religions and politics of the time.

Some of the largest and most elegant gardens were commissioned by rulers or noblemen as tangible expressions of their power or religious leanings. The 14th Century Saihoji garden *(pages 20-21)*, was built in a burst of religious fervor by a Kyoto nobleman. The Temple of the Golden Pavilion, on the other hand, was one of many luxurious gardens built by warrior-class shoguns eager to adopt the lifestyle of the old aristocracy.

During the turbulent 15th and 16th Centuries, when rulers were too busy with civil wars or political intrigues to construct gardens, Zen temples became sources of great garden art. Smaller, but no less inspired than the gardens of the ruling class, these spare, symbolic compositions of sand and stone *(pages 24-27)* were partly a reflection of religious asceticism, partly a reaction to the political strife. They were sanctuary gardens, for quiet contemplation.

Another contemplative art—the tea ceremony—also flourished in the 15th and 16th Centuries, gaining popularity especially among the warrior class, for whom the tranquil ritual of drinking tea in rustic gardens provided a welcome respite from military pursuits. Later incorporated into civilian life, the tea garden provided inspiration for some elements of what may be the most magnificent of all Japanese gardens: the 17th Century strolling garden at Katsura Detached Palace in Kyoto *(pages 30-31)*. Katsura offers so many delights that some Japanese say they could spend a lifetime there.

At Katsura, an oak column with its bark provides a subtle transition between the inside of the Shokin-tei teahouse and the natural beauty that is outside.

Consecrated by nature

Two extremes in garden design exist side-by-side at Saihoji, a temple in Kyoto. In the 14th Century, a wealthy nobleman commissioned a Buddhist priest to rebuild the temple and its grounds. The priest, Muso Kokushi, a recent convert to Zen, created a traditional pond garden ringed by pavilions, teahouses and flowering cherry trees and, on a hillside above the pond, a garden composed solely of huge stones. The pond garden echoes the style of earlier pleasure gardens; the rock garden presages later Zen dry-landscape designs.

Great granite boulders step down
a steep hillside at Saihoji, evoking the
sight and sound of rushing water.
Six centuries of weathering have only
intensified the image.

Over the centuries nature has layered
the banks of Saihoji's pond with
more than 40 varieties of moss,
giving it a subdued, unearthly beauty.
The garden's pavilions are long
gone, casualties of Japan's civil wars.

A garden for earthly delights

In 1397, in the hope of spending his declining years removed from the cares of state, the Shogun Ashikaga Yoshimitsu built a spectacular retreat—a three-tiered pavilion that hung over the glassy waters of a mirror-smooth lake. Its gardens, modeled after those at Saihoji *(pages 20-21),* were meant for strolling and contained constantly changing views. Alas, Yoshimitsu's retirement was cut short by his death only two months after the garden's completion in 1408.

Originally built in the 14th Century but destroyed by fire in 1950, the Golden Pavilion was replaced by this exact replica and newly adorned with a shimmering surface of gold leaf to fit its ancient name.

Gardens in the abstract

Under the influence of the ascetic Zen Buddhist sect, lavish pond gardens designed for temporal delights gradually gave way to waterless gardens designed for spiritual discipline. Made of rocks, sand and a minimal amount of vegetation, some of these "dry gardens" simulated streams, cascades or undulating ocean waves *(pages 26-27)*. Others—like the 16th Century Ryoanji garden below—were more abstract. Because the viewer must complete the scene, the meaning of these abstract gardens is fixed only by the imagination.

Composed of nothing but 15 mossy stones set in groups of two or three in a sea of raked gravel, the garden at Ryoanji has for centuries defied attempts to assign it any single meaning. The ingenious designer is unknown, although the garden is often credited to Soami, a talented designer of the era.

In the Tofukuji monastery garden, checkerboard squares of moss and stone end in an undulating line like the froth of a receding wave. Though built in 1935, the garden follows ancient Zen principles.

A boat, represented by geometric shapes, sails through waves

An imaginary river flows between mossy banks and swirls around a bend in this 16th Century garden at Shinnyoin temple. To evoke the water's rippling flow, the rocks are arranged in an overlapping fish-scale pattern.

of clipped azaleas in a 17th Century Zen seascape at Daichi.

In this tiny courtyard garden at Daisenin temple, scale and perspective are used so skillfully that the rocks and gravel create the impression of a river coursing between towering cliffs and rushing beneath a low bridge.

These enigmatic cones of sand in a courtyard garden at Daitokuji temple once served a ceremonial purpose. When important persons arrived, sand was sprinkled along the path in a symbolic act of purification.

Tranquil places for tea

While the tea ceremony was originally devised by Zen monks as a religious ritual, the mood of the ceremony, with its emphasis on spiritual refreshment, soon gained it wider adherence. Schools arose to provide instruction not only in the refined art of preparing and drinking tea, but in the creation of a suitable setting for this activity. One of the greatest instructors was Sen Rikyu, the tea master whose precepts govern the design of the rustic garden of the Urasenke teahouse in Kyoto, shown here.

Planned as a place for withdrawal from worldly cares, the sun-dappled Urasenke tea garden—glimpsed here through the main entrance—is separated from its Kyoto environs by a thick wall of wood and plaster.

Olive, pine and cedar trees, as well as bamboo grass, edge the path to the tea master's residence in the outer garden. The garden is divided into inner and outer sections to create an increasingly restful mood.

Located in the outer garden, a roofed bench, or koshikake, provides a place for guests to assemble before the ceremony. The green-bamboo broom hanging on a column is used to keep the area meticulously clean.

The teahouse itself is made of rough plaster, natural wood, uncut stone and thatch. To remind guests of the importance of humility, Rikyu introduced the low door, which had to be entered on hands and knees.

A bamboo dipper rests atop an ancient stone basin filled with clear water for guests' ritual ablutions. The basin is set on a bed of pebbles called umi, or sea, connecting this basinful of water with the ocean.

A garden fit for a prince

In 1620, Prince Hachijo, uncle to the Emperor, decided to build a country house along the Katsura River, southwest of Kyoto. Katsura palace eventually occupied a site of some 11 acres. Borrowing liberally from Japan's existing garden tradition, Hachijo scattered villas and teahouses around a large pond and connected them with a meandering path artfully placed to reveal hundreds of different, often unexpected, views. For his friends' amusement, the prince also added a "toy mountain," a "little wood on the hill" and a "bridge that joined two islands," features he knew they would recognize from Lady Murasaki's popular novel, *The Tale of Genji*. Though Hachijo died before Katsura was completed, he is credited with creating this landmark garden, which sums up then-current ideas in garden design and anticipates the "strolling gardens" of the future.

Cutting through a row of hedges, one path at Katsura emerges onto a small peninsula at whose tip is a beautifully pruned pine tree. Beyond the tree, across the pond, can be glimpsed the Shokin-tei teahouse.

Rounding the teahouse and looking back on it from across the pond, the stroller's wide-angle view embraces the same pruned shrub and stone lantern that occupied center stage when seen from inside the teahouse.

Steppingstones carry the stroller across a pebbled peninsula where the view of Shokin-tei includes an arched stone bridge.

Putting principles into practice 2

Few gardeners have the space or money to build an Emperor's pleasure grounds, but many have discovered that the principles of Japanese design can be extremely useful in creating handsome and practical gardens of modest size. They fit the mode of modern living and are pleasing to the eye all through the year. The Japanese approach is particularly suited to contemporary houses oriented toward outdoor living, one reason this style is so popular on the West Coast. But the ideas are just as adaptable for a city brownstone or a Cape Cod clapboard cottage.

If the notion of establishing a Japanese garden in the United States seems unnatural, perhaps you have stereotypes in mind; you do not need to have a pagoda, or flowering cherry trees reflected in a lake. Nor do you have to eliminate your flower beds or lawn. Some of the most appealing of the gardens done in the Japanese spirit have been started in small, even out-of-the-way problem areas, perhaps places handicapped by poor soil or lack of sun. Without disrupting much of your existing landscape, you can experiment, for example, with a little viewing garden as a welcoming note near the entrance to your home. Or try an intimate enclosed landscape just outside your bath or bedroom, or one adjoining an outdoor sitting area or in a narrow side yard. After living with a tiny Japanese garden for a while, you may find it so congenial that you will want to expand it.

Japanese gardens are entrancing in small spaces because they accomplish so much with only a few materials; they constitute a kind of horticultural shorthand in which each element does more than you expect of it. In designing such a garden, you have only three basic materials to consider. One is stone: rocks, cobbles and various kinds of gravel and sand. The second is water—either real water, in the form of a pool, stream or waterfall, or water that is implied by an arrangement of rocks, gravel and perhaps a small bridge. The third component, of course, is plants: the low, slow-growing evergreens

A delicate azalea bloom floating in a rock-studded stream serves to summarize the quintessence of a Japanese garden: a composition of tranquil beauty that is shaped from water, stone and plants.

and the light, contrasting accents supplied by a lacy Japanese maple or a stand of slim bamboo. To these basic elements you may want to add three others—paths to permit strolling through the garden, enclosures provided by fences, and such embellishments as a stone lantern, a water basin or a small garden shelter.

PRINCIPLES OF DESIGN The elements can be assembled in many ways, but in sorting out the possibilities, it is well to bear in mind the basic maxims of Japanese garden design:

● View your design in terms of its lines and textures for maximum effect. Do not fall back on a bold display of color; the best Japanese gardens have muted palettes, largely green, gray, brown and beige. Splashes of flowers or changing leaf colors can be used sparingly as seasonal accents, but man-made objects of wood or masonry look best unpainted.

● Establish a focal point—perhaps a handsome weatherworn rock, a graceful tree, a garden pool or a sparkling cascade—and let it dominate your design (though never from the exact center of the composition). Use restraint as you add other elements so that they complement the focal point rather than compete with it. This is particularly important in a small garden, where the use of only a few elements contributes to a feeling of spaciousness.

● Strive for a composition that is asymmetrical, yet remains balanced. An open, arching tree placed to the right of center, for example, might be balanced by the solidity of a low rock to the near left. Place rocks, shrubs and other elements in a natural way; a useful concept in grouping is an imaginary triangle with unequal sides, the triad long employed by the Japanese to achieve dynamic but balanced effects. Such triangles, with three of the elements of a composition at their apexes, are used in both horizontal and vertical planes to create pleasing three-dimensional designs *(page 35)*.

● To achieve a sense of spaciousness and serenity, let the horizontal lines be dominant—low rocks that are rounded or flat, expanses of water or raked gravel, plants with strong horizontal branching patterns or a prostrate growth habit. Use vertical counterpoints only occasionally to eliminate monotony; too many verticals give the garden a restless look, especially if placed singly.

● Avoid strong lines that lead directly away from an observer or directly across his view. A path, a bridge or the longer dimension of a pond will seem more interesting and add an illusion of greater depth if it follows a roughly diagonal course toward the back.

● Do not reveal everything at once. A steppingstone path or a stream bed is more enticing if it leads behind plantings or rocks to suggest that it continues indefinitely.

Guideposts for grouping

In a Japanese garden, stones, plants and man-made objects are precisely grouped in pairs or in odd-numbered combinations. Elements within each group are interrelated. To attain maximum variation within a group, the Japanese apply the principle of asymmetry; that is, they make sure that when only two elements appear, the objects are not of the same size or volume, and when three or more elements are arranged, they form imaginary triangles with unequal sides. These triangles are formed on both the vertical and horizontal planes, which keeps the composition from looking flat.

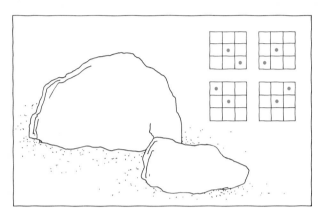

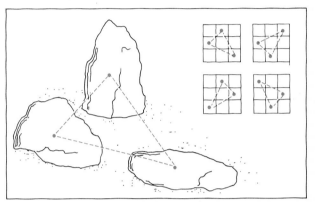

When you work with a pair of elements (stones, plants, man-made objects or any combination of these), select the ones with different sizes or volumes. Arrange the elements at an angle (insets) from the main viewing area, creating some depth between them. Avoid setting them end to end or side by side in a straight line.

When you group three elements, use stones or plants of different sizes or volumes. The largest or most prominent will become the focal point of the arrangement. To create the illusion of depth, position the elements so that they form an imaginary triangle of unequal sides, whether viewed from the front or from above (insets).

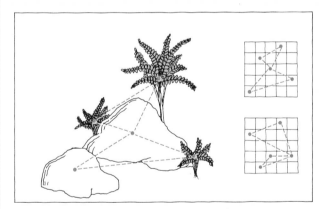

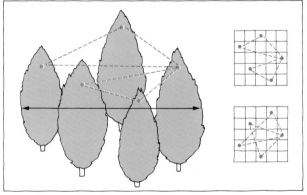

When combining stones and plants in a group of five or more, use only one or two plant species. Select plants that have different shapes but are naturally compatible—two mountain plants, for example, or two woodland plants. Use rocks as a quiet backdrop. Arrange the parts to form the invisible triangles shown in the drawing and insets.

Tall trees, which attract attention when standing alone, form more restful compositions when five of them are grouped so that their combined width (arrow) exceeds their height. Use trees of unequal height and arrange them so that any three will form an uneven triangle when seen from the front or from above (insets).

In planning your garden, you can ensure better results and fewer unforeseen problems if you draw it on paper first. Measure the area with a tape rule, including the main dimensions, the location of adjoining house windows and doors, and major existing features like walks, driveways, fences and trees. Note any low area that might require drainage—or that could be used for a small artificial stream or pool—as well as any high area that might provide a focal point with an artificial waterfall or a grouping of rocks and plants. If you plan to excavate, check for hidden obstacles like underground pipes or a septic field. As a guide for choosing plants, note which parts of the garden receive full sun, partial sun or no direct sunlight at all.

TESTING THE PLAN

Transfer this information onto graph paper; depending on the size of your garden, let one or more squares equal a foot. Then place tracing paper over the layout and start sketching your ideas for the placement of plants, paths, rocks and pools. Rather than erasing and correcting a scheme that is not working out, place another sheet of tracing paper over the first and refine the design. When you have arrived at a promising plan, rough out the main elements in the garden itself with stand-ins—lengths of rope or garden hose to delineate the edges of a path or a pond, stakes of various heights to indicate shrubs and trees, newspaper and cardboard cartons to show where rocks will go, anything that will help you visualize how the

THREE BASIC STONE SHAPES

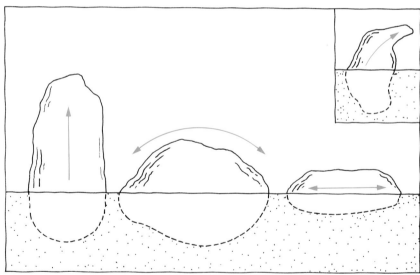

Most Japanese-garden stones are selected from one of three basic shapes, each of which conveys a different feeling. The vertical thrust of a tall stone—two or three times taller than it is wide—creates a sense of excitement. *A medium stone, about as tall as it is wide, gives an impression of restfulness. A stone that is low to the ground suggests peacefulness. Besides the basic form, stones may have unusual shapes (inset).*

elements will fit together. Record changes on your sketch; you will undoubtedly want to make more adjustments later, but the exercise will enable you to make a list of the materials you need.

Whether your garden is to be a simple but classic dry landscape, or is inspired by a tea-garden or a hill-and-pond design, much of its basic structure and ultimate dramatic effect will depend on your use of stone. There is a great difference between a Japanese garden and an English-style rock garden. Both recall scenes from nature, but the English garden seeks to duplicate natural rock-and-plant formations, while the Japanese garden extracts only the essence of such a scene, treating rocks and plants as symbolic, artistic elements. To the Japanese, and to Westerners who adopt their approach, rocks are more than beautiful; each has its own intrinsic quality, its own special character, texture, color, patina and what is called "vigor"—its innate lines of force.

Japanese gardeners approach rocks with reverence. Just as there are plant nurseries in other countries, Japan has rock nurseries where a gardener goes to seek precisely the stone he needs to express a desired symbolism or artistic effect. Choices are not made casually; a buyer may examine many, reflecting on their merits and discussing their possibilities for hours, even returning several times before a sale is made. Particularly valued are rocks that suggest some natural or legendary association—mountains, islands, waterfalls, turtles, cranes, tigers, hares, boats and the like. Unusually large and beautiful rocks, shaped by nature into stunning patterns, have sold for as much as $10,000 each.

Most Western gardeners settle for less exalted rocks that are easier to find and a lot less expensive. If you live in a rocky region, you may find what you need on your own property or on that of a neighbor only too glad to have you cart it away. Plant nurseries and landscape contractors often have sources, and the classified pages of your telephone directory may list suppliers of natural rock, quarried and crushed rock, gravel and sand under the heading "Stone."

When you look for rocks, keep a few criteria in mind. Most important is the character of a particular stone in relation to its garden use. The Japanese favor metamorphic rocks like granite, gneiss and schist for their picturesque qualities—dark, densely textured, often grained, weathered or mottled with moss or lichens. These are preferred over lighter-colored sedimentary rocks like limestone or the more colorful, pitted volcanic rocks, though these too can be used if they are the only ones available. Japanese gardeners seek stones that express a definite terrain—rugged, angular rocks to suggest the wildness of mountains, cliffs and waterfalls,

ROOTING A STONE

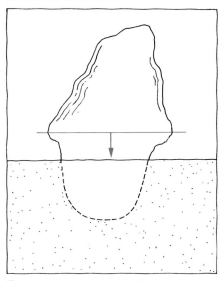

To make a stone appear to be a natural outcropping, embed its least attractive end as deep as its widest dimension (red line). If that does not provide enough height, set the stone higher and plant around it.

A CHOICE AMONG ROCKS

or stones smoothly rounded and polished by water or glacial action for a garden stream bed or a pond's border.

In keeping with the Japanese taste for asymmetry, rocks are typically used singly or in odd-numbered combinations, though sometimes in pairs. An especially handsome rock may be made a focal point, such as a symbolic island in a pond or dry landscape, or a transitional element just outside a door to lead the eye into the garden, or an accent at the bend of a stream. Three-rock groups offer more possibilities; a large rock, a medium-sized rock and a small, low rock *(page 36)* can be arranged in many different ways. The potential combinations multiply rapidly if the compositions are enlarged to include even more rocks.

SETTING UP A ROCK GROUP

Since rocks give stability as well as drama to a garden, it is essential that they have ample visual weight and are seen to be firmly rooted to the ground. A common error is to scatter rocks that are too small loosely on the surface. A rock must not only be securely anchored against teetering, toppling or settling; it must *look* solid and secure. To achieve this, many Japanese landscapers set a rock into the ground to the depth of its spread line—the point of greatest girth—to give the maximum appearance of stability *(page 37);* others bury at least a third of any rock.

When you have determined the best setting for your largest rock, excavate to the necessary depth and tamp the bottom of the hole; if the soil is unstable or the rock very heavy, make the hole a bit oversized and line the bottom with concrete. When the underlayment is hard, have the crane hoist the rock over the excavation and lower it, while someone swings the rock so the side you want to display in your composition is facing in the desired direction. To keep the hoisting rig from scarring the rock, make sure chafing gear is used—pieces of wood, thick nylon cord or several layers of folded burlap inserted under the chains. When the rock is just above its resting place, use small, flat stones as wedges to prop it into alignment and to make it easier to withdraw the chains. Then fill in around the rock with smaller stones, rubble and subsoil. Finish with topsoil if you intend to plant close to the rock. Then place secondary rocks in similar fashion until your design is completed.

SAND, GRAVEL AND STONES

If your garden is to be a dry landscape, you can fill in around the rocks not only with plants but with small stones, gravel or coarse sand. Cobbles, rounded stones 2 to 6 inches in diameter, are appropriate to suggest the course of a winding dry stream bed or a stretch of rocky beach. They can also be used, as they often are in Japan, in decorative bands under the eaves of a gutterless roof, to keep dripping rain from furrowing the ground and splashing up mud.

For larger flat areas, many Japanese gardeners blanket the bare earth with a finer stone material to keep the ground dry and neat and to serve as a background that unifies the design. Although this is sometimes called sand, do not use fine white beach or builder's sand; it records every footprint, blows or washes away, and can be unpleasantly glaring. A better choice is fine gravel, coarse decomposed granite, or crushed rock about ¼ inch in diameter—up to ½ inch if the surface will often be walked on. These materials come in many colors, from tan to blue to almost black, but the best color for most gardens is a soft off-white or light gray, providing a neutral background for the darker hues of rocks and plants.

Spread the gravel or other material to a depth of 2 or 3 inches and rake it smooth. To keep it from scuffing or washing where it does not belong, contain it with metal or plastic garden edging or, more handsomely, with unpainted redwood strips set on edge and held in place with short wooden stakes, much as you would edge a path *(below)*. The gravel will act as a mulch to retain moisture around plant roots during summer heat, reducing the need for watering. Weeds that manage to push through it will be easy to pull. To eliminate weeds even more effectively, lay a membrane of plastic film or builder's tar paper under the gravel, piercing it with holes 6 inches to a foot apart to let rain water drain through. The membrane

CONTAINING A GRAVEL BED

LAYING OUT AND BUILDING A SAND GARDEN

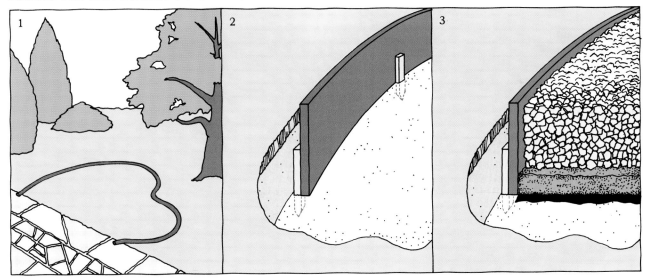

A so-called sand garden is actually made mostly of gravel, which holds its place and pattern better. Outline the garden with a hose or rope and mark the edges. Then excavate to a depth of 3 inches and tamp the bottom.

To contain the gravel filler, edge the area with thin, pliable wood strips wide enough to extend about ¼ inch above the outside soil. Hold the edging in place with stakes driven deeply enough to be hidden by gravel.

Cover the tamped soil with a sheet of weed-proofing plastic punctured at 3-foot intervals so water can drain through. Then add a ½-inch layer of coarse sand to anchor the top 2½-inch layer of gravel. Tamp and level.

will smother weed seeds in the soil and discourage new ones from taking root; it will also allow you to use a thinner covering of gravel.

To calculate how much gravel to order, multiply the length and width of the garden area to be covered to get its square footage, then multiply by the depth of the gravel in fractions of a foot ($\frac{1}{6}$ for a 2-inch layer, $\frac{1}{4}$ for a 3-inch layer) to get the amount needed in cubic feet. Divide by 27 to convert the figure into cubic yards, the measure in which you will place your order.

AN ILLUSION OF WAVES

Once installed, you can keep the gravel neat by smoothing it occasionally with the back of a steel garden rake. If you would like to suggest water in this dry landscape, make parallel wavy or rippled lines *(page 42)* with the tines of the rake. Even better is a special pattern rake made by cutting a sawtooth edge into an inch-thick board and mounting it on a long handle *(below)*.

A small viewing garden along these lines can be built in any level area where an intimate landscape is desired; if you like, add a pair of low shrubs and a small tree chosen to fit into the area without making it seem crowded. But if you have more space, you can consider a garden that you can stroll in, one with low, landscaped mounds, a path, a pool, perhaps even a stream and waterfall. The classic Japanese *tsukiyama,* the hill garden with or without a pond, abbreviates a view of faraway mountains and lakes or valleys. The low hill, or group of hills, is placed at the rear of the garden and is built of material excavated to make the pond or valley and path in front. Groups of rocks at the base of the hills add visual weight and stabilize the mounded soil. The pond should be irregular in shape, as ponds naturally are, with miniature bays and promontories; if it is

A GROOVING TOOL

To create grooved patterns in gravel (page 42), make a rake from a board at least $\frac{3}{4}$ inch thick and 3 inches wide. For simple designs in a large area, a rake head about 15 inches long will speed the job; for smaller areas or intricate patterns, choose a board half that length. To serrate the edge, cut V-shaped notches 1 $\frac{1}{4}$ inches deep and 1 $\frac{1}{4}$ inches wide. The rake will produce deeper grooves and more pronounced ridges if you deepen and square these indentations (inset). Nail a 4-foot pole to the board as a handle, strengthening it with braces positioned so the back of the rake can be used to smooth the gravel before making patterns.

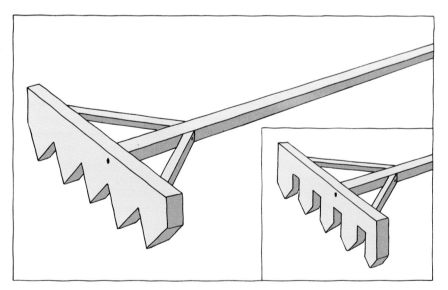

large enough it may contain one or more small islands or rocks representing islands. A waterfall and stream may link the hills with the pond, adding the musical sound of running water.

For a very small pond, really a reflecting pool, you can buy a shell of rigid plastic reinforced with glass-fiber mesh. Such shells come in irregular shapes up to about 12 feet long and are both durable and very easy to install. Try to find one that is dark gray or black; it will fit unobtrusively into the garden and give brilliant surface reflections with an illusion of considerable water depth. (Shadows cast on the water's surface by nearby rocks and plants also add to the illusion of depth.)

Almost as easy to install, and less expensive, is a flexible pool liner made of polyvinyl chloride (PVC) woven with nylon for greater strength. You can buy such a liner in almost any size; again, a dark color is best. Outline the pool you plan with a garden hose, then dig a bowl-shaped depression inside, sloping the sides to a depth of about a foot (at least 2 feet if you plan to have waterlilies or goldfish). Put the dark topsoil and the lighter-colored subsoil in separate piles for use in building mounds. Remove roots or stones that might puncture the plastic, smooth the bottom by bouncing a tire on it, then line it with an inch or so of sand. Stretch the liner tautly across the top, weighting its edges in place. Use the garden hose to fill the center of the liner with water, which will gradually stretch the plastic down and mold it to the hole's contours. When the pool is full, trim off excess plastic and conceal its edges with rocks and plants.

FLEXIBLE POOL LINERS

Subsoil and topsoil from the excavation can be used to build a mound behind or on one side of the pond. With rocks and plants added later, it becomes a natural setting for a small waterfall emptying into a stream that winds down to the pond. Such a system can be powered with a recirculating pump that uses the same water over and over, pumping it from the pond through concealed piping to the waterfall source. For a small installation, you may need only a submersible pump with a capacity of 200 or 300 gallons an hour. Set it in the pond, lead flexible plastic tubing to the waterfall source, then string the waterproof cable from the pump to a grounded electrical outlet and plug it in.

The appearance of the waterfall will depend on the volume of water supplied and the shape of the rock over which it drops. In front of a small collecting pool fed by the pump, a single rock is set to form the lip of the falls. A flat, smooth stone called a mirror stone creates a broad, sheetlike flow. Or you may choose a stone that has ridges and pockets to cause the water to sparkle and jump as it descends. One with a point projecting upward at the lip will divide the flow into two

SHAPING A WATERFALL

cascades. One with a deep V-shaped groove in its forward edge will funnel the water into a narrower, more powerful stream; if there is a large enough volume of water the stream will be pitched out from the rock to yield a foaming, glittering display.

In addition to the mirror stone, a classic Japanese waterfall has other specific rocks. Vertical flanking stones, one generally higher than the other, are set on either side, projecting to frame and contain the cascade. Two lower, smaller base stones are set like buttresses in front of the flanking stones. In the stream at the base of the falls may be a wave-dividing stone; it splits the water into still more agitated patterns. To look and sound like a waterfall, the cascade should drop in the clear for at least a foot. If the terrain permits, it can be several feet high or it may descend in many splashing steps.

To complete your miniature watercourse, you must make the stream bed waterproof. Its irregularities and the constantly moving water suggest the use of concrete. With the pump turned off, line the bed with 2 inches of coarse crushed rock, about an inch in diameter,

Raked designs for gravel gardens

The Japanese have used rakes to keep their gardens tidy since ancient times, but it was not until the Middle Ages that ingenious gardeners began to incorporate raked lines—left behind in pebbled ground covers—into the garden design.

Zen priests, who used the patterns to simulate water in their dry temple gardens, developed the corrugated art form to perfection. Some patterns are shown below; opposite are methods for inscribing designs on such gravel canvases.

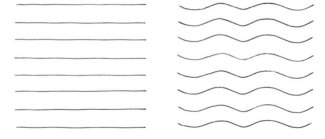

Raked patterns can be appreciated as abstract designs, but the Japanese traditionally use these designs to evoke watery settings. Straight lines represent calm water,

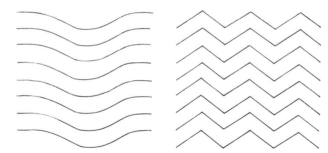

small waves suggest a gently flowing stream, and larger waves indicate fast-moving water or waves breaking. The zigzag pattern symbolizes a fish net cast across the sea.

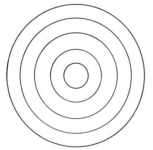

Among traditional patterns based on the circle are concentric circles, which represent either raindrops striking a pond or fish coming to the water's surface; a swirl

pattern, symbolizing a whirlpool, convenient for use in a confined space; and overlapping semicircles, which call to mind ocean waves or surf breaking on a rocky coast.

then dust on a layer of coarse sand that will sift among the stones to form a solid base. Firm this layer by tamping it with the butt end of a wooden post. On top of this base, pour about 2 inches of concrete, embedding 2-inch wire mesh in it for strength. Use a stiff mix of 1 part portland cement, 2 parts sharp builder's sand and 3 parts gravel by volume, mixed with just enough water to give a consistency that will stick to the sides of the stream bed. Trowel the mix into place on the bottom and up the sides of the bed. For a more natural look, you can press small river stones into the concrete while it is still soft; to get a good bond, soak the stones in a bucket of water so they will go in wet. Cover the finished stream bed with burlap or straw and keep it moist for a week to cure the concrete.

When this basic construction is finished, your Japanese garden will look distressingly like a cross between a rock pile and a waterworks. But this is only the skeleton of a garden, waiting to be fleshed out. It will take the final elements—trees, shrubs and other plants—to make your Japanese garden truly enchanting.

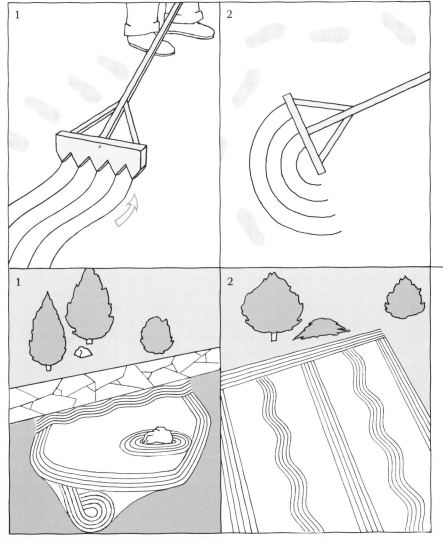

ETCHING ON GRAVEL

1. *Patterns are inscribed in coarse sand or fine gravel with a saw-toothed wooden rake (page 40). To make wavy patterns, pull the rake behind you over a level surface, applying pressure on one side, then on the other. Use the flat back of the rake to erase footprints.*

2. *To make a circular pattern, treat your rake like a compass, fixing one end tooth in place and pivoting the rake around it until the design is complete. For any pattern, begin at the garden's far edge.*

STYLING THE BORDERS

1. *The Japanese have developed a number of principles for using raked patterns. The garden at the far left suggests a body of water, and waves are placed where they would logically occur in nature, lapping against beaches and around a rock-bound island.*

2. *In the angular garden at near left, straight-lined patterns emphasize the rectangular lines and are placed to echo the garden's contours. Wavy central patterns contrast with the other designs. In both of the gardens, flat unraked areas serve as foils for patterned areas.*

Summoning up the sights and sounds of water

Water and stones are essential elements in a Japanese garden. The water can be real—dripping into a stone basin, burbling along a shallow, pebble-strewn stream, splashing into a pool fed by a waterfall. Or it can be merely suggested by an arrangement of raked gravel and stones, as in the sea of gravel opposite. But whether real or implied, water supplies the sense of cool tranquility so important to Japanese landscape design.

In these watery landscapes, stones of all sizes are used, from pea-sized gravel to boulders weighing several tons. Sometimes they define the watercourse, separating water from dry land. Sometimes, as in the gravel sea, they are symbols. Tall stones suggest cliffs and mountain peaks; two upright stones set closely together in a dry garden can suggest a waterfall. Low stones simulate hills and low mountains or, in a dry garden, islands. Small, smooth cobblestones may represent a waterworn beach or riverbed. This symbolism, however, is never intrusive: the stones are chosen and placed to look as though nature had put them there.

In the Western interpretations of Japanese water landscapes that appear on the following pages, these ideas about stones and water have been translated with remarkable fidelity. Although the gardens are foreign in concept, their economy and simplicity suits them well to American life styles. Many help solve landscaping problems, transforming a corridor garden at the side of a house, a backyard swamp or a city plot ringed with skyscrapers into a restful retreat. Even the top of an unused parking deck is reborn with the aid of a Japanese-style waterfall (page 48).

Typically, these gardens require almost no maintenance, for only a few species of plants are used in their designs. Flower beds, which require constant tending, are nonexistent, and dwarf evergreens keep pruning and autumn cleanup to a minimum. The dry gardens, of course, approach the ultimate goal in low-maintenance gardening, requiring only an occasional raking or even vacuuming to keep them as pristine as the day they were made.

Gravel, raked in wavelike patterns and studded with boulders, creates a tranquil seascape within sight of three high-rise apartment buildings in Philadelphia.

Only a suggestion

In a dry Japanese landscape, gravel and rocks are handled in various ways to suggest the presence of different kinds of water. For the illusion of a sea or large lake, for example, fine gravel is laid in an irregular shape and dotted with boulder islands; the sea's surface is then raked in patterns that suggest waves and whirlpools. For a pond, smooth round pebbles or cobbles are set close together on a bed of fine gravel, suggesting still water, while coarse gravel or elongated stones imply a rushing river or stream.

Boulders and the stark trunk of a Japanese black pine rise from the raked surface of a gravel garden in Seattle. Weighted wires on the pine's branches are training them to dip downward.

This dry garden follows the path of a former stream whose waters now flow through storm sewers. Rocks were added to intensify the feeling of a water course, and plants line the banks.

Creating the real thing

Whenever a pond, stream or pool appears in a Japanese garden, it must seem to be there naturally, without human intervention. A stream meanders, following the natural contours of the land, with pebbles and small rocks placed in its bed at key points to create eddies. A pond's concrete edges are disguised with rocks and plants, and perhaps with a flowering tree, trained to lean over its surface to cast its reflection onto the water. To accentuate this naturalism, the water's source is always indicated, frequently with a waterfall.

More than 65 tons of rocks were brought to the top of a concrete parking deck to create this small landscape whose interest is centered in two pools connected by a waterfall.

Japanese maples overhang the rocky banks of a man-made watercourse that consists of a 4-foot waterfall and two pools linked by rapids. The lower pool is stocked with carp.

A man-made stream flows between
smooth rocks toward a pond. Its right
bank is planted with azaleas, its left
with baby's tears, a flowering quince
and a tamarix juniper.

Natural streams supply the water
for this artificial pond carved from a
swamp. The massive glacial rocks
that edge the pool were already there,
but the evergreens were added.

Plants with an Oriental heritage 3

Not long ago an American lady returned from Japan where, like a lot of visitors to that country, she had fallen in love with the gardens. She longed to re-create some of their beauty back home, but despaired of finding the right Japanese plants. After poking around a couple of local nurseries, however, she was delighted to discover many of the very same species she had admired in their native habitat, plus a few others that, while not strictly Japanese, looked enough like Japanese equivalents to round out her theme.

Though the lady was agreeably surprised, her experience was not unusual. Thanks to the efforts of earlier visitors to Japan— amateur botanists and professional plant hunters—much of the country's rich flora is widely available in North America.

Many of the best varieties of these and other Japanese plants are included in the illustrated encyclopedia in Chapter 5 *(page 97)*. Most are readily obtainable, but remember that many native American plants are not much different from their Oriental cousins, and make perfectly acceptable substitutes. The inclusion of a few plants native to your region can, in fact, help to make the garden even more authentically Japanese. One of the cardinal principles of Japanese landscaping is that plants should blend into their surroundings: if a pine grove is seen over a garden wall in Kyoto or Osaka, the same kind of pine tree will almost invariably be included within.

Also, you do not need many plants to create a Japanese garden. The Japanese themselves frequently use only one or two species as major plantings, with one or two more for accents. It is not unusual to see a garden consisting of a single picturesque pine and a group of azaleas, with lots of empty space between the two. Actually, this empty space is important: it balances the weight of the plants, but more than that, it has an intriguing shape. A consciousness of the shape of space lies behind much of the intricate pruning Japanese gardeners practice on their plants *(pages 54, 56 and 59)*. In one kind

Westerners prize the Asiatic lotus for its serene beauty, but the flower has additional significance in the Orient. Buddhists view the flower's rise from the mud as a symbol of spiritual ascent and purity.

of pruning, for example, the intention is to open up the tree or shrub so that layers of space are visible between its branches. The space is there to enhance the natural shape of the branch—but it is also there for itself alone.

Of all the plants in a Japanese garden, the most basic are the evergreens; along with rocks and water these provide the garden's framework. Indeed, some traditionalists feel that as much as three quarters of the garden should be made up of material of this kind. Not only do evergreens shape the garden through the year but their darker presence provides a backdrop for the lighter, brighter colors of flowering plants and autumn foliage. A predominantly evergreen garden need not, however, be monochromatic. Evergreen species differ in color from yellow-green to blue-green and even almost black, and in addition offer the seasonal colors of bright green needles and cones in spring, with—in some species—the reds and smoky blues of fall berries.

UBIQUITOUS BLACK PINES

In most Japanese gardens the unchallenged evergreen favorite is the Japanese black pine, widely considered the best of trees. A native of the coastal regions of the windswept Japanese islands, the black pine has stiff-needled, dark green foliage, deeply fissured black bark and a bold, often dramatically irregular, habit of growth. These characteristics give it, in Japanese eyes, a rugged masculine

ROUNDING A SHRUB, TAMAZUKURI FASHION

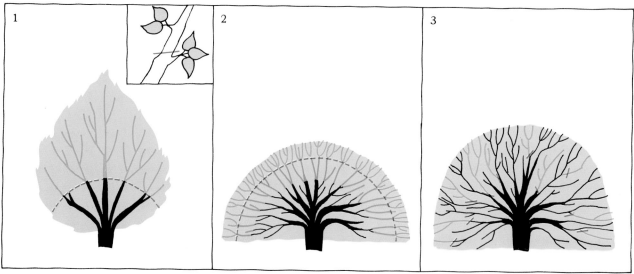

To make a low, evenly rounded mound from a shrub such as an azalea or privet, first cut back the shrub to half its height (dashed line) in early spring or after it flowers. Cut each branch just above a node (inset).

Prune or pinch back new growth each spring to keep the shrub's shape. Leave one or two new buds, leaves or leaf clusters on each branch. If the shrub is growing vigorously, prune it another time in late autumn.

In four or five years, when a shrub becomes so filled with small branches that air no longer circulates freely and light does not penetrate, thin by cutting back as many as a third of the branches (red bars).

appearance. In traditional Japanese design it is often the center of interest in a dry-landscape garden or in a pond garden, set on a peninsula where its misshapen branches overhang the water.

Another great favorite is the Japanese red pine, which takes its name, like the black pine, from its bark color—a dusky orange-red. Slender, softer-looking and more difficult to grow than the black pine, it is considered a feminine tree and is often used as a foil to the black pine's masculinity. In classic gardens the two were often planted together around the edge of a pond. One particularly popular variety of the red pine, the Tanyosho pine, is a picturesque tree with a low, broad, flat-topped shape. Left to grow naturally, it reaches a height of 10 feet, but with pruning it can be kept shorter and its height and breadth roughly equal.

DWARFS AMONG THE CEDARS

Along with the pines, the mainstays of a classic Japanese garden are the cryptomerias, or Japanese cedars. These tall, stately conical trees, long valued for their aromatic wood, also come in smaller and even dwarf versions that are much more appropriate to garden use. The cedars have small, dense, blue-green needles that can be trimmed and pruned into rounded, decorative shapes, and in winter, given the right mix of weather conditions, the foliage turns a bronze green.

Similar to the cedars in general appearance, but with different foliage, are the false cypresses. These too are narrow conical trees that normally grow quite tall but are available in a number of smaller and dwarf varieties. The foliage of the false cypresses is glossy and scalelike, sheathing branches that grow in cupped and twisted sprays, playing lively tricks with light and shadow. One of the most desirable species is the dwarf Hinoki false cypress, which seldom grows more than 4 feet tall and has dense, dark green foliage. Sawara false cypresses are also popular, combining compact size with unusual foliage; in some versions the needles are threadlike and have gold-colored tips.

Other needled evergreen trees frequently found in Japanese gardens are the slow-growing and often picturesquely branching yews, in both their upright and spreading dwarf forms, and the related podocarpus, with its dense, pendulous branches. Finally there are the junipers, which in Japan, as in America, are used not only as trees but as shrubs, and in their low-growing, creeping varieties, as ground covers.

DECIDUOUS TREASURES

In contrast to the evergreen trees, which dominate the Japanese garden and give it an aura of permanence, deciduous trees provide more transient pleasures. They are used for their distinctive foliage and flowers, and for the tracery of their bare winter branches,

Points on pruning pines

Most pine trees form tiers of branches that radiate from their trunks like wheel spokes. As a tree matures, the weaker branches of each tier break off or die because of wind, snow, insect attacks or lack of sunlight. Thus the tree gradually trades its Christmas-tree shape for a weatherworn, asymmetrical one.

Japanese gardeners prefer the aged, asymmetrical shape, which they consider visually more interesting. They prune young trees to encourage and hasten such shaping. Pruning also controls the size of the tree. Initially the tree looks denuded, with only thin tufts of needles on each branch. But after several years, the foliage thickens until each bough becomes a heavy, dense mound of needles fanning out in clusters.

WHERE AND WHEN TO CUT

1. *To prune a pine tree in the Japanese style, remove all weak or unwanted branches (red bars), spacing the branches to keep one from shading another directly below it. Ideally, viewed from above (inset), the lowest branches will receive as much sunlight as the upper branches. Retain a branch emerging from any outer curve in the trunk. Branches that need shaping or slowed growth can be anchored parallel to the ground.*

2. *Prune all branchlets that point down (red bars). A sparse branch needs no further pruning (inset, left) but if many branchlets exist, remove those that point straight up as well as down (inset, right).*

3. *Each spring, when the candles of new growth are about five inches long, snap off the top half of each vertical candle and the top third of each horizontal one (red bars). Remove all that point downward.*

4. *To keep the pine looking as if it were carrying clouds of needles, repeat the candle pruning every spring. Remove any branchlets that crowd a branch or grow too rapidly (inset). Keep the desired shape in mind as you prune.*

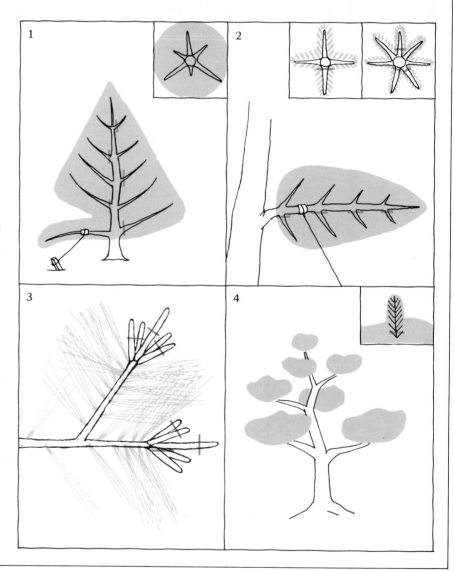

which decorate the snowy landscape with calligraphic patterns—and also let in sunlight when it is most welcome.

Outstanding among the Japanese deciduous trees are the maples—small, slow-growing, with graceful shapes and delicately cut leaves. The true Japanese maple has star-pointed leaves that are red in the spring, green in the summer and orange-red again in the fall. But over the centuries the Japanese have developed hundreds of different varieties. Some remain red throughout the growing season; others are gold or pale pink fading to almost pure white, and in many varieties the leaves are variegated. Among the most exotic are the threadleaf maples, with leaves so deeply cut they resemble lace. One of the laciest of them, *Acer palmatum dissectum atropurpureum*—surely one of horticulture's grandest names—has red-purple leaves that turn brilliant crimson in the fall; its apt common name is Red Lace Leaf Maple

The color of maple foliage is so important to the Japanese that they go to elaborate lengths to help nature along. They have discovered, for instance, that an ideal spot to achieve the most beautiful reds is a bright spot near a pond, where the air is humid and the soil is always slightly moist, because moisture, soil acidity and sunlight enhance the hue. Lacking a pond, they place the trees in a depression, where the soil dries out less rapidly than it does on a rise; and in the heat of the summer they mist the delicate twigs daily. Since the best reds also result from exposing the tree to the maximum day and minimum night temperatures, they place maples where they get the morning sun, to warm them, but are shaded from the afternoon sun, whose heat would be likely to linger on in the leaves past sunset.

Other deciduous trees included in Japanese gardens for their colorful foliage are the ginkgo and Japanese ash, whose leaves turn clear gold in the fall; and the Japanese zelkova—a disease-resistant relative of the American elm—whose autumn foliage is a soft apricot color. Also grown for its splendid color is the katsura tree, whose leaves are purple when young and in the fall turn scarlet and yellow. But the katsura grows so tall, 50 feet high, that it is seldom used in any but the largest gardens. Another tree admired for its color but used infrequently is the weeping willow, whose distinctive drooping foliage is yellow in the spring and again in the fall. But the tree grows so fast and its roots are so invasive that they must be pruned annually to keep them within bounds. Also, in Japan the weeping willow's swaying branches are associated by impressionable youngsters with ghosts, so thoughtful gardeners, out of courtesy, often refrain from using them.

To many gardeners, Japanese or otherwise, the most colorful of the Japanese deciduous trees are those that flower in the spring. And probably the most breathtaking of these spring-flowering trees are the cherries. After centuries of crossbreeding, some 200 varieties exist, with blossoms ranging in color from white to deep pink, and in shape from single whorls of petals to ball-shaped multipetaled types. One of the best known is the early-blooming Yoshino cherry, whose annual display brings thousands of tourists to Washington, D.C., each spring, and also inspires cherry-viewing festivals in Kyoto and other cities in Japan. Another favorite is the Kwanzan cherry, which has masses of deep-pink flowers that bloom along upright branches resembling the outstretched fingers of a hand. And for its many admirers, there is nothing to match the weeping Higan cherry, with its graceful drooping branches and light-pink flowers.

THE SPRINGTIME BLOOMS

Other spring-flowering trees cherished by Japanese gardeners include Japanese apricots and crab apples, which belong to the same genus as the cherries, as well as the flowering quinces and the Kousa dogwood. The latter puts forth clouds of large white blossoms about a month later than its American cousin, followed by large red berries, resembling raspberries, that are relished by birds. And though most magnolias are too tall and boldly florid for Japanese tastes, one exception is the star magnolia, a slow-growing tree of moderate size that bears fragrant, delicately petaled flowers and has dense, dark green foliage that turns bronze yellow in autumn.

Just as numerous as the choice of trees for a Japanese garden is the choice of shrubs. Many of them are simply low-growing versions of the popular Japanese evergreen trees—yews, junipers, cryptomerias, false cypresses. But a far greater number are broad-leaved evergreens—Japanese boxwoods, hollies, barberries, aucubas, ardisias, fatsias, andromedas and gardenias. Probably the one most frequently used is the evergreen azalea, particularly the azaleas that have small leaves and grow naturally in dense, compact forms. Unlike Western gardeners, however, who grow azaleas for their riot of color, Japanese gardeners traditionally use them architecturally. They shear them into soft mounds that suggest the contours of hills, mountains, rocks or the waves of the sea.

SMALL SHRUBS AND LARGE

Deciduous shrubs also have their place in the Japanese garden. Like deciduous trees, they are used primarily as counterpoints to the evergreens, to provide the seasonal color of flowers and autumn foliage. Many of them are familiar to Western gardeners—forsythia, kerria, viburnum, spirea, hawthorn, winter hazel and witch hazel, to name just a few. But the Japanese species tend to be more modest in size and bloom than hybridized Western varieties. One exception is the Japanese tree peony, a plant whose history goes back to the time when it was cultivated only in temple gardens. The silky flowers of the tree peony have been hybridized into single- and double-flowered forms of magnificent size, as much as 5 inches across, in an incredible range of subtle colorings—pink, white, ruby red, magenta, rose, yellow, salmon.

Another group of distinctively Oriental plants that are often used in counterpoint to the evergreens are the bamboos. These giant grasses with their vertical lines and airy foliage make perfect foils for the evergreens' dense-spreading branches. But the Japanese love them for many other reasons as well. They like the contrast of their foliage against rocks and their reflections mirrored in still water.

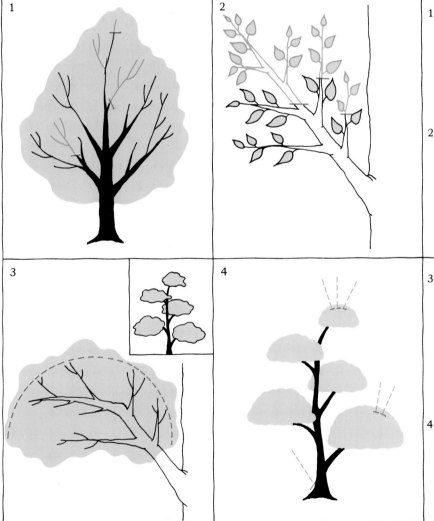

BROAD-LEAVED PRUNING

1. *To prune a broad-leaved evergreen tree such as a Japanese photinia in the Japanese style, cleanly cut off weak or unwanted branches at the trunk or at a branching point (red bars). Cut off the tree's central leader to control its height and thicken its trunk.*

2. *In order to encourage horizontal branching, cut back the branch to an outward-facing branchlet. Then cut back all vertical branchlets so that you have only two or three leaves remaining on each.*

3. *To shape foliage on branches of small-leaved trees into the decorative mounds known as tamazukuri, in early spring shear the top of each branch into an oval shape (dashed line). If the leaves are large or if you wish to shape the branches into uneven and more naturalistic mounds (inset), prune only the strong vertical shoots.*

4. *Maintain the shape of the tree by removing any suckers that sprout from the base of the tree or from branches. Cut back runaway vertical shoots so they are ½ inch below the oval outline of the mound.*

They delight in the rustling sound their leaves make in the wind and the shadows they cast against rice-paper shoji screens. In spring they cut the edible young shoots, which are considered great delicacies, and in fall they harvest the full-grown canes to use for fences and household goods, knowing this keeps the bamboo from overwhelming the garden.

CONTROLLING BAMBOO

Bamboos are in fact very vigorous plants. A shoot of one variety has been known to add as much as 4 feet a day to its height, and the running bamboos, which spread horizontally by means of underground stems, will send up shoots, which the Japanese call "bamboo children," as much as 100 feet away. The latter type must often be cordoned off by planting it inside some sort of barricade—a section of concrete pipe, a chimney flue or, for larger groupings, a barrier of 18-inch-wide plastic or galvanized metal buried in the earth like a subterranean fence.

The Japanese sometimes plant dwarf bamboos like *Sasa pygmaea* as ground covers, a category of plants that plays an even more important role in Japanese garden design than it does in America. Unlike American gardeners, however, the Japanese seldom blanket expanses of ground with low-growing plants, preferring instead to use them selectively, in small areas, as a contrast for the grittiness of gravel, for example, or as a naturalizing element against the base of a rock or the edge of a pond. Tucked around shrubs, they also hide bare, weak-looking stems. But what they do best is make the transition from trees or shrubs to the ground seem less abrupt.

One of the most popular ground covers in Japan is aspidistra, because it grows in shade and because its stiff bladelike leaves are a favorite plant material for *ikebana* arrangements. Other choices for shade that are more familiar to American gardeners are ferns, Japanese spurge—better known as pachysandra—and asarum, or wild ginger, which has shiny, heart-shaped leaves. For sunny locations the Japanese use nandina, blue flags and bellflowers. But the classic Japanese ground cover is moss. In one famous garden designed in Kyoto in the 13th Century, more than 20 different kinds of moss carpet the ground in cloud patterns ranging in color from emerald green to a deep rich bronze.

THE BEAUTY OF MOSS

Mosses can be a lovely addition to the garden—sheathing the trunks of trees, softening the contours of stones, simulating the dry bed of an old watercourse. But incorporating them into an American garden is not always easy. In Japan, where the climate is humid, mosses grow naturally, but in most parts of the United States they must be constantly misted and watered. In addition, few American nurseries carry mosses. For most gardeners the simplest solution to both problems is to use a mosslike substitute whose needs are less demanding. Two that are readily available are moss sandwort, also called Irish moss, a low-growing evergreen ground cover with needle-like foliage that can be grown in full sun and light shade, and a similar plant, *Pyxidanthera barbulata,* commonly called—although it is not a moss—flowering moss.

Since many true mosses are native to North America, however, you might want to try collecting and transplanting the real thing from the wild. First make note of the conditions under which it is growing—in soil, on a rock, in sun or partial shade. Then lift it by sliding a knife blade or spatula underneath the matted growth and gently pry it up. Place the clumps in a container large enough to hold them flat, and cover them with a moistened newspaper. Replant them as soon as possible. If they are to grow in soil, scratch the soil surface and set each clump in place, pressing it down firmly. If they are to grow on a rock, mix up a mudlike slurry of garden soil and smear this over the rock; then press the moss onto it.

Mosses spread rapidly once established and if they are laid checkerboard fashion, with spaces between clumps, the gaps should soon be filled. For a while, until new growth appears, water the moss several times a day. After it is established, water it only when a loss of fresh green color indicates it is suffering from drought. Keep dead

TRANSPLANTING WILD MOSS

BRANCH-BENDING TECHNIQUES

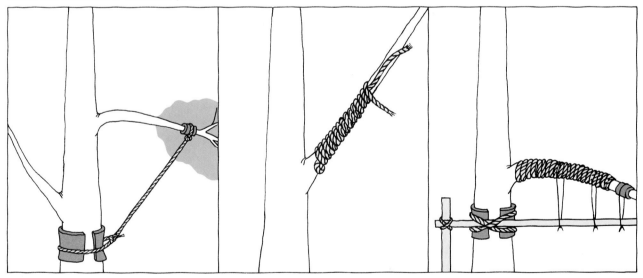

To train a tree's branch to grow horizontally, anchor it with a rope to its trunk or to a stake in the ground. Use a pad from a tire or hose to avoid cutting into the bark. Branches may need two to four years of anchoring.

To keep bark from separating when a branch is bent on a sappy tree, first wrap the branch with rope. Place the rope along the branch, stretching it toward the trunk, then wrap both branch and rope. Tie the loose ends.

Gently bend the wrapped branch toward the ground. While a helper is holding the branch, tie it at intervals to a support, then tie the support to the trunk. If added strength is needed, brace the support with a vertical post.

leaves off the surface, as these smother the plants. But in winter, if the moss is exposed to drying winds, cover it with a temporary layer of straw or pine needles, as the Japanese do.

Finally, in planning your Japanese garden, you may want to consider some plants not normally associated with Japanese landscaping. Vines are an example; the Japanese in fact frequently use vines as a decorative covering for fences and walls, just as Western gardeners do, and they also train them over rustic garden structures of bamboo or weathered wood—arbors and pergolas fitted with benches for pleasant sitting. Japanese and Chinese wisteria are favorite vines for this purpose, but also used are Japanese versions of akebia, bittersweet, clematis, honeysuckle and jasmine.

You may also wish to consider a few flowering annuals and perennials. As a class, these colorful plants are generally relegated to cutting gardens in Japan, where their evanescent beauty can be plucked at its peak for indoor flower arrangements. But there are exceptions. A major one is the Japanese iris, less flamboyant than its Western cousins but remarkable for its rich blues and purples and the purity of its whites. Few Japanese gardens that include any sort of water are without an iris or two growing at the water's edge, and in dry-landscape gardens they are often similarly used, to make the illusion of water more real. One variety, the *Iris kaempferi,* which is naturally dry when dormant, is usually grown in containers and removed from the garden for winter storage. But the smaller *Iris laviegata,* a bog plant by nature, is left in the garden all year round.

MAINTENANCE CHORES
Once established, the plants in a Japanese garden will require much the same kind of maintenance that they do in any other garden. However, since the accent is on permanence, there will be far less of the usual flower-bed tending, and the use of mulches, gravels and ground covers will reduce the weeding chore. You may have to water the garden occasionally in periods of drought, and perhaps feed the plants—though too much fertilizer will defeat your purpose; Japanese plants should be kept in scale. Indeed, the main chore will probably be pruning.

The true Japanese gardener prunes not only to keep his plants neat and well-proportioned but to bring out their inherent beauty, to emphasize the character of a particular plant, to reveal the grace of its branches silhouetted against the sky or dipping toward the surface of a pond. And you will be pruning to sculpt the plant to suit the garden's overall design.

The Japanese have many pruning techniques, most of them centuries old. Evergreens, for example, are often pruned in horizontal layers, opening up spaces between their branches so the structure of the tree and the laciness of its foliage are revealed. Black pines are often pruned to accentuate their rugged, wind-buffeted shapes, nandinas to emphasize their delicacy, crape myrtles to complement their roundness. Pruning of this kind not only enhances the tree's appearance but improves its health, by admitting light to the lower branches. Pruning also allows sunlight to reach plants growing beneath the tree. And in some cases it introduces a view of the moon or a distant mountain through the branches.

SLOWING THE GROWTH RATE

Intensified naturalness is the purpose of this kind of pruning, but sometimes liberties are taken. For instance, the Japanese will often slow a vertical branch's growth by training it to move laterally, either by tying it to stakes below the branch, or by attaching stones to the midpoint of the branch, forcing it to grow outward.

The ultimate goal of all these pruning techniques is a kind of airy grace. But the Japanese also practice another sort of pruning whose goal is bushiness. Called *tamazukuri,* meaning "making round," its intention is to capitalize on the natural density and compactness of a tree or shrub. The customary forms of *tamazukuri* are low, rounded and cushiony—and they can be, despite their small size, the garden's strongest design element. Sometimes these tuffet shapes echo and accentuate the shapes of nearby stones, sometimes they soften the ragged edges of rocks. Often a series of them, diminishing in size across the garden, suggest a view of mountains receding into the horizon.

THE RIGHT TIME TO PRUNE

All of these various forms of pruning have their appropriate subjects, but there are certain general rules that apply to all plants. The best time to prune is generally right after the leaves fall, when you can see the structure of the branches better. Especially to be avoided is spring pruning of plants like dogwoods and maples, which bleed profusely if cut when their sap is rising. Similarly, flowering plants that bloom on the current year's growth should ideally be pruned in the late fall, so as not to interfere with the formation of new buds. On the other hand, plants like forsythia and azalea, which form flower buds in the preceding year, should be pruned as soon as possible after the flowers have faded.

Having chosen your plants and trained them to fit into the context of Japanese garden design, you may find them yielding some unexpected dividends. This is especially true if you live in a cold climate. The Japanese say that a garden blooms twice—the second time in winter, when the pond is frozen and snow settles gently on branches, leaves and rocks. And indeed, the serenity of a Japanese garden is never more apparent than it is in the quiet hours of a snowy January dawn.

Fascinating immigrants from the Far East

The beauty of Japanese plants—from the satiny shimmer of a camellia to the gnarled elegance of a Japanese black pine—has fascinated Western gardeners for centuries. As early as 1694, Engelbert Kaempfer, a German doctor and naturalist with the Dutch East India Company, returned from Japan with a collection of azaleas, camellias and tree peonies that stunned botanists in Europe. Kaempfer gathered his plants surreptitiously and at great personal risk, for shoguns sharply watched the movements of early European traders and explorers. One plant collector was thrown out of Japan for obtaining maps of the islands. Other collectors were in mortal danger of encountering the daimio, feudal princes who believed it their patriotic duty to kill foreigners.

Despite such obstacles, a slow but steady stream of plants trickled from Japan into Europe and eventually across the Atlantic. That trickle became a flood after Commodore Matthew Perry appeared in Tokyo Bay with American warships in 1853, forcing Japan to open trade with the West. Japanese bamboos, azaleas, hydrangeas, hostas, evergreens, lilies, peonies and flowering fruit trees all found adopted homes overseas. Today many Western gardeners regard these plants as native, using them liberally in landscapes without realizing their Japanese origins. The camellia *(opposite)*, for example, has become so entwined with the folklore of the American South that its Japanese heritage (camellias first arrived in America about 1820) is all but forgotten.

When choosing plants for a Japanese-style garden, look first among authentic imports, such as those that appear on the following pages. But keep variety to a minimum. Many Japanese gardens contain only one or two species of plants; a simple stand of evergreens shading a lichen-covered rock is sufficient to suggest a temple garden. Remember too that a plant should suit its surroundings. A tree with a rough, weathered appearance, such as a Japanese black pine, should be grown in a garden that reflects a rugged mountainside or seashore—not a calm woodland glen.

*The plump flower of the camellia symbolized happiness in
ancient Japan to everyone but the samurai, who saw in the
short life of the flower intimations of their own mortality.*

Blushes of color

Bowing to the Oriental tradition of simplicity and subtlety in landscape design, Japanese gardeners use colorful shrubs sparingly as seasonal accents. First come the fiery spring flowers of azaleas and Japanese quince, followed by the beautiful summer blooms of crape myrtle and hibiscus. In autumn, chrysanthemums spill showers of color from stone pots, while shrubs like nandina show off their scarlet berries. Winter shifts the emphasis to decorative evergreen foliage, such as the speckled leaves of Japanese aucuba.

Several Kurume azaleas, first introduced into America in 1915, frame a man-made waterfall. The azaleas are pruned low to emphasize the restfulness of their spreading forms.

Tree peonies, such as this double-flowered species, are traditionally grown in a sand or rock garden.

The brilliant autumn berries of evergreen nandina last into winter's snows, attracting hungry birds.

In early spring, a Japanese quince blazes with red-orange blossoms. The fruit is small, green and hard.

A Japanese aucuba displays the speckled leaves that earned this shrub its nickname: gold-dust tree.

Seasonal favorites

Japanese landscape architects traditionally add one or two deciduous trees to a garden, valuing them for their flowers and foliage. Treasured above all others are the cherry, whose blossoms are Japan's national flower; the cutleaf maple, whose orange leaves warm the autumn landscape; and the apricot, whose early blossoms are a harbinger of spring. Cherries, which are thought to look best in first light, are often placed where the rising sun shines through their fragile petals; maples where the noonday sun sets their leaves aglow.

*Two autumnal cutleaf maples complement each other across
a sea of gravel and fallen leaves. One is pruned symmetrically,
the other asymmetrically, its shape balanced by rocks.*

*A weeping Higan cherry tree hangs a curtain of blooms
over a hillside. To better appreciate the blossoms, the Japanese
may train trees in shrine gardens to arching trellises.*

The ageless evergreens

Evergreens predominate in Japanese gardens, their year-round beauty evoking a soothing sense of timelessness. They serve mainly as background plants, but some are singled out for ornamental pruning. Those with fascinating shapes, like the tender bamboo *(pages 72-73)*, technically an evergreen, and the rugged black pine, are pruned to emphasize their natural silhouettes. Others with dense foliage are clipped into tight rounded shapes, representing such landscape elements as boulders, clouds or distant hills.

Standing out in stark relief against the white and gray of winter, a black pine (foreground) exudes the windswept strength that earned it the Japanese nickname, "man tree."

*Pruned in a Japanese style called tamazukuri, the rounded,
cushion-like shapes of these junipers carry the eye across
a garden to its far sides as if they were visual steppingstones.*

A clump of black bamboo, thinned and stripped of lower foliage, reveals shiny canes. The Japanese prize bamboo for its grace, for the rustling sound it makes in the wind and for the shadows it casts on rice-paper screens.

Delicate finishing touches 4

In many Japanese gardens, a pleasing composition of natural materials—plants, rocks and water—is all that is needed to make a satisfying design. Indeed, the addition of anything else to a small garden or one with spare lines could damage the serenity that every Japanese garden should evoke. There are, however, a few manmade elements that can make such a garden more useful and enjoyable if they are introduced with imagination and restraint.

Some of these are practical as well as esthetic. Paths, steppingstones and bridges let you stroll through the garden and enjoy it close-up. Fences or walls offer privacy while providing a backdrop for a garden's featured elements. Certain traditional Japanese accessories like stone lanterns light the way at night while emitting a welcoming glow. And finally, simple shelters recall the Japanese motif of the teahouse and also provide pleasant places to relax.

Paths in a Japanese garden are not laid out on the straight and narrow as a means of getting from place to place. Like the other elements, they are intended to offer esthetic experiences in themselves. Their materials are chosen carefully and related to the surroundings; paths are laid out to add contrasting textures and colors to the composition and to choreograph movement, luring the stroller to explore, stopping him at one place to admire a handsome tree, at another to look into a pond or listen to water trickling.

Paths can be made of such familiar materials as crushed stone, gravel, wood chips or shredded bark. But those in classic Japanese gardens are almost always arrangements of stones—either the wandering steppingstones called *tobi-ishi* or a wider ribbon of cut-stone pavement called *nobedan*.

Steppingstones, as contrasted with paths worn in bare earth, were introduced in the 16th Century as an essential part of the teahouse garden. They led the visitor from the entrance through a narrow wooded passageway to a rustic stone water basin, where he

Shaped like memorial reliquaries found in Buddhist temples of the Far East, this stone pagoda is displayed in a Long Island garden as a waterside ornament. Black-pine boughs temper the dramatic shape.

performed ritual ablutions, then on to the small teahouse itself. The stones kept his clogs or slippers clean as they slowed his pace.

Paths engaged more and more of the Japanese landscaper's interest, and certain conventions of design emerged. In time, each path became a work of art, expressing a character and vitality all its own. Even a short path was made lively by varying the size of the stones and using them in rhythmic groups. A set might follow a 1-2 pattern of single stones alternating with two stones placed close together. Or a staggered pattern such as 1-1-2, 1-2-1, 2-2-1 or 2-3 might be used. Still other sets arranged stones in sweeping curves or angled them in zigzag patterns like the wild-goose setting or the plover setting, named after the flying patterns of the birds.

SELECTING STEPPINGSTONES

The steppingstones of some classic Japanese gardens are imposing indeed: massive rocks that rise several inches above the ground and are sunk as much as a foot into it. But for a contemporary gardener working alone, such stones are hard to find and move. Also, they are likely to be out of scale in a modern garden. It is enough to find reasonably flat, medium-sized stones of a single, durable kind of rock or to settle for cut stones sold at building-supply yards. The stones should be at least 18 inches in diameter to accommodate a stroller's foot and at least 3 inches thick; they can then be embedded in the ground on tamped soil to prevent tipping but will protrude enough to be visible and keep shoes dry. The spacing of stones can be varied, but to make walking easy, stones should not be more than 4 or 5 inches apart. The easiest way to determine spacing is to walk casually over the course, noting where your feet fall *(opposite)*.

SLOWING THE PACE

When planning a path, remember that an irregular or curving course leading from one point of interest to another will create a leisurely mood and make the garden seem larger. If the path's far end is hidden by plantings, that too will suggest that the garden is larger than can be seen at a glance. At points of emphasis—a stopping place with a special view, a change of direction at a curve, an intersection of two paths—set a larger stone, 2 feet or more in diameter. To make your pattern even, place major stones first, then work outward, linking them with smaller stones until the path is completed. Set most of the stones with their longest dimension crossing the path; this provides an unhurried look and makes it easier to fit the stones into a pattern around a curve. Try to give each stone some relationship to its neighbors; a stone with an indentation in its leading edge, for example, can nest visually with one that has a protuberance on its facing edge.

If the stones are heavy, you can simply dig a shallow hole for

Pathways struck in stone

Over the centuries, the Japanese have developed steppingstone paths in a wide range of styles. Whatever the style, some practical considerations apply in laying it out. For safety, choose flat or slightly convex stones that will not trap water. Make certain the rocks are thick enough to rest solidly in the earth and wide enough to accommodate a foot easily. Then, for comfortable strolling, let your own gait be your guide to the stones' placement.

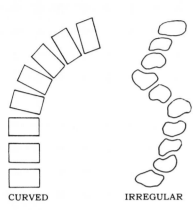

CURVED

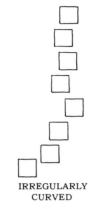

IRREGULAR

IRREGULARLY CURVED

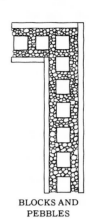

BLOCKS AND STONES

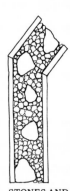

BLOCKS AND PEBBLES

STONES AND PEBBLES

LAYING STEPPINGSTONES

1. *To add a steppingstone path to your garden, plan a route leading to close-up views of choice plants or rocks. Drive stakes at convenient intervals and connect them, using powdered chalk or twine. Remove a strip of turf twice as wide as the stones you have chosen; add more soil if necessary and tamp it down.*

2. *To make footprints visible, scatter sand over the path, then walk down the path several times at a leisurely pace, always beginning at the same point. Circle where your footprints cluster. Cut paper patterns shaped like your stones and put them over the circles. If the spacing seems satisfactory, set the stones in place.*

3. *Outline the first stone's shape in the soil, remove the stone and dig a hole to fit. After you have laid two or three stones in their holes, lay a board across them, adding or removing dirt under each until all are level and at the same height, projecting at least 2 inches above the surrounding soil.*

4. *With all stones in place, tamp soil in around the stones with a stick. Spray with a hose to clean the rocks and settle the soil.*

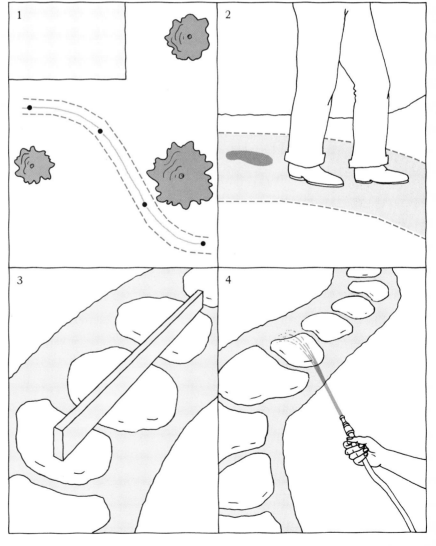

An ancient Japanese device— originally used to frighten deer and wild boars away from gardens— produces such a pleasantly surprising thump that it is a fixture in many modern gardens. The shika odoshi (deer scare) is a bamboo pipe that pivots, seesaw-fashion, over a support. One end rests on a stone or wood block; the other is a reservoir that slowly fills with water until the weight of the liquid forces the pipe to tilt, spilling its contents. Once empty, the shika odoshi springs back to its original position, producing a hollow thump as it strikes the block.

each, twisting the stone and adding handfuls of soil that you tamp in with a stick until the stone is solidly set. But such bedding will be easier and more reliable if you excavate an extra inch to make space for a layer of coarse builder's sand. In colder climate zones, if you have a poorly drained area, you may need to protect the stones against frost heaving by digging 4 inches down and putting in a 3-inch layer of crushed rock or gravel before topping with sand. If steppingstones cross a ground cover of gravel, as in a dry-landscape garden, set the stones on sand so their tops will be about an inch above the surrounding surface when the gravel is raked into place.

For wider paths that will let you walk without paying so much attention to where you place your feet—an entrance walk, for example, or a terrace paralleling the back wall of the house—you can use one of the many patterns of inlaid-rock or cut-stone pavement that the Japanese call a *nobedan*. This can be a pattern of steppingstones and smaller cobbles bordered by cut-stone edging, steppingstones combined with pairs of long rectangular offset stones, irregular or square-cut flagstones, precast concrete paving blocks, roof tiles set on edge, or almost any combination of these.

Since the masonry units of a *nobedan* are heavy, they will stay in place if you simply lay them on a bed of tamped soil or sand. Butt them together with narrow joints filled with more soil or sand, spread with a broom and washed into the cracks with the fine spray from a hose. Start with the larger units and those along the edges, then fill in gaps with smaller stones. Use stakes, string and a carpenter's level to keep the paving straight-edged and of uniform height.

In setting stones of the *nobedan*, compose the path's sides first. Place each edging stone so it maintains a straight outer edge in relationship to the stone before it. As you fill in the center, keep the width of the joints between stones roughly consistent.

If a path intersects a stream bed, either wet or dry, you can cross it with steppingstones. Choose bulky stones that are flat enough to step on, broad enough to remain securely in place and tall enough to match the level of the path on either side. Or you can build a bridge. To look as if it belongs in the garden, a bridge should be located at a logical place—where a path crosses a stream or where peninsulas reach toward each other from the edges of a pond.

Keep the bridge unobtrusive and in scale with the rest of the garden. The high-arched, red-lacquered bridges sometimes associated with Japanese gardens, are, in fact, Chinese in origin. Most Japanese garden bridges are low and simple in design, made of unpainted natural materials such as stone slabs or wooden planks. They are designed so they can be appreciated both from a distance and while they are being used. Such a bridge is always built at an angle to the major view, to give an illusion of greater garden depth and also to make it possible to see the span and supports in relation to the pond or stream bed below. Views from the bridge are also taken into account; some bridges zigzag casually across to prolong the stroll with a fresh glimpse of the garden at each turn.

One of the simplest, most dramatic bridges is nothing more than a single, massive slab of stone, either natural or cut. In Japan, a cut slab is sometimes shaped into a subtle arching curve. A slab bridge is laid over a narrow part of a stream bed and is imbedded in either bank, supported by other rocks. There are no handrails so warning stones are usually set at each corner of the bridge. Imitation stone bridges can easily be made of concrete. A shallow wooden form, flat or slightly arched, is built so it will be connected at each corner with holes dug for foundation piers. Then concrete is poured for slab and piers. The sideboards can be left in place and stained a dark color or removed after the concrete has hardened. The bottom boards are almost invisible and can be left in place.

A ROCK FOR A BRIDGE

Even easier to build is a bridge made entirely of wood. For crossing a small stream you can use one strong plank—a length of 2-by-12 or 3-by-12 unfinished redwood, cedar or other rot-resistant wood, or a long piece of construction timber treated with a preservative. Place the plank with at least 18 inches imbedded in either bank. To make a wider, more substantial span, use a pair of 2-by-10s or 2-by-12s set side by side. Nail two or three crosspieces on the undersides. Longer, more elaborate bridges can be built by sinking pairs of preservative-treated wood pilings into the stream bed to hold two or more spans. Bolt crosspieces to these pilings 6 inches below their tops, then nail planks on the crosspieces.

A more rustic bridge can be made of peeled or unpeeled logs. Lay a pair of strong young tree trunks 2 or 3 feet apart so they stretch from bank to bank. Across them, nail shorter logs or half-logs butted together to form a corduroy span. The bridge can be left this way or turned into an earth bridge, a *dobashi,* by attaching side pieces of more logs, timbers or tied reeds, then topping the walkway with a few inches of mixed soil and gravel tamped into place.

MAKING AN EARTH BRIDGE

The same kind of pilings that support long bridges can also retain banks under bridges and around the edges of ponds. Rot-resistant posts of cedar or redwood are cut to even or uneven lengths, sharpened at one end, butted together and driven into the ground. Soil is then filled in behind the miniature sea wall they form.

Enclosures in the Japanese garden are regarded with the same creative eye as pathways and bridges and are of equal importance in the design. In Japan space is very limited, so houses and gardens are closely integrated. Enclosures define outdoor areas, provide privacy and filter out distracting views and sounds. This is done in a variety of ways—with screens of trees, tall hedges, mounds of earth, sometimes masonry walls. Next to a living screen, the most common and practical solution is to build a fence, and the Japanese have raised fence building to the level of an art.

MATERIALS FOR FENCING

Fences are made of bamboo canes, pine laths, saplings, tree branches, bush stalks, reeds, woven strips of bark, rough planks, even boards charred by fire and brushed to emphasize the grain.

For a fence around a modern Japanese-style garden, a basic framework can be built of 4-by-4 posts set 6 or 8 feet apart and connected with lines of 2-by-4 rails nailed across the top and near the bottom. To retard rot belowground, use posts of rot-resistant redwood or cedar, or pressure-treated timbers. For a 6-foot fence, a height that gives privacy without producing a claustrophobic feeling, select posts 9 feet long so 3 feet will be anchored in the ground. Mark the line of the fence with stakes and string, and use a posthole digger to excavate narrow holes deep enough for a 3-inch layer of gravel for drainage. Then set each post on the gravel and fill around it with gravel and soil, tamping the mix firmly and using a carpenter's level on the front and side of each post to make sure it remains vertical. Guided by a level string, nail the 2-by-4s between the posts to form the lower rail and on top of the posts to form the upper one.

This basic framework can be filled with many kinds of handsome materials. One of the most popular fences for gardens in both Japan and the United States is the board-and-board pattern, in which vertical boards of uniform width, 6, 8 or 10 inches, are overlapped and nailed alternately on opposite sides of the frame. This design presents an equally pleasing appearance on both sides, yields a deep shadow pattern, and provides reasonable privacy while letting air circulate through. Let the unpainted wood weather to a rich natural color—redwood will turn brownish-black, cedar silvery gray. If you prefer not to wait for the raw wood to mellow by itself, apply a weathering stain or a darker natural wood stain.

BUILDING WITH BAMBOO

For a more distinctively Oriental look, you can panel the fence frame with bamboo instead of boards or use decorative sections of bamboo in a fence otherwise surfaced with boards. Japanese designers do not hesitate to mix materials as long as they are compatible, to vary the height of a fence to conceal something ugly or to let in more sunlight, or even to omit a panel to frame a distant view.

Cut the tops of lengths of bamboo just above a solid joint so rain and dirt will not collect inside. Space them along the frame, butting

Delicate frames for gardens

In Japan, where house walls typically open wide onto gardens, many homeowners enclose their property with tall fences of wood, reeds, brush or bamboo—delicate panels that provide needed privacy while blending with the natural setting. However, the Japanese do not confine their fences only to a garden's edge. They often install airy latticework panels within a garden to separate different areas of use. One of the most specialized of these interior fences is the "sleeve"—a panel that conceals utility areas or provides a textural backdrop to basins or plants.

BEAUTIFUL BARRICADES

Bamboo uprights, lashed alternately to opposite sides of a horizontal frame, create an open mesh (1). The Japanese use low versions of this fence to divide garden areas and taller versions, with small trees in front, to mark garden perimeters. For greater privacy, the solid fence (2) combines bamboo uprights with unpainted wooden boards. Spaces at the top and bottom allow for ventilation while making the fence seem less forbidding.

The corrugated fence of golden canes (3) can be used as a low divider or a tall garden wall, adding textural interest to either location. Less sturdy but just as handsome is the fence of ready-made bamboo shades hung in a wooden frame (4).

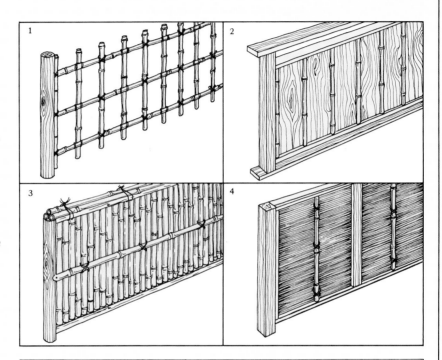

The "sleeve" fence is so named because it projects from the house like a sleeve from a kimono. Often placed beside the front door, it serves as a visual baffle, hiding from view such utilitarian objects as a children's seesaw or a rack for drying clothes. While this fence can be made in a variety of materials and designs, it is customarily a single panel, twice as tall as wide: a 3-foot "sleeve" is 6 feet high. Here, the top is curved, but it could also be uneven or straight—an option open to all Japanese fences with unframed tops.

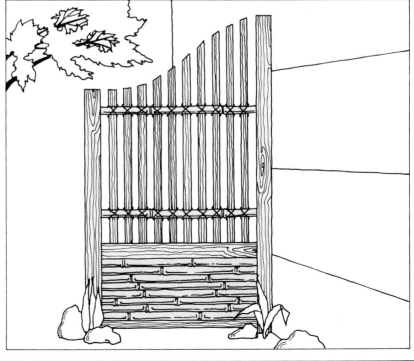

them together for maximum privacy or leaving gaps for an airier effect. To avoid splitting canes, drill holes for the nails, and take care not to crush the bamboo with your hammer. You may prefer to lash the canes in traditional Japanese style (page 83). Use a heavy, dark polyester or nylon twine. Gardeners in Japan take pride in using one of several classical knots, but any neat method of tying, such as a square knot, will do if it is used consistently. Cut ends of twine are tucked out of sight or left to dangle. Or you can use short lengths of flexible rust-resistant wire of an unobtrusive color. Twist the ends together on the back side of the fence, cut them off short and bend the stubs so they will not snag or scratch. To prolong the life of bamboo, keep the bottom of the paneling at least 3 inches above the ground. You may also want to give the canes a coat or two of clear sealer, but use a flat finish rather than the shiny kind.

Lightweight materials like bamboo are also appropriate for the low, open sections of fence that are used to define areas within a garden—to set off a corner from conventionally landscaped areas, for example, or to conceal a service area or cutting garden. One of the most useful designs is the abbreviated *sodegaki,* or sleeve fence, so called because it extends out like a kimono sleeve from the house. Seldom more than 5 feet high and 3 feet long, a sleeve fence is used not to enclose an area but to hide an unwelcome sight or to provide a

THE BASICS OF BUILDING BAMBOO FENCES

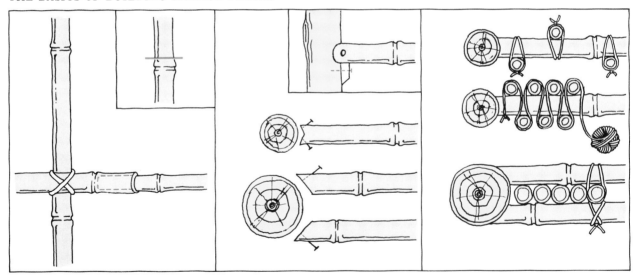

To lengthen horizontal bamboo fence poles, insert the tip of one cane into the hollow base of another. Cut vertical poles just above a membrane-covered joint (inset) to keep rain and dirt from entering the cane.

To make a fence frame, cut a v into a cane end, drill holes and nail the cane to the post. Strengthen the union with chucks (inset). For a double-pole variation, cut the end of each cane at a slant.

Fill in the fence frame by lashing canes to horizontal supports, or by weaving a cord over and under closely spaced canes. For a double-pole frame, drop canes between the poles, tying them at intervals.

backdrop for a particular view. It is usually constructed at a right angle to the house to relate it to the garden and to give one room a measure of privacy and a view of its own. At its simplest, a *sodegaki* may be a latticework of bamboo canes lashed together, perhaps supporting the tracery of a morning glory or other vine. (To find a retailer who sells bamboo—usually a window-shade manufacturer—look under "Bamboo" in a classified telephone directory.)

To complete your garden enclosure, you may need a gate. It is the Japanese fashion not to create a barrier but rather to extend a sense of welcome within polite limits. Often a gateway is only two tall posts, one on either side of the opening, sometimes connected a foot or two above head level with a rail. Should a more conventional gate prove necessary, it should be as simple as possible and in character with the fence, either a repetition of its pattern or a variation on the theme. Fences without gates are not exceptional, but be wary of gateways without fences. The freestanding Oriental-looking archways sometimes seen in Western Japanese-style gardens are derived from ceremonial gateways used to signify entrances to Shinto shrines. They are not used in residential gardens in Japan.

Much the same can be said about other ornaments seen in Western versions of Japanese gardens. All too often they add up to what one landscape architect calls the Disneyland effect. Many of Japan's finest classical gardens have no ornaments at all, relying solely on the ornamental qualities of plants and rocks. There are a few objects, however, that can lend charm to a garden if they are used sparingly, spaced carefully and placed logically.

One artifact that has a time-honored place in the Japanese garden is the stone water basin, long associated with the cleansing ritual of the tea ceremony. Place in an intimate corner, its splash can add a cooling note, especially in a garden that has no other water in the form of a stream or pond. Water basins are of two kinds—the *chozubachi,* up to 4 feet tall and often placed near the veranda of the house, and the *tsukubai,* a lower version set in the tea garden and used in a bending position as a gesture of humility. Either type is appropriate, but the *tsukubai,* associated with the tea ceremony, is more popular and easier to integrate into a small garden.

The finest old stone basins are of granite or other hard rock, either hollowed naturally by the force of a mountain waterfall or carefully cut into bowl shapes by artisans. Such treasures are rare and costly, but many suppliers sell reproductions cast in concrete.

Place the basin in a cool corner of the garden, then make it a focal point with plants and stones. Typically a *tsukubai* is the key element in a group of rocks arranged around a water-catching bed of

TWO TWINE LASHINGS

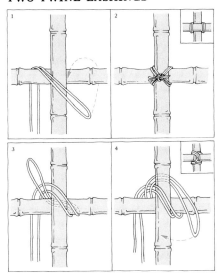

To lash bamboo poles together for a garden fence, use dark-colored jute as the Japanese do, or substitute rot-resistant polyester cord. Loop a double strand of cord across the intersecting poles and thereafter tie in either a box-style or intertwined lashing. To tie in the box style, bring the cord under the vertical pole (1) and back across the vertical pole (arrow), tying the ends together in a square knot (2).

To tie the more intricate intertwined lashing, carry one end of the cord across the back of the intersecting poles, right to left. Pull it through the loop on the left side (3), then carry it behind the vertical pole (4), over the right-hand horizontal pole. Finally, tie the two ends of the cord in a square knot, as for the box-style lashing.

smaller stones called a "sea." The basin is set at the rear, with its rim notched or its top tilted so that water will spill into the sea when it overflows. Traditionally, a bit forward and to the left of the basin is a lower stone on which the user may put his personal belongings or, at night, a lantern. Forward and to the right is another low stone for a bucket of hot water in winter. In front, steppingstones lead to a large, flat stone on which to stand and bend while ladling water from the basin. Smaller stones complete the circle, forming a retaining wall around the sea, which is lined with small stones to conceal a drain.

The basin can be replenished with fresh water from a bucket, but many gardeners build a piping system so water can trickle and splash while the garden is in use. The water can be introduced into

PLACING A WATER BASIN

1. *The Japanese combine the tea garden's water basin with a group of rocks. In front of the basin a flat stone is provided for a guest to stand on. This rock is separated from the basin by a pebble-filled hollow called the sea. One stone to the left is provided to hold a lantern; a lower one to the right is for a bucket of hot water in winter.*

2. *As the side view shows, the basin dominates the grouping. The basin's edge should be about a foot from the ground and tilted slightly forward so any spills fall into the sea. The lantern stone is a few inches lower than the basin, the bucket stone a few more. The front stone is 2 feet from the basin's center and 2 inches high.*

3. *To provide shade and to keep the water cool, plant a small tree or shrub behind the basin. Add ferns, dwarf bamboo or other low plants on the sides.*

4. *If you prefer, you may use an alternate arrangement by placing the basin in the sea. In either case you can add running water with a hose connecting a hidden faucet to a bamboo post that is fitted with a flume. If water will be trickling constantly to add a pleasant sound to your garden, install a drain.*

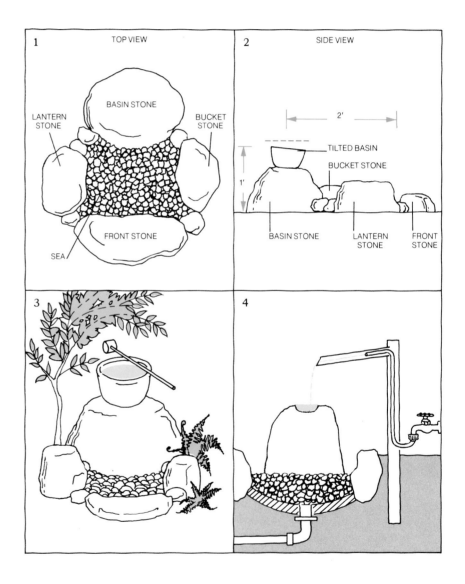

the basin through a *kakei,* a hollow bamboo flume designed to suggest in miniature the sight and sound of a mountain waterfall.

Often associated with a water-basin grouping is a traditional stone lantern, or *ishidoro.* Long used in Buddhist temples and Shinto shrines, where they have burned ceremonially since ancient times, stone lanterns were introduced into Japanese gardens in the 16th Century to light the way to the teahouses at night. Lanterns too are available in reproductions in cast concrete. Designs vary from the tall milepost kind, named after road markers along Japan's old highways, to short, squat *yukimi* lanterns with mushroom-shaped roof lines. These lanterns catch decorative caps of snow in winter and balance on graceful spreading legs.

Although many gardeners never illuminate them, stone lanterns look best if placed where they would be expected to cast light: near a water basin, along the turn of a path, next to a gateway, or at water's edge where the shape would be reflected. In most gardens a single lantern is enough. The sense of perspective will increase if the lantern is partially obscured by the tracery of a nearby branch. Place a low lantern on a large, flat rock with its weight evenly distributed; the pedestal will enhance the lantern's importance.

In the evening an illuminated stone lantern gives a soft, pleasant effect. The Japanese prefer the warm glow of a candle or an oil-wick lamp. To diffuse the light and keep the breeze from blowing out the flame, they may insert little windows of rice paper on balsawood struts. Since these do not last long, some people substitute frosted glass or use a lamp with a small glass chimney. If you plan to light your garden often, you can run a low-voltage garden wiring system to the lantern and fit it with a low-intensity bulb.

Finally, if your garden is large enough, you may want some sort of shelter, arbor or pavilion modeled along Japanese teahouse lines. It can be a structure large enough for entertaining or simply a shady retreat, consisting of an umbrella-like roof atop a log post stripped of its bark and furnished with a bench.

TEAHOUSE-TYPE SHELTERS

Whatever the structure's design, it should, like other elements in the garden, be kept in scale with its surroundings, and only natural materials should be used: unpainted or stained wood for posts and beams; bamboo, rushes or earth-colored plaster for walls; wood shingles, boards or thatch for roofing. In some gardens, such a shelter can do double duty, concealing a tool house or potting shed. But more likely you will simply locate it at the end of a winding path toward the back of your garden, a private, special place where you can go to relax on a summer afternoon, to read a book or to contemplate the beauty of your Japanese-style landscape.

Artistic accents with ancient traditions

In Japan, a land laced with rivers and streams, even the earliest gardens included a bridge or two as a matter of necessity. It was not until the 16th Century, however, when the tea ceremony came into vogue, that three other additions to the garden became popular: stone basins for ritual cleansing of body and spirit, steppingstone paths to keep guests' feet dry during the walk to the teahouse, and lanterns to light the way at night. Today the Japanese continue to include these elements in their gardens, though now mainly for their decorative effect. Indeed, steppingstones, bridges, stone lanterns and basins have become so identified with Japanese garden design that Western designers, too, consider them indispensable finishing touches, as demonstrated in the Japanese-style gardens of the United States shown here and on pages that follow.

These elements must be used in the Japanese manner. Otherwise, writes one expert, the result can be "something that is vulgar and totally in contradiction to the simplicity, naturalness and subtle composition of the tasteful Japanese garden."

The designers of these Western gardens have gone back to Japanese tradition for inspiration and guidance, choosing humble materials—weathered rock, bamboo, unpainted wood—for their finishing touches, and suiting the style of lanterns, basins, bridges and walkways to the size and character of the gardens. The ornate and imposing *kasuga* lantern on page 88, the arched wooden bridge on page 94 and the geometrically patterned path of square flagstones on pages 92-93 all add grace to sophisticated gardens. Squat lanterns, walkways of uncut stone and a hand-carved granite bridge *(page 95)* harmonize with more rustic settings.

Once selected, these man-made elements have been placed where they blend most naturally into the garden's composition and the contours of the terrain. They have been placed where their own contours are often partly hidden by a cascade of flowers or a filigree of branches—for, to the Japanese, beauty is best revealed to the imagination when it is half concealed from the eye.

No longer used for ablutions, this ancient stone basin still refreshes the spirit. Besides its visual appeal, it provides the soothing sound of water falling from a bamboo spout.

Lamps for contemplation

Originally, Japanese temple gardens were lit with ornate pagoda-roofed lanterns, like those used in China, but over the centuries Japanese artisans developed hundreds of lantern styles of their own. Tall lamps are traditionally placed under trees, to illuminate their branches, and lower lamps beside walkways and steps to light the way. Some lanterns are reserved for use beside pools for their flickering reflections. And the snow-viewing lantern has an especially wide brim to collect a decorative mound of new-fallen snow.

Although cast from concrete instead of carved out of stone, this modern lantern incorporates the traditional five demountable parts— pedestal, platform, light box, roof and finial.

One of the best known of the classic lanterns is this imposing pagoda-roofed kasuga style, named for the Buddhist temple at Nara, where these lamps were lit as a mark of devotion.

Carved by hand but wired for electricity, this modern granite lamp (left) has been positioned, in accordance with Japanese practice, so its light illuminates a flight of steps leading into a California garden.

A squat lantern with overhanging roof and tripod base casts light on a turn in a garden walk bordered with low-growing ivy, podocarpus, Japanese hemlock and slender-leaved rhododendrons.

The Japanese place this plump lantern near the water's edge, where its shape is said to resemble that of a resting goose. In a garden in New York, the lantern has an electric bulb and translucent windows.

Pathways for meandering

According to one old account, a 16th Century tea master was inspired to create the first steppingstone path after he saw a shogun's devoted attendants spreading their garments along a muddy garden path to keep the shogun's shoes clean. Today there are hundreds of variations, but most paths can be categorized as *tobi-ishi,* in which natural stones are set into the ground in repeating patterns; *nobe-dan,* paved, straight-edged paths inlaid with natural and cut stones; or *shiki-ishi,* paved walkways of cut, geometrically shaped rock.

Steppingstones dwindle down to single file as the gravel path narrows in this California garden. In the wider part, bright-green baby's tears underscore the similarity between the pathway and an arroyo.

Water-washed flagstones from California rivers file across this pond. The pathway's casual appearance belies an elaborate man-made substructure: concrete and metal pilings brace the stones.

For this California version of
a nobedan path, the designer has set
smooth river rocks into a bed of
concrete, tempering the formality of
the straight-edged design with the
informality of the paving materials.

This modern variety of the traditional
shiki-ishi path substitutes concrete
disks for the conventional cut-
stone slabs. The path, the black pebble
"beach," and even the pachysandra
ground cover echo the water's curve.

For the tobi-ishi, or steppingstone path, in this New York garden, the designer has chosen square and rectangular cut stones to

contrast with rounded planting islands, and has set the stones in a curving line designed to lead the eye through this composition.

Bridges for reflection

Interested less in getting quickly to the other side than in lingering over a watery expanse, the Japanese build curves into their steppingstone bridges and angles into bridges made of planks. One of the most distinctive Japanese bridges—the *yatsuhashi*, or "eight plank" style—is traditionally composed of eight platforms that zig and zag across a stream to take advantage of a series of views. Even bridges that take a more direct route to the opposite shore—bowed stone slabs or arching spans—invite reflection on the watery world below.

This variation on the yatsuhashi bridge defies conventional notions of what a bridge should span: after leading visitors on a zigzag tour over a leaf-strewn pond, it casually returns to the shore near where it began.

An arching bridge of weathered redwood spans this California pond. One contemporary addition to the timeless scene is the lantern-like device at upper right; a raccoon alarm, it goes off when marauders are near.

In this garden bordering a bird sanctuary, a hand-carved granite bridge serves two functions. It spans the water, but the bowed slab also leads the eye to the "borrowed view" of the arching hills beyond.

An encyclopedia of Japanese plants 5

To Western eyes there is something decidedly exotic about the look of a Japanese garden, so it may come as a pleasant surprise to discover that its plants are quite familiar. Many trees and shrubs regularly used in American gardens are of Japanese origin. Obvious examples are flowering cherries and cut-leaved maples. Indeed, a number of much-hybridized plants, such as the ubiquitous hosta, are the product of Japanese horticulturists, who have been tinkering with plant genetics for centuries.

Creating a Japanese garden on American soil does, however, call for an awareness of certain differences between the two countries. Though Japan and the United States occupy roughly the same latitudes, from the 30th to the 45th parallel, their climates are not the same. Japan is a string of mountains rising from the sea. Constantly bathed in mists and fog and with an annual rainfall of 64 inches, it has the humidity of the tropics, although winter temperatures sink to freezing or below. The growth habits of Japanese plants reflect these climatic conditions.

In the encyclopedia that follows all the plants listed are native Japanese species or species that have been used in Japanese garden design for centuries (some are native to the Asian mainland). They have been chosen for their adaptability to the North American climate and for their general availability. Most will be stocked by local nurseries; others can be acquired through nurseries that specialize in particular kinds of plants. If a Japanese plant is unavailable, do not despair. Substitute an American equivalent, planted and pruned in the Japanese style.

To aid you in your choice, climate zones are given for each plant, keyed to the map on page 151, and for quick reference there is a chart of plant characteristics on pages 152-153. The entries are listed alphabetically by their Latin botanical names, and cross-referenced by common names.

Japanese plants include a Kaempferi iris and (clockwise from upper left) black pine, threadleaf maple, bamboo, juniper, felt fern, Keisk rhododendron, pachysandra, painted fern, scouring rush and mimosa.

NIKKO FIR
Abies homolepis

THREADLEAF JAPANESE MAPLE
Acer palmatum 'Dissectum'

A

ABIES

A. firma (Japanese fir, Momi fir); *A. homolepis*, also called *A. brachyphylla* (Nikko fir)

Because of their great size—they grow to a height of 100 feet or more—these native Japanese evergreens are generally used only in large gardens, as background or single specimen plants. They have a naturally conical shape formed by stiff, horizontal branches and are frequently pruned to encourage these branches to grow outward at regular intervals, like the spokes of a wheel. Both species have stiff, flat needles and upright cones. Both grow very fast when young, 1½ to 2 feet a year, making them useful as filler plants that can be quickly replaced when they become too large. Neither fir is particularly suited to city conditions, being damaged by polluted air, but the Nikko fir is the more tolerant of the two. The Nikko fir also accepts heavy pruning and is often grown in pots.

The Momi fir grows to 150 feet. With age, it loses its lower branches. The light-green needles are ⅝ to 1½ inches long with notches in the rounded tips. The smaller branches are grooved on the undersides and slightly fuzzy. Cones are yellow-green, 3½ to 5 inches long, and appear only on the upper branches. The Nikko fir reaches only 100 feet, but its branches spread more widely, 25 to 30 feet across. It has dark green needles, 1 to 1½ inches long, silvery on the underside, with rounded, slightly notched tips. The younger branches are shiny and deeply grooved; the growing tips at the ends of the branches are round and white and are often marked with resin. On older branches the gray bark peels off in thin shreds, revealing pink-orange areas underneath. The cones are up to 4 inches long and 1½ inches in diameter. Borne on both upper and lower branches, they are purple when young, but with age they turn brown. Among other forms of the Nikko fir are *A. homolepis scottiae*, a dwarf; *A. homolepis tomomi*, which has fewer branches and shorter needles; and *A. homolepis umbellata*, whose cones are green when young.

HOW TO GROW. The Momi fir is hardy in Zones 6-9; the Nikko fir in Zones 5-9. Both do best in deep, moist, well-drained acid soil, pH 5.5 to 6.5. Plant in a location sheltered from winter winds. Feed in the spring if foliage is pale by scattering any garden fertilizer around the tree. Mulch in the summer with an organic material such as shredded bark, bark chips or peat moss to keep the soil cool and moist. Firs need little or no pruning to maintain their natural conical shapes, but if irregular side shoots do appear, they can be removed in the spring. If the top is broken, select one new shoot to replace it, and remove competing shoots. Propagate firs from seed sown in a cold frame and wintered over there; in the spring transplant seedlings to a shaded, sheltered location for several years before moving them, in the early spring or fall, to the garden. Mature firs more than 8 or 10 feet tall are difficult to transplant.

ARBORVITAE See *Thuja*

ACER

A. japonicum (full-moon maple); *A. palmatum* (Japanese maple)

Gardeners and poets praise the maples of Japan. In autumn, their delicate, brilliant foliage is ablaze on slopes, near ponds or against fences and evergreens—in any place that sets off their color. Cultivated and crossbred for centuries, they are available in hundreds of varieties.

The full-moon maple grows rather slowly, becoming round

with maturity; a 4- to 5-foot tree will reach 15 feet in 10 years, eventually growing 20 feet tall. The smooth, 3- to 6-inch leaves are finely cut into seven to 11 lobes. Light green in spring, they change to a ruby red by fall.

The Japanese maple and its varieties are small, dainty trees that grow even more slowly than the full-moon maple; a 4- to 5-foot tree increases only 6 or 8 inches a year, ultimately reaching 10 to 20 feet. Its arching branches sometimes dip almost to the ground and may need to be supported by stakes when young. The 2- to 4-inch leaves have fewer divisions, but are more deeply indented than those of the full-moon maple. Arranged on branches in flat sprays, the leaves give the Japanese maple a lacy, graceful appearance.

Although delicate in form, the Japanese maple is a hardy tree, seldom damaged by smoke or other air pollutants. It adapts well to pruning and its branches are often thinned to accentuate its graceful shape. It is easily transplanted.

Among the many varieties, a particular favorite is the threadleaf Japanese maple, *A. palmatum dissectum,* which has very deeply cut fan-shaped leaves and gnarled, pendulous branches; it grows only 8 to 12 feet tall and about 9 feet wide. Like the species, its leaves are bronze in spring, green in summer and red in autumn.

HOW TO GROW. The full-moon and Japanese maples are hardy in Zones 5-9, although early-spring frosts in northern areas may damage new growth, which appears before that of most other maple species. They do best in a moist, fertile soil, supplemented with peat moss or leaf mold. Partial shade seems to enhance their color. In northern parts of their growing area, the intermittent shade of taller trees that block the midday sun is ideal; in southern areas, constant light shade is necessary. Plant maple trees in the spring, preferably in the form of balled-and-burlaped stock, in their original soil. Prune in fall or winter. Propagate from seed, but seedlings may not duplicate the parents' coloration.

ADONIS

A. amurensis (Amur adonis)

The dainty Amur adonis, with feathery foliage and golden yellow flowers, is related to the buttercup. In Japanese gardens, it is planted next to rocks or under trees, where its flowers provide early-spring color. It is a low-growing perennial, 9 to 15 inches tall, with large cup-shaped flowers, 2 inches across, that bloom at the tips of the stems. The flowers appear before the leaves have unfurled. The leaves are segmented and fernlike, 3 to 6 inches long; they die back to the ground early in the summer.

HOW TO GROW. Amur adonis is hardy in Zones 3-7. It will grow in almost any kind of soil but prefers one that is rich, well drained and supplemented with peat moss. It does best in partial shade, reacting adversely to intense heat, but it may be planted in full sun in cool coastal and mountain regions. Set out plants when they are dormant, from midsummer through fall, spacing them 12 inches apart. Propagate in the spring from seeds or by dividing clumps.

AKEBIA

A. quinata (five-leaf akebia)

The smooth foliage of the five-leaf akebia climbs gracefully over walls and trellises in Japanese gardens. Often planted for shade, this semievergreen vine twines vigorously around any support, growing into a dense mass of leaves and stems 20 to 40 feet long. It screens fences, wires, covers rainspouts or grows as a thick ground cover. The vine should be placed carefully, however; it sends out runners and underground shoots that can choke nearby shrubs and plants.

For climate zones, see map, page 151.

AMUR ADONIS
Adonis amurensis

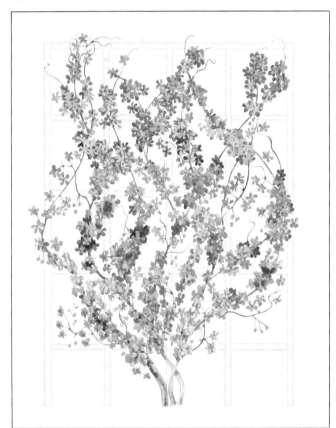

FIVE-LEAF AKEBIA
Akebia quinata

PINK SILK TREE
Albizia julibrissin rosea

JAPANESE ANEMONE
Anemone japonica

This species of akebia, native to China, Korea and Japan, is named for its large leaves, each one divided, like a hand, into five shiny, rounded leaflets 3 to 5 inches long. The vine bears fragrant purple flowers, about ½ inch across, in early spring. They bloom at night, combining separate male and female blossoms in each cluster; however, the clusters are frequently hidden by the leaves. The flowers are followed by purple berries.

HOW TO GROW. The five-leaf akebia is hardy in Zones 4-10, its leaves remaining green year round from Zone 7 south. The vine thrives in either partial shade or full sunlight in a light, well-drained soil. Set out plants in early spring, spacing them about 2 feet apart. Fertilize in spring with an all-purpose garden fertilizer, and prune to keep the size within bounds in early spring and as needed. Propagate from cuttings, by root division or from seeds.

ALBIZIA

A. julibrissin (silk tree, mimosa)

In summer, when plants are in bloom, the silk tree is often the center of interest in a Japanese garden, especially when it is planted against a dark background to dramatize its fluffy pink flowers and tiered horizontal branches. When planted at the base of a small hill, this deciduous tree is often trained so its branches overhang the mound. It frequently has multiple trunks but can be pruned to a single trunk while it is young.

The fernlike 9- to 18-inch leaves consist of dozens of ¼- to ½-inch leaflets that hang down on cool evenings. Ball-shaped 2-inch flowers are borne in clusters up to 8 inches across. In autumn the tree produces flat pealike pods about 6 inches long. The silk tree grows rapidly; a 5-foot tree will become 10 to 15 feet tall in three to five years. It eventually reaches a mature height of 25 to 35 feet, with a spread equaling its height. Native to Japan, the silk tree is often called a mimosa.

The pink silk tree, *A. julibrissin rosea,* is a smaller variety; a 6-foot plant will reach 10 to 12 feet in height in three or four years. Its maximum height is usually 15 to 20 feet. The flowers, which are a deeper pink than those of the silk tree, form somewhat smaller clusters.

HOW TO GROW. Silk trees grow well in Zones 8 and 9; the pink silk tree is more cold resistant and can be grown in Zones 6-9. Both types grow best and flower most profusely in full sun and well-drained soil, though they tolerate partial shade and poor or alkaline soil. They can also withstand windy locations. Young trees bought balled and burlaped with their roots in their original ball of soil should be planted in spring. Prune trees in late winter or in fall, after the leaves have fallen. Propagate by seed or root cuttings.

ALMOND, FLOWERING See *Prunus*
ALTHEA, SHRUB See *Hibiscus*
AMUR ADONIS See *Adonis*
ANDROMEDA, JAPANESE See *Pieris*

ANEMONE

A. japonica, also called *A. hupehensis japonica* (Japanese anemone)

The Japanese anemone, a perennial grown for its late-summer flowers, is actually a native of China—Hupeh, the source of one of its Latin names, is a Chinese province—but it is considered one of the classical plants of Japanese gardening. Traditionally it is grown in the shade of trees or against dark rocks, where the clear, light colors of its flowers can best be appreciated. Sometimes plants listed as *A. japonica* are actually hybrids of this plant and *A. vitifolia* (grape-leaved anemone), a Himalayan species; this hybrid is taller than either parent, up to 5 feet, and is generally too large for use in a Japanese garden.

The Japanese anemone grows to a height of 2½ to 3 feet. It has slender, branching flower stalks and deeply cut dark green leaves that form a 12-inch mound of foliage. The 2- to 3-inch-wide flowers are generally pink or mauve, though there is also a white variety. For Japanese gardens single-flowered varieties are considered more suitable than those with double flowers. The Japanese anemone is long-lived, and if left undisturbed it grows more beautiful with age. It is best not to move the plant except for propagation.

HOW TO GROW. The Japanese anemone is hardy in Zones 5-10. It will grow in almost any soil, but does best in a moist, well-drained loam, supplemented with peat moss. Partial shade is necessary, especially during midday heat. In Zones 5 and 6 protect the plants in winter with a 6-inch mulch of salt hay or other organic material. Propagate in the spring by seed or division, or by root cuttings taken in the fall. Cut stems down to the ground in late fall, after flowering ends.

ARALIA, JAPANESE See *Fatsia*
ASH, JAPANESE MOUNTAIN See *Sorbus*
ASH, KOREAN MOUNTAIN See *Sorbus*

ASTILBE

A. arendsii (hybrid astilbe, false spirea); *A. japonica* (florist's spirea, silver sheaf); *A. simplicifolia*

In Japan, astilbes are often grown beside pools, where their roots get the constant moisture they need and their fluffy flower heads are reflected in the water. All are perennials, blooming in midsummer, their many tiny flowers forming long, graceful plumes at the ends of the stems. *A. arendsii* hybrids have a complicated parentage that goes back to Chinese and Japanese originals. They grow 2 to 3 feet tall and have shiny copper-green leaves that divide into many deeply cut leaflets; the flower plumes are 8 to 12 inches long. These hybrid astilbes come in many varieties, distinguished chiefly by color. Among the recommended white forms are Deutschland and Avalanche; in pink forms, Rosy Veil and Peach Blossom are favorites, while Red Sentinel and Fanal are good red varieties.

A. japonica, a Japanese species, grows 1 to 2 feet high, with leaves similar to those of *A. arendsii*. The 8- to 10-inch flower plumes are typically white, but in some cultivated forms they may be purple or yellow. *A. simplicifolia,* also from Japan, grows only 6 to 12 inches high, with correspondingly smaller flower plumes, 4 inches long, which may be white or pink. The leaves of this species are simpler in form, being single deeply cut ovals.

HOW TO GROW. Astilbes are hardy in Zones 4-8, and grow in almost any moist, well-drained garden soil. They do best in partial shade but will tolerate sun if they are watered frequently during the heat of the summer. Set out plants in fall or spring, spacing them 12 to 18 inches apart. Feed them once a year, in spring, by scattering a low-nitrogen fertilizer such as 0-20-20 around them. Astilbes multiply rapidly and should be dug up and divided every two or three years; before replanting them, replenish the soil with peat moss and a dusting of fertilizer.

ATHYRIUM

A. goeringianum pictum, also called *A. niponicum pictum* (Japanese painted fern)

A colorful fern with red-purple stalks and ribs and gray-green fronds, the Japanese painted fern is often the only

ASTILBE
Astilbe arendsii 'Rosy Veil'

JAPANESE PAINTED FERN
Athyrium goeringianum pictum

For climate zones, see map, page 151.

plant material used in a dry rock-and-gravel garden, where it is grown in clumps next to rocks. It is also grown along the paths of tea gardens, where its multicolored foliage contrasts with the shaded surroundings. The spear-shaped fronds grow 6 to 18 inches tall, unfurling in late spring and lasting until fall, when they turn yellow and die. A Japanese native, this fern spreads slowly; new growth rises from a thick, creeping stem, or rhizome, just below the ground surface.

HOW TO GROW. Japanese painted fern is hardy in Zones 3-8 but needs a secluded spot, protected from wind north of Zone 5. It does best in light to open shade in a moist, well-drained acid soil, pH 5.5 to 6.5. Use a soil mixture consisting of 1 part garden loam, 1 part builder's sand and 2 parts peat moss or leaf mold. Plant rhizomes in the spring or fall, setting them just beneath the surface of the soil. During the growing season, keep the soil moist but never soggy. Normally ferns do not need to be fertilized but if leaves yellow in spring or midsummer, scatter fish-meal fertilizer around them. In spring, before new growth starts, remove dead fronds. If the plants become crowded, selectively move some of them.

AUCUBA

A. japonica and varieties (Japanese aucuba, Japanese laurel)

Japanese aucuba, a broad-leaved evergreen shrub, is admired for its dramatic foliage, which often has yellow or white markings. It thrives in shade and is frequently planted against house walls or under trees, where it provides a colorful accent. If female plants are grown near males, the sprays of tiny brownish-purple blossoms that decorate branch tips in early spring are followed by 2- to 3-inch clusters of red berries that usually remain on the plant all winter. Because these exceptionally hardy plants will thrive in salt air and in dust and smoke, they make excellent shrubs for city and seashore locations.

Japanese aucubas grow rapidly, reaching a height of 15 feet or more in 10 years, but they may be contained with moderate pruning; also there are compact varieties that grow only 2 to 3 feet tall. The original species from the Orient has leathery dark green leaves up to 7 inches long. Varieties with yellow or white markings come in several forms: *A. japonica variegata*, known as the gold-dust tree, has yellow specks on its foliage. The leaves of Picturata have bright yellow centers with dark green edges, while Sulphur reverses the order and has leaves with green centers and yellow edges. Crotonifolia has white-spotted leaves.

HOW TO GROW. Aucubas are hardy in Zones 7-10 and slightly northward of Zone 7 if given a sheltered location. They do best in light to deep shade in moist, well-drained soil. Established plants can withstand drought, but too much sun will burn the leaves. Set out plants in spring or fall. To stimulate new growth and more berries, sprinkle cottonseed meal lightly beneath plants in early spring, but do not scratch it in, as this disturbs the shallow roots. Pruning to improve the plant's shape is best done in early spring, but light pruning can be done at any time. On variegated kinds, remove any branches with solid green leaves. Propagate from cuttings taken in spring or by seed.

AZALEA See *Rhododendron*

B

BABYLON WEEPING WILLOW See *Salix*
BALLOONFLOWER See *Platycodon*
BAMBOO See *Phyllostachys*
BAMBOO, BLACK See *Phyllostachys*
BAMBOO, FISHPOLE See *Phyllostachys*

JAPANESE AUCUBA
Aucuba japonica 'Picturata'

BAMBOO, GOLDEN See *Phyllostachys*
BAMBOO, HEAVENLY See *Nandina*
BAMBOO, SACRED See *Nandina*
BARBERRY, JAPANESE See *Berberis*
BELLFLOWER, CHINESE See *Platycodon*

BERBERIS
B. thunbergii (Japanese barberry)

Despite its prickly thorns, the Japanese barberry has many things to recommend it for Japanese gardens: colorful autumn foliage, bright red berries, sprays of delicate flowers in spring and dense foliage that can readily be pruned into tight, rounded shapes. Though it is sometimes used as a hedge, a single Japanese barberry may form the focal point for some area of the garden. This medium-sized deciduous shrub, native to the southern and central islands of Japan, grows 4 to 7 feet high, with arching branches that may spread as much as 6 feet. Its oval leaves, 1 inch long, are yellowish-green during the summer, reddish-orange to purple in the fall. The cup-shaped yellow flowers, 1/3 inch across, hang in small clusters along the branches, as do the oval 1/2-inch-long red berries that follow. Unless birds eat them, these berries may last through the winter, dropping only the following spring when the flowers appear. The new branches of Japanese barberry have a yellowish tinge, but at maturity the wood takes on a purple-brown hue.

HOW TO GROW. Japanese barberry is hardy in Zones 4-10, growing in almost every part of the United States. It is remarkably adaptable, withstanding deep cold, pollution and even poor soil, provided the soil is well drained. The shrub does best in sunny areas but can tolerate shade. Plant Japanese barberry in late fall or early spring, setting hedge plants 1 to 2 feet apart. Pruning is not normally required to preserve its naturally graceful shape, but pruning and shearing to produce a hedge or a topiary shape should be done in late spring and when necessary to preserve the shape. Propagate from seeds, planted in the fall, or from cuttings taken in spring, midsummer or winter. Some species of this shrub are alternate hosts of black stem rust of wheat and are not grown in areas of the country where wheat is a major crop.

BETULA
B. platyphylla japonica (Japanese white birch)

Planted in small clumps near the boundary of a Japanese garden, Japanese white birches create a woodland look. Native to Japan's cool highlands, these deciduous trees are valued for their ruffled, paper-thin white bark. In winter, the bark patterns are particularly striking if the trees are set in front of darker evergreens. The Japanese white birch is often pruned into a symmetrical cone shape.

These birches grow rapidly; within 10 years, a 6-to 8-foot tree will reach a height of 20 feet or more. The trees may eventually become 60 to 75 feet tall. The 1½- to 2½-inch pointed oval leaves turn yellow in fall. The American canoe birch, *B. papyrifera*, is similar in appearance and can be used as a substitute if the Japanese species is difficult to find.

HOW TO GROW. Japanese white birches grow best in Zones 4-6; farther south, their growth is stunted by prolonged summer heat. They require full sunlight and grow in any moist soil, but do not plant them where they would be exposed to strong winds. Buy balled-and-burlaped trees—with roots in their original soil balls—and plant them in the spring. Like other birches, the Japanese white birch may be attacked by two serious pests. The birch leaf miner eats the interiors of leaves, which become blotched and brown. The bronze birch borer infests the inner bark of branches; brown tips on upper

JAPANESE BARBERRY
Berberis thunbergii

JAPANESE WHITE BIRCH
Betula platyphylla japonica

For climate zones, see map, page 151.

LITTLELEAF BOX
Buxus microphylla

COMMON CAMELLIA
Camellia japonica

branches are often the first sign of infestation. Prune these birches in summer or fall only, since at other times the trees may bleed excessively. The species is propagated by seed.

BIRCH See *Betula*
BISHOP'S HAT See *Epimedium*
BLACK BAMBOO See *Phyllostachys*
BLACK PINE, JAPANESE See *Pinus*
BOSTON IVY See *Parthenocissus*
BUTTERCUP WINTER HAZEL See *Corylopsis*

BUXUS

B. microphylla (littleleaf box, boxwood)

A favorite evergreen shrub for *tamazukuri*—round pruning—littleleaf box is valued for its naturally low, compact form. It is used alone, tucked against rocks, or massed for formal hedges. If left unpruned, its dense small leaves, ⅓ to 1 inch long, form billowing irregular mounds. This long-lived Japanese native grows very slowly; at maturity, in about 25 years, it reaches 3 to 4 feet in height and spreads 2 to 3 feet wide. Wintergreen, a Korean variety, is a good substitute for littleleaf box in northern gardens because it stays green in very cold weather when other boxes may turn brown.

HOW TO GROW. Littleleaf box is hardy in Zones 6-9 and does well in either full sun or partial shade. It thrives in almost any well-drained moist soil but grows best in soils supplemented with peat moss or leaf mold. Plant in spring, setting hedge plants 1½ to 2 feet apart. Mulch with a 1-inch layer of chunky peat moss, wood chips or peanut shells. During the first summer, until plants become established, water frequently and spray the foliage with the garden hose. To strengthen weak plants, scatter cottonseed meal beneath them in early spring, but do not disturb the soil, as the boxes have shallow roots. Prune in early spring before new growth starts. To shape into tree form, select one central leader and cut all other upright shoots to the ground; remove weak or crowded branches, opening up the center of the tree to the light. For hedges and round-pruned specimens, shear in early spring for the first several summers to stimulate branching; thereafter, trim in spring and summer to maintain shape. Propagate additional plants from cuttings taken in the spring or summer.

C

CAMELLIA

C. japonica (common camellia); *C. sasanqua* (sasanqua camellia)

For centuries the Japanese have grown camellias in their gardens, admiring them for their year-round glossy dark green leaves and profusion of large waxy flowers. Sometimes Japanese gardeners use them as hedges, sometimes as ornamental trees, pruning them to accentuate their shapes. Far less delicate than generally believed, these shade-loving evergreens withstand salt air and polluted city conditions. Their 2- to 5-inch flowers come in pink, red or white, or in mixtures of these shades; the blooms may be single or multipetaled. The thick, glossy leaves are 2 to 4 inches long.

In Japan, Korea and China, common camellia may reach a height of 45 feet or more, but in North America it usually grows 6 to 10 feet tall in 15 years and rarely exceeds 15 feet after 20 to 25 years. Some varieties, called early-blooming, flower in midfall; late-blooming types flower in midspring. Sasanqua camellia, which may become 15 to 20 feet tall in its native Japan, becomes only 6 to 8 feet tall in most American gardens, taking 10 years to reach that size. It blooms from early to late fall.

HOW TO GROW. Camellias thrive in humid areas of Zones 7-9. They grow best in partial shade in moist, well-drained, slightly acid soils with a pH of 6.0. Although some hybrid varieties can tolerate full sun and less humidity, plants in the northern limits of the growing zones need a location protected from the drying effects of cold air and winter sun. In Zones 7 and 8, plant outdoors from spring to fall; in Zone 9, plant in any season. To conserve moisture, provide a permanent 2- to 4-inch mulch of pine needles, wood chips or ground bark. In dry, hot weather, hose down plants to prevent buds from dropping off. In spring, scatter cottonseed meal or special rhododendron-azalea-camellia fertilizer beneath plants. Prune camellias after flowering, in late fall or spring, depending on the variety's period of bloom. Propagate from stem cuttings of new growth, taken when that growth has just ended in late spring.

CAMPHOR TREE See *Cinnamomum*
CAPE JASMINE See *Gardenia*
CEDAR, JAPANESE See *Cryptomeria*
CELANDINE, TREE See *Macleaya*

CEPHALOTAXUS

C. harringtonia, also called *C. drupacea* (Japanese plum yew, cow's-tail pine)

The Japanese plum yew, a native evergreen, is a small shrubby tree that is often massed to serve as a hedge or screen in a Japanese garden. It grows slowly, only 4 to 6 inches a year, reaching an ultimate height of 30 feet. Its multiple stems and arching branches give it a naturally informal shape, but it responds well to pruning, and in small gardens this shape can be readily controlled. The needles are soft, flat, dark green and 1½ to 3 inches long; they have sharp tips and are waxy blue on the undersides. Because they grow along the entire branch, back to the trunk, the tree has a thick, rounded appearance. Male and female flowers are borne on separate plants, just as they are on the plum yew's close relative, the Japanese yew. These flowers appear in the fall and are followed by oval green fruits, about 1 inch long, which turn purple when ripe, a process that takes two years. In addition to the parent species, Japanese plum yew comes in several varieties suitable for various landscaping situations. One, *C. harringtonia fastigiata,* has stiff, erect branches and a more columnar shape.

HOW TO GROW. Plum yew is hardy in Zones 6-10 but grows best in areas with cool, moist summers. It thrives in full sun or partial shade, and in deep, moist, well-drained slightly acid soil with a pH of 6.0 to 6.5. Plant in spring or fall in the permanent location chosen, as Japanese plum yew is difficult to transplant. To grow for hedges or screens, set plants 2 to 3 feet apart. Prune during the summer to maintain size or control shape. If a natural appearance is desired, the only pruning necessary will be occasional trimming of the branch tips. If foliage becomes pale or turns yellow, feed the tree in spring with cottonseed meal scattered around its base. Propagate additional plants from cuttings taken in the fall, or from seeds planted in the fall and wintered over in a cold frame.

CERCIDIPHYLLUM

C. japonicum (Katsura tree)

As the Japanese garden represents an appreciation of order, the Katsura tree is a natural expression of that order, with branches that spread upward in conical symmetry. A deciduous tree, its size limits its use to only large gardens —a 6- to 8-foot tree will reach 20 to 25 feet in five or six

JAPANESE PLUM YEW
Cephalotaxus harringtonia

KATSURA TREE
Cercidiphyllum japonicum

For climate zones, see map, page 151.

CHINESE REDBUD
Cercis chinensis

JAPANESE QUINCE
Chaenomeles japonica

years and eventually will reach a height of 40 to 60 feet.

A native of Japan, the tree is grown for its foliage as well as its form. Its shiny, rounded 2- to 4-inch leaves cast dense shade. Newly unfolded leaves are tinged with red in early spring; they turn a deep blue-green in summer and change to shades of red and yellow in the fall. The Katsura tree bears inconspicuous male and female flowers on separate trees; the fruit, a winged capsule, appears in autumn. Male trees usually have a single trunk, while female trees may have several. Female trees also tend to have a more spreading form than the cone-shaped males. The dark brown bark shreds along the trunk and branches of older trees, giving an interesting texture.

HOW TO GROW. The Katsura tree is hardy in Zones 4-9. It does best in moist, well-drained soil. It will tolerate damp and alkaline soils as well, but should not be planted in dry soil. In Zones 7-9, young trees need shade during the hottest part of the day. In Zones 4-6 full sun is preferable, but the tree can also be planted in partial shade. Prune in autumn after the leaves have fallen. The Katsura tree can be propagated by seed or by cuttings taken in spring.

CERCIS

C. chinensis (Chinese redbud, Chinese Judas tree)

The Chinese redbud, valued by the Japanese for its early-spring flowers, is often placed in front of a building or in a corner of the garden where it stands out in a still-wintry landscape. A small tree or large shrub in Japan, the Chinese redbud grows as a shrub in North America, with a mature height of 4 to 8 feet. When most other plants are still dormant, clusters of ¾-inch rosy-purple flowers are covering the upward-spreading branches and even the main stems. The Chinese redbud first blooms when it is four to five years old. As the flowers fade, 3- to 5-inch heart-shaped leaves unfold, hiding the 5-inch seed pods that follow the flowers. In autumn, the leaves turn yellow before falling.

HOW TO GROW. Chinese redbud grows in Zones 6-9 in well-drained, sandy soil; it will not tolerate moist, heavy soil. It does best if given shade during the hottest part of the day and with protection from wind. Plant container-grown or balled-and-burlaped plants in spring. Avoid bare-rooted redbuds, since they frequently do not survive. Young Chinese redbuds can be successfully transplanted in early spring. Pruning is very rarely required. The shrubs are propagated by division, cuttings or seed.

CHAENOMELES

C. japonica (Japanese quince); *C. speciosa*, also called *C. lagenaria, Cydonia japonica, Pyrus japonica* (flowering quince)

In Japan the quince is admired for its fragrant, extremely early flowers, which may open in mid-January if weather conditions are favorable. A low-growing, wide-spreading deciduous shrub, it tolerates pruning so well that it is a classic subject for bonsai. In the garden, it is often pruned to a single stem and grown as a small tree. Alternatively, it is grown in rows as a hedge, its dense foliage and thorny branches intertwining to form an effective barrier.

The Japanese quince grows only 3 to 4 feet tall, but it spreads 5 to 7 feet; the flowering quince grows 5 to 6 feet tall with an equal spread. Both species have shiny oval leaves, 1½ to 3 inches long, and thorns so long they sometimes appear to be small branches. The flowers, which appear before the leaves, are 1 to 2 inches wide and bloom in clusters of two to four blossoms. On the Japanese quince, they are red-orange; on the flowering quince, they may be white, pink or red, depending on the variety. Both species produce hard round green aromatic fruit in the fall, about 2 inches in diameter.

HOW TO GROW. The Japanese and flowering quinces are hardy in Zones 4-10, withstand pollution, and grow well in almost any soil. To produce prolific flowers, they require full sun. If you plant in the fall you will benefit from their early-spring bloom; set hedge plants 2½ to 4 feet apart. Prune after the flowers have faded, shaping plants into tree forms or hedges. Propagate from cuttings taken in the spring or midsummer, or by suckers or seed.

CHAMAECYPARIS
C. obtusa (hinoki false cypress, Japanese false cypress); *C. pisifera filifera* (thread sawara false cypress); *C. pisifera squarrosa* (moss sawara false cypress)

The hinoki and sawara false cypresses are among the most important trees in Japan. Their wood, aromatic and long lasting, is prized for fine cabinetry, and as garden trees they fill many functions, depending on their size. The tall form can define a garden's boundary or mark such features as a pathway or a garden gate. Dwarf forms, which range from 1 to 3 feet high, are grown in the shade of taller trees or among rocks, and may be pruned into rounded cushion shapes; they are also popular for bonsai.

In Japan the taller forms of hinoki and sawara false cypress become towering cone-shaped trees that are more than 100 feet high, but in North American gardens their average height is about 30 feet. Hinoki false cypress grows somewhat more slowly than sawara false cypress, but neither adds more than 10 inches to its height in a year. Both have flat fanlike leaves that cling to the branches like scales, and interesting reddish-brown bark that shreds off in long, narrow strips. Both also bear tiny round brown cones, ¼ inch across, in sprays along the branches.

Cultivated varieties of these two trees vary greatly in foliage color and habit of growth, as well as in size, from the original species. In the species the leaves are green, streaked with silver on the undersides, and the branches are horizontal with upswept tips. But some varieties have stiff or pendulous branches, and new growth at the branch tips may be white or yellow, giving the tree a dappled appearance. Two attractive sawara false cypress varieties are the thread sawara, with long, drooping cordlike foliage; and the moss sawara, with plumelike gray-green foliage that turns bronze in the fall. Both varieties are tree forms, the thread sawara becoming 20 feet tall, the moss sawara, 30 feet tall. All of the false cypresses are adversely affected by salt air, pollution and winter winds.

HOW TO GROW. False cypresses are hardy in Zones 5-8 and grow best in cool, moist air. They thrive in sun or partial shade, in hotter areas preferring the latter. Plant them in spring or fall in a moist, well-drained, slightly acid soil with a pH of 6.0 to 6.5. To prevent new plantings from drying out, mulch with an organic material such as shredded bark, 2 inches thick. Feed each spring by sprinkling cottonseed meal around the base. False cypresses can be pruned in spring to limit size and to increase branching and fullness. If a single trunk is desired, remove competing shoots. Propagate from seed sown in spring or from cuttings taken in fall.

CHERRY, JAPANESE CORNELIAN See *Cornus*
CHERRY, JAPANESE FLOWERING See *Prunus*
CHERRY, ORIENTAL See *Prunus*
CHERRY, POTOMAC See *Prunus*
CHERRY, WEEPING HIGAN See *Prunus*

For climate zones, see map, page 151.

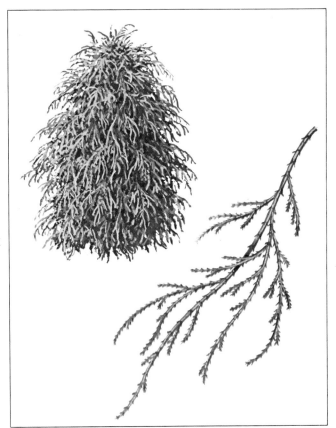

THREAD SAWARA FALSE CYPRESS
Chamaecyparis pisifera filifera

MOSS SAWARA FALSE CYPRESS
Chamaecyparis pisifera squarrosa

DECORATIVE CHRYSANTHEMUM
Chrysanthemum morifolium 'Always Pink'

ANEMONE CHRYSANTHEMUM
Chrysanthemum morifolium 'Yellow Divinity'

CHERRY, YOSHINO See *Prunus*
CHINA FIR See *Cunninghamia*
CHINESE JUDAS TREE See *Cercis*
CHINESE REDBUD See *Cercis*

CHRYSANTHEMUM

C. morifolium (florist's chrysanthemum); *C. niponicum* (Nippon daisy)

Chrysanthemums have been cultivated in the Orient for thousands of years, and in Japan they have come to symbolize longevity. A stylized 16-petaled chrysanthemum is the official insignia of the Japanese Emperor, while lesser members of the Emperor's family wear chrysanthemum insignia containing 14 petals. Possibly because of the mystique surrounding it, the plant has special importance in a Japanese garden. It is often elaborately trained by pinching back and disbudding to form pyramids and cascades of bloom, some of which require extensive bamboo understructures. But it is also allowed to grow more naturally. Few gardens, in fact, are without at least one example of this major flowering plant of the Japanese autumn.

The florist's chrysanthemum probably originated in China centuries ago. It comes in many sizes and shapes, but its flowers all have the same basic arrangement: they are made up of a band of outer petals, called ray florets, and a circle of inner petals, called disc florets. In double-flowered forms, the ray florets are so numerous that they almost hide the disc florets. And there are other forms in which the ray and disc florets are not easy to distinguish from each other. In some, the ray florets curve inward and overlap to form large globelike blooms; these are said to belong to the incurve class. In others, the ray florets curve backward in the manner of the petals of an aster, and are classed as decorative or aster-flowering blooms. There are also forms in which the ray florets are spoon-shaped, quill-shaped, threadlike or spider-like. And there is a class called anemone in which five overlapping rows of ray florets surround a dome-shaped center of disc florets. In all these flowering types, the colors range from white and yellow to purple and dark red.

The plants themselves are 1½ to 3 feet tall, with a stiff bushy habit of growth. The leaves are 3 inches long, gray-green, hairy and thick, with deeply cut edges. The entire plant has a strong, distinct odor that is not unpleasant but not fragrant either.

The Nippon daisy, a native of Japan, is also a dense bushy plant but is somewhat smaller; it grows from 1½ to 2 feet tall. The flowers have white outer petals and greenish-yellow disc petals, like those of the common daisy, and are about 3 inches across. The leaves are 3½ inches long, dark green and thick, but only the tips of the leaves are notched.

HOW TO GROW. Florist's chrysanthemums and Nippon daisies are tender perennials, hardy in Zones 6-10, but in colder climates they are often grown in pots, sunk in the garden and lifted for wintering under mulch in a cold frame. They thrive in almost any well-drained garden soil, but moisture is important; they should be watered during dry spells. For permanent outdoor plantings, set rooted stock in the ground in early spring, spacing plants 1 to 2 feet apart. Mulch with a 2-inch layer of organic material, such as peat moss, to discourage weeds and preserve moisture. To get bushier plants and more flowers, pinch back the tips of new growth until the middle of summer to force more side branches, unless you want fewer but larger flowers. In that case, pinch off all except the terminal bud on each stem. Propagate by dividing roots in spring, or from cuttings of new growth, also taken in the spring.

CINNAMOMUM

C. camphora (camphor tree)

Important for its aromatic wood that is used in fine cabinetry, the camphor tree is one of the largest plants in Japanese landscaping. A broad-leaved evergreen with a rounded crown that is twice as wide as the tree's height, the camphor tree becomes 100 feet tall in temple gardens, but in more restricted situations its height is more often 40 to 50 feet. Usually grown for its ornamental value, it is occasionally pruned into shrub form or sheared into a tall hedge.

Camphor trees are densely covered with dark green shiny oval leaves, up to 5 inches long. These drop off in early spring but are quickly replaced by new leaves that are an attractive red when young. In spring the tree bears 2- to 3-inch spikes of yellowish-white flowers followed by black berries the size of peas. Camphor trees grow slowly and withstand pollution well. However, their dense shade and extensive root system may create problems, as may the disposal of their nondecomposing leaves.

HOW TO GROW. Camphor trees are hardy in Zones 9 and 10 and thrive in either full sun or light shade. They do best in a well-drained, moist sandy soil. Plant before new growth begins in the spring and keep young trees watered well so roots penetrate deeply. Feed with a light sprinkling of cottonseed meal in the spring. Camphor trees are seldom bothered by pests or diseases, but their leaves may become pale in cool weather. If used as a hedge, they may be regularly sheared when actively growing. Otherwise prune in fall, removing lower branches to create walking space under the trees and thinning out branches to allow some light to penetrate the dense foliage. Propagate from seeds sown when ripe or from cuttings taken in the spring or summer.

CLEMATIS

C. florida (cream clematis); *C. orientalis,* also called *C. graveolens* (Oriental clematis)

Compared to the boldly colored hybrid forms of clematis found in many North American gardens, these two Asiatic species are charming but low-key. The flowers of cream clematis are creamy white with a green center stripe down the back of each petal-like sepal; the blooms of the Oriental clematis are yellow. In Japanese gardens these vines twine around stone pillars or over bamboo trellises.

Cream clematis may be evergreen in mild climates but otherwise is deciduous. It grows 8 to 12 feet tall, with three-part lance-shaped leaves, each leaflet 1 to 2 inches long. The flowers are 2 to 3 inches across, with oval, slightly pointed sepals; their period of bloom is midsummer. Oriental clematis reaches a height of 10 to 15 feet. Its deciduous three-part leaves are composed of narrow leaflets, ½ to 2 inches long, that give the plant a fernlike appearance. The fragrant flowers are small, 1½ to 2 inches across, with sepals that end in pronounced points; they bloom abundantly in the fall. Silky silver-gray seed pods follow the flowers and remain on the plant for several months.

HOW TO GROW. Clematises are hardy in Zones 5-10 and thrive in a well-drained fertile soil that is neutral to slightly alkaline, pH 6.8 to 7.5. A cool, moist, shaded location is essential, especially in hot, dry areas. Plant clematis in the spring or fall, placing the growing point 2 inches deep. Fertilize in the spring with a light sprinkling of bone meal and dust the soil lightly in the fall with ground limestone. Mulch in summer with a 2- to 3-inch thick layer of organic material and in winter, with pine boughs.

Clematises should not be pruned for two years after planting, and thereafter only to maintain shape. Prune cream

LARGE INCURVE CHRYSANTHEMUM
Chrysanthemum morifolium 'Yellow Nob Hill'

CAMPHOR TREE
Cinnamomum camphora

For climate zones, see map, page 151.

ORIENTAL CLEMATIS
Clematis orientalis

JAPANESE DOGWOOD
Cornus kousa

clematis, which blooms on old wood, after flowering; prune Oriental clematis, which blooms on new wood, in the early spring. As plants become heavy, both types need to be tied to supports. Propagate additional plants from stem cuttings taken in midsummer or from seeds started in the fall and wintered over a cold frame.

COMMON CAMELLIA See *Camellia*
CORNEL, JAPANESE See *Cornus*
CORNELIAN CHERRY, JAPANESE See *Cornus*

CORNUS

C. kousa (Japanese dogwood, Japanese strawberry tree); *C. officinalis* (Japanese cornelian cherry, Japanese cornel)

The Asiatic dogwoods are prominent in Japanese gardens. Planted near the house as a specimen, the bushy Japanese dogwood bears flowers on the upper side of its branches. The Japanese cornelian cherry is frequently situated in garden corners where its blossoms are the first sign of spring. Both deciduous trees can be located near the base of a hill, where their spreading branches, pruned to accentuate their arching shape, will follow the line of the hillside; or they can be placed against dark backgrounds in order to intensify their pale flowers.

The Japanese dogwood is native to both Korea and Japan. It reaches a maximum height of 15 to 20 feet and spreads 8 to 10 feet wide. Great quantities of snowy-white flowers, 3 to 4 inches across, cover its horizontal branches in early summer, about a month later than native American dogwoods bloom. The bark of the tree peels in oddly shaped patches, disclosing paler bark beneath. Its leaves, which unfold before the flowers, are pointed ovals, 4 inches long, that turn scarlet in fall. In autumn, the Japanese dogwood bears red, strawberry-like fruit.

The Japanese cornelian cherry is a dense shrubby tree that grows slowly when young, but the rate increases with time, and the tree eventually reaches a height of 15 to 25 feet. Clusters of ¾-inch yellow flowers blossom at the tips of branches in early spring, before the oval 3-inch leaves appear. Oval red fruits, resembling cherries, ripen in summer.

HOW TO GROW. Both the Japanese dogwood and the Japanese cornelian cherry are hardy in Zones 5-8. They tolerate partial shade but do best in full sun and grow in any moist, rich soil, even adapting to such wet places as pond borders. The Japanese dogwood may be pruned in early spring, but keep pruning to a minimum as wounds heal slowly. The cornelian cherry should not be pruned until after blossoms fade, since the flowers appear on the previous year's growth. Propagate from seeds or from cuttings of mature wood taken in late summer.

CORYLOPSIS

C. pauciflora (buttercup winter hazel); *C. spicata* (spike winter hazel)

Buttercup and spike winter hazels, both native to Japan, are grown primarily for their early-spring flowers, which bloom long before most other deciduous shrubs show any sign of life. In Japanese gardens they are generally used as single accent plants, although occasionally they are seen massed in rows along the sides of houses. Both species are 5 to 6 feet tall with oval, deeply veined, dark green leaves that turn gold in the fall; those of the buttercup winter hazel are 2 inches long, while the leaves of the spike winter hazel are 4 inches long. On both species, the leaves unfurl after the flowers. Winter hazel flowers are fragrant, yellow and bell-shaped, about ½ inch long, and are borne in drooping clusters on smooth, silky young branches. The clusters of the buttercup winter hazel are relatively sparse, containing only two or three flowers; those of the spike winter hazel have six to 12 flowers and dangle as much as 6 inches.

HOW TO GROW. Winter hazels are hardy in Zones 6-9. They do best in a moist, well-drained acid soil, pH 5.5 to 6.5, enriched with peat moss or leaf mold, and thrive in either full sun or partial shade. Set out plants when they are dormant, in the fall; in northern areas, choose a protected site so extreme winter cold will not kill flower buds or a late frost damage the early blooms. Prune after flowering to keep a plant from growing too large. Propagate from cuttings of young wood taken in the spring or from cuttings of mature wood taken in late summer.

COTTON ROSE See *Hibiscus*
COW'S-TAIL PINE See *Cephalotaxus*
CRAB APPLE See *Malus*
CRAB APPLE, JAPANESE See *Malus*
CRAPE MYRTLE See *Lagerstroemia*
CREAM CLEMATIS See *Clematis*

CRYPTOMERIA

C. japonica (Japanese cedar, cryptomeria); *C. japonica nana* (dwarf Japanese cedar)

Growing as a narrow cone, Japanese cedar is a large evergreen tree, becoming 50 to 60 feet tall within 30 years. It is used extensively to form tall hedges around large Japanese gardens. Tightly packed along the branches, the inch-long needles may be bright green or green tinged with blue. During winter in cold regions the foliage turns bronze. The round 1-inch cones last for several years on the tree. The trunk is covered with shredding reddish-brown bark that reveals the yellow inner wood, which has a pungent fragrance. Young plants grow rapidly, adding 2 to 3 feet each year. The Japanese cedar is sensitive to salt air and pollution and cannot withstand harsh winter winds or hot, dry summer winds.

The slow-growing dwarf Japanese cedar forms a mound that becomes about 3 feet in height and 5 feet across in 25 years. Dark green in summer, the dense foliage becomes dull green or bluish in winter. With its slightly drooping branches, dwarf Japanese cedar is attractive planted as a specimen or in a container. Globosa Nana is a variety that is cone shaped when young but becomes globe shaped in maturity.

HOW TO GROW. Japanese cedars are hardy in Zones 8-10 and in coastal areas of Zone 7. They do not do well in areas with extremes of hot or cold temperatures and should be planted in a spot that is protected against wind. They grow fastest when given full sun, but can be planted in partial shade if rapid growth is not desired. A moist, well-drained slightly acid garden soil is ideal. Work cottonseed meal into the soil under the trees each spring. Mulch plants in the summer, using an organic material such as shredded bark to keep the soil moist and weed-free. Pruning, which is seldom necessary, should be done in the spring. Remove competing side shoots if a single trunk is desired. Plants are easily transplanted when young. Set out in spring or fall and keep the soil evenly moist for the first year. Sow seeds as soon as they ripen or take cuttings in the summer to propagate.

CUNNINGHAMIA

C. lanceolata, also called *C. sinensis* (China fir)

Growing to a mature height of 75 feet or more, this tall native of China is an evergreen tree with a broad cone shape and horizontal branches that droop slightly at the tips. In

For climate zones, see map, page 151.

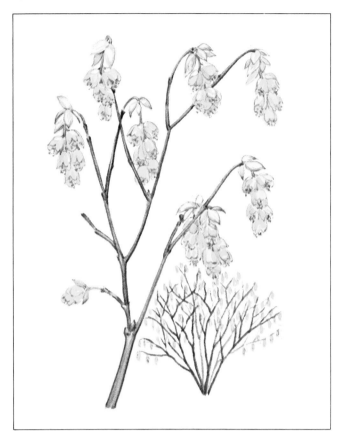

SPIKE WINTER HAZEL
Corylopsis spicata

JAPANESE CEDAR
Cryptomeria japonica

CHINA FIR
Cunninghamia lanceolata

JAPANESE FELT FERN
Cyclophorus lingua

Japan it is traditionally planted at shrines and temples and is at its best as a focal-point specimen in a large garden. The sharp, stiff 2- to 2½-inch needles have white bands on the undersides and are arranged in spirals along the branches. In the winter, the needles may turn from green to bronze. Trees retain their lower branches, even when old. With age, the rough brown outer bark peels off to reveal red inner bark. Globelike cones, 1½ to 2 inches across, are borne in clusters on the upper branches. Young trees increase by 2 or 3 feet each year and reach a height of 20 to 30 feet in about 25 years. The variety Glauca has blue-green foliage.

HOW TO GROW. China fir is hardy in Zones 7-10. If the tips of the branches are damaged by cold, they fall off and are replaced by new growth later in the year. The China fir is unusual among conifers in its ability to recover from injury; new shoots will sprout from the roots or stump of a tree that is cut down or killed to the ground by a severe winter. Plant in full sun or light shade and in any well-drained acid soil. Since the wood is brittle, the Chinese fir must be protected from strong winds to prevent the trunk from snapping. If foliage becomes yellowish, fertilize in the spring with cottonseed meal. Prune in the spring to limit growth, maintain shape or remove dead branches. The China fir may be transplanted in spring or fall. Propagate by seeds or cuttings started in spring or summer.

CYCLOPHORUS

C. lingua, also called *Niphobolus lingua* or *Pyrrosia lingua* (Japanese felt fern, tongue fern)

Japanese felt fern, named for its fuzzy, tongue-shaped fronds, is often classed as a climbing plant in Japan. When placed at the base of rough-barked trees, its creeping stems will cling to and climb the trunk. More conventionally, it is used against rocks and in the shade of larger plants. Its leathery dark green fronds, 9 to 15 inches high, are densely covered on the undersides with hairs and scales. The plants spread moderately fast, remain green all year long and unlike most ferns, can tolerate drought, once established. The fronds of one variety, Corymifera, the crested felt fern, are forked at the tip; there is also a variegated kind.

HOW TO GROW. Japanese felt fern is hardy only in Zone 10, in Southern California and Florida. It thrives in light shade in moist, well-drained slightly acid soil with a pH of 6.0 to 7.0. An ideal soil mix is 1 part garden loam, 1 part builder's sand and 2 parts leaf mold or peat moss. Plant any time, placing ferns at the depth they were previously growing. Normally ferns do not need fertilizer but if leaves yellow, scatter fish-meal fertilizer around them in spring or midsummer. Propagate by dividing the creeping stems or by sowing spores that develop on the backs of fronds.

CYPRESS, FALSE See *Chamaecyparis*

CYRTOMIUM

C. falcatum (Japanese holly fern, holly fern)

The arching fronds and shiny, dark green holly-like leaflets of the Japanese holly fern provide dramatic shape and year-round color next to rocks, under trees or at the foot of a wooden bridge. Its leathery, 3- to 5-inch leaflets pack fronds that become 1 to 2½ feet tall and up to 9 inches wide. New growth unfurls in spring from a silvery cover. The variety Rochfordianum has wider, more deeply toothed leaflets, up to 2 inches across. Japanese holly fern, native to most of tropical Asia, spreads rapidly and is easier to grow than most ferns; it tolerates wind, polluted air and occasional drought.

HOW TO GROW. Japanese holly fern grows in Zones 8-10. It

does best in partial shade but it will tolerate sun and thrives in moist, well-drained acid soil with a pH of 5.5 to 6.5. An ideal soil mixture consists of equal parts garden loam, builder's sand and peat moss or leaf mold. Plant at any time, placing ferns at the depth they were previously growing. Normally ferns do not need to be fertilized but if leaves yellow, scatter fish-meal fertilizer around plants in spring or midsummer. Propagate by sowing spores that develop on the backs of leaflets or by division.

D

DAISY, NIPPON See *Chrysanthemum*

DAPHNE
D. odora (winter daphne)

Although native to China, winter daphne is widely used in Japanese gardens either singly or in scattered groups, often by the water's edge where its bright flowers are reflected. These evergreen shrubs grow rapidly to a maximum height of 3 to 5 feet in about five years and have a natural globular shape that may be accentuated by pruning. They have stiff oblong leaves, 2 to 3 inches long, and very fragrant pale purple flowers that bloom in clusters at branch tips in late winter and early spring. The variety Alba bears white flowers; Marginata has yellow-edged leaves. The bark and leaves of all winter daphnes are poisonous if eaten.

HOW TO GROW. Winter daphne is hardy in Zones 7-9. It grows best in partial shade but tolerates sun in cool and coastal areas. It thrives in moist, well-drained soil. In frost zones, plant the shrubs in spring or early fall; elsewhere, plant them at any time. To keep the soil moist and cool, provide a permanent mulch, 2 to 4 inches deep, of wood chips, chunky peat moss or ground bark. In spring, scatter cottonseed meal or rhododendron-azalea-camellia fertilizer beneath plants; if the soil becomes too acid, add ground limestone. Winter daphnes are difficult to transplant except when very small and container grown. Prune after spring flowering. Propagate from cuttings of mature growth taken in late spring or early summer.

DAY LILY See *Hemerocallis*

DEUTZIA
D. gracilis (slender deutzia); *D. scabra*, also called *D. crenata* (fuzzy deutzia)

A centuries-old favorite in Japan, the deutzia is prized for its white flowers, which cover the plant like snow in spring and early summer. It is often grown as an informal hedge because it tolerates pruning and clipping well, its twiggy branches quickly responding with new growth. In winter the tracery of bare branches traps snow in interesting patterns, as does the plant's peeling reddish-brown bark. Slender deutzia grows 2 to 4 feet high, with arching stems and a narrow, pointed leaves 2 to 2½ inches long. Its 3- to 4-inch flower clusters are white in the species, but there are also many cultivated varieties with flowers of pink, yellow and rose through purple. Fuzzy deutzia grows rapidly to a height of 6 to 8 feet, with a spread of 4 to 6 feet. It has hairy pale green leaves, 2 to 4 inches long, and tiny bell-shaped flowers that bloom in 2- to 3-inch clusters. Fuzzy deutzia is available in many cultivated varieties, some double flowered, others with blooms of pink, lavender or rose. Pride of Rochester has double white flowers with pale pink outer petals.

HOW TO GROW. Slender deutzia is hardy in Zones 4-9, fuzzy deutzia in Zones 5-9. They grow in either full sun or partial shade in a moist, rich soil. Plant them in spring,

HOLLY FERN
Cyrtomium falcatum

WINTER DAPHNE
Daphne odora

For climate zones, see map, page 151.

spacing hedge plants 2 to 2½ feet apart. In cold areas, the tips of deutzia branches suffer from winterkill and must be pruned in the spring. Other pruning, to maintain a neat appearance, should be postponed until after flowering since deutzia blooms are borne on the previous year's growth. When pruning for appearance, remove the oldest stems at ground level. All deutzias are pest and disease resistant.

DOGWOOD See *Cornus*
DOGWOOD, JAPANESE See *Cornus*

E

EAST INDIAN LOTUS See *Nelumbo*
ELM See *Ulmus*
ELM, CHINESE See *Ulmus*
ELM, JAPANESE See *Ulmus*

ENKIANTHUS

E. campanulatus (redvein enkianthus); *E. perulatus* (white enkianthus)

These Japanese members of the heath family have been used in Japanese gardens for centuries. They are valued for their shrubby growth, which is easily pruned into low, rounded shapes, and for their attractive flowers, foliage and bark. The flowers are bell shaped and dangle in clusters beneath the leaves; the foliage turns bright red in the fall; and the young bark is smooth, with a reddish tinge. They are often grown singly as specimen plants or in rows as a hedge.

Redvein enkianthus has creamy white flowers, ⅝ inch long, patterned with a network of red veins; they bloom in late spring. The leaves, which cluster at the ends of stems, are dull green, 1½ to 2 inches long, with finely toothed edges. In mild climates, this shrub may grow 20 feet tall, but in cold areas its mature height is between 6 and 8 feet; at this height its spread is 3 to 5 feet. White enkianthus, a smaller plant, grows only 6 feet high, with a spread of 3 to 4 feet. It has pure white flowers, ½ inch long, which bloom about a week before those of redvein enkianthus. The bright green leaves, 1 to 2½ inches long, typically turn scarlet in the fall but this coloring is sometimes mottled with yellow. Both species are tolerant of pollution and city growing conditions, but intolerant of being transplanted and once in place, should not be moved.

HOW TO GROW. Redvein enkianthus and white enkianthus are both hardy in Zones 5-9. Both grow best in a moist, well-drained acid soil, pH 5.0 to 6.0, similar to that needed by azaleas and rhododendrons. They do well in full sun or light shade. Plant in early spring or late fall; for hedges, set plants 2 to 3 feet apart. When clipping enkianthuses into hedges or ornamental shapes, prune new growth after spring flowering, but pruning is generally not required to maintain the plants' natural shape. Propagate from cuttings taken at any time of year, even in winter when the shrubs are dormant. Move young plants to their permanent location in the garden when they are two or three years old.

EPIMEDIUM

E. diphyllum; E. grandiflorum, also called *E. macranthum* (bishop's hat, long-spurred epimedium)

Epimediums are often seen in classical Japanese gardens at the water's edge, where their overlapping heart-shaped leaves soften rocks or simply hide the ground. Their foliage is attractive in all seasons—in spring the new leaves are tinted with pink or red; in summer they are marked by beautiful veins; in fall they turn bronze and may remain all winter if the plant is in a protected location. In addition, the epimediums produce interesting flowers made of four petal-like spreading sepals with four cup-shaped true petals in the center; these dangle in clusters at the end of wiry stems.

E. diphyllum, a native Japanese plant, is a dwarf species growing only 6 to 8 inches high. Its leaves are 2 to 3 inches long, and its flowers are white, ¾ to 1 inch across; it blooms in early spring. Bishop's hat, native to Korea as well as Japan, also has 2- to 3-inch-long leaves, but grows 9 to 12 inches high and has 1-inch-long flowers in colors ranging from white and yellow to rose and violet, depending on the variety. It blooms in late spring and early summer. Epimediums spread by means of creeping underground stems, the rhizomes, to become sizable clumps, but this growth is slow.

HOW TO GROW. Epimediums are hardy in Zones 3-8. They do best in partial shade and a rich, moist, well-drained soil supplemented with peat moss or leaf mold. Plant them in fall or spring, spacing them 8 to 10 inches apart. In early spring, clip plants back to ground level to dispose of old leaves, which might interfere with new growth. Propagate by dividing the rhizomes in midsummer.

EQUISETUM
E. hyemale (common scouring rush); *E. scirpoides* (dwarf scouring rush) (both also called horsetail)

Horsetails are reedlike evergreen plants with hollow, jointed stems. They are widely used in Japanese gardens by the edge of a pool, among rocks or in the shade of trees; the Japanese value them for their thin vertical lines and unusual cones that grow at the tips of fertile stems in summer. The bright green stems have many black-ringed joints, which sometimes sprout tiny branches. The cones, which contain spores, first appear brownish-green, then turn yellow as they ripen. Common scouring rush grows up to 4 feet tall, suitable for a low border. Dwarf scouring rush becomes only 6 inches tall; its twisting stems form tangled mats that are well suited for a ground cover. Both species spread rapidly by underground stems, or rhizomes, and are difficult to eradicate once established. The stems can be cut at any time for indoor arrangements. The abrasive silica contained in the stems makes them a popular scrubbing agent in Japan.

HOW TO GROW. Horsetails grow in Zones 3-8 in partial shade. They do best in constantly moist to wet soil with a pH of 6.0 to 7.0 but can tolerate drier conditions once established. Prepare the soil by mixing 1 part soil, 1 part builder's sand and 2 parts leaf mold or peat moss. To prevent spreading, plant clumps in pots and sink the pots to their rims in the garden or contain the rhizomes by placing metal barriers underground around the desired growing area. Propagate by dividing plants or by sowing spores as soon as they are ripe.

EULALIA GRASS See *Miscanthus*

F

FALSE CYPRESS See *Chamaecyparis*
FALSE SPIREA See *Astilbe*

FATSIA
F. japonica, also called *Aralia japonica* and *A. sieboldii* (Japanese aralia, Japanese fatsia)

The Japanese aralia is a tender evergreen shrub with large, fan-shaped leaves and spreading branches, like those of a tree. In Japan, this treelike shape is encouraged, often with pruning, and the plant is placed under larger trees or where its branches will overhang embankments or water. It grows fairly fast, reaching a height of 4 to 8 feet in three to five years. In its native Japan, it may become 15 to 20 feet

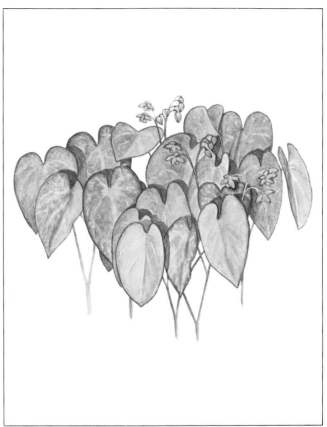

BISHOP'S HAT
Epimedium grandiflorum

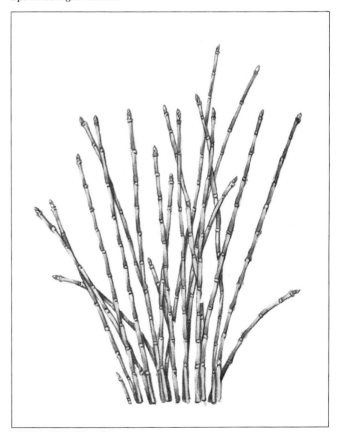

DWARF SCOURING RUSH
Equisetum scirpoides

For climate zones, see map, page 151.

JAPANESE ARALIA
Fatsia japonica

tall. The deeply cut, leathery leaves with seven to nine lobes grow 6 to 16 inches wide and extend horizontally from the stems. In late fall, small white flower clusters bloom in sprays 9 to 18 inches long at the tips of the branches; they are followed by tiny inedible black berries. One variety, *F. japonica albo marginatus* has white-edged leaves; another, *F. japonica aureo variegata* has leaves with gold markings. All forms tolerate salt air and city pollution.

HOW TO GROW. Japanese aralia is hardy in Zones 8-10. It grows best in moist, well-drained soil and in partial to deep shade but tolerates sun in coastal areas and near the northern limits of its hardiness. Plant in spring or fall. Fertilize at two-month intervals all through the year by scattering 5-10-5 fertilizer or cottonseed meal beneath plants. Prune in the early spring, shaping the shrub into tree form by cutting off leggy branches to about 6 inches from the ground. Propagate from seed or from cuttings taken in the spring. Japanese aralia is easy to transplant.

FELT FERN, JAPANESE See *Cyclophorus*
FERN, JAPANESE CLIMBING See *Lygodium*
FERN, JAPANESE FELT See *Cyclophorus*
FERN, JAPANESE HOLLY See *Cyrtomium*
FERN, JAPANESE PAINTED See *Athyrium*
FERN, TONGUE See *Cyclophorus*
FIR See *Abies*
FIR, CHINA See *Cunninghamia*

FIRMIANA
F. simplex, also called *F. platanifolia* (Chinese parasol tree, phoenix tree)

Since antiquity, the Chinese parasol tree's immense leaves have shaded garden teahouses. The branches are frequently pruned in layers to emphasize their naturally regular arrangement and to reveal more of the shiny gray-green bark, which in winter makes the leafless tree attractive. It is suitable for either single or mass plantings.

A native of both China and Japan, the Chinese parasol tree grows rapidly. In five years, a 5- to 6-foot tree will be 12 to 15 feet tall. Eventually the tree will reach 40 feet or more with a spread equal to its height. The foot-wide leaves account for the tree's common name, since each casts a large pool of shade. The leaves are deeply divided into three to five sections. In early summer, 12- to 18-inch clusters of greenish-white flowers appear. They are followed in autumn by 4-inch fruit pods that split into four or five petal-like sections, revealing seeds clinging to the edges of each section. The tree is fairly resistant to air pollution.

HOW TO GROW. The Chinese parasol tree grows best in frost-free areas of Zones 9 and 10. In the cooler parts of Zone 9 it will suffer some frost-damaged branches that will require pruning. The tree does well in a sunny site, in almost any moist, well-drained soil. Shallow roots make the tree susceptible to wind damage, so it should be planted in a sheltered location. Propagated from seed, it is easy to establish.

FISHPOLE BAMBOO See *Phyllostachys*
FIVE-LEAF AKEBIA See *Akebia*
FLORIST'S CHRYSANTHEMUM See *Chrysanthemum*
FLORIST'S SPIREA See *Astilbe*
FLOWERING CRAB APPLE See *Malus*

FORSYTHIA
F. japonica makino (makino forsythia); *F. suspensa* (weeping forsythia) (both also called golden bell)

In a Japanese garden, forsythias are planted in an open

CHINESE PARASOL TREE
Firmiana simplex

space or against the backdrop of a low hill where their bright yellow flowers are most conspicuous in early spring. Makino forsythia and weeping forsythia, two species widely used, have rambling, gracefully arching branches whose tips may touch the ground. Native to Japan, makino forsythia grows to about 5 feet in height; weeping forsythia, a Chinese species, may reach 10 feet, with a width of up to 15 feet. Before the leaves emerge in spring the branches of both are covered for their entire length with flaring, short-stalked flowers. The Japanese often cut the branches for indoor flower arrangements. Makino forsythia and weeping forsythia have 3- to 5-inch oval leaves with toothed edges. Like other forsythias, these two are fast-growing shrubs that are remarkably adaptable to adverse growing conditions; they withstand the air pollution of cities and can be successfully grown in seaside locations. They are also long-lived. A 50-year-old specimen may still be attractive and bloom profusely.

HOW TO GROW. The makino forsythia is hardy in Zones 6-9; the weeping forsythia is hardy in Zones 5-9. They grow well in almost any kind of well-drained soil in full sun or partial shade. Pruning should be done immediately after flowering, since flower buds will form on the new growth of that season for bloom the following spring. Each year, taking care to preserve the natural form of the plant, cut several four- or five-year-old branches to within 4 inches of the ground to encourage new growth. Both species are propagated by cuttings taken at any time of year except in winter, or by division.

FULL-MOON MAPLE See *Acer*
FUNKIA See *Hosta*

G

GARDENIA

G. jasminoides, also called *G. grandiflora* (gardenia, Cape jasmine); *G. jasminoides radicans* (creeping gardenia)

Since ancient times gardenias have been grown in Japanese tea gardens for their dark evergreen leaves and very fragrant waxy white flowers. These tender shade-tolerant natives of Japan and China are used individually against rocks and along streams or are planted in rows for hedges. They grow moderately fast but their size can readily be controlled with pruning. Cape jasmine becomes 3 to 5 feet tall in three to five years and bears 2½- to 5-inch blooms. Its 3- to 4-inch leaves are normally solid green, but one variety, *G. jasminoides aureo variegata,* has yellow markings on its foliage. Creeping gardenia, a smaller variety of the same species, grows only 6 to 12 inches tall but spreads up to 3 feet wide. It has 1-inch flowers encircled by 1-inch leaves. In areas where night temperatures do not fall below 65°, gardenias usually bloom in spring and summer, occasionally producing a few blooms in fall.

HOW TO GROW. Gardenias are hardy in Zones 8-10. They grow in full sun or partial shade and do best in moist, very acid soil, pH 4.5 to 5.5. In frost zones, plant gardenias in the spring after the danger of frost is past; elsewhere, plant at any time. Set them in the ground at the same depth at which they were previously growing. Prevent shallow roots from drying out with a permanent 2-inch mulch of wood chips, sawdust or ground bark. From spring through late summer, feed the plants once a month with a balanced fertilizer such as 20-20-20 or with cottonseed meal. Remove faded blooms to encourage more flowers. Prune to shape after flowering, removing as much as two thirds of the new growth in order to produce bushier plants. Propagate additional plants from cuttings of new growth.

For climate zones, see map, page 151.

WEEPING FORSYTHIA
Forsythia suspensa

GARDENIA
Gardenia jasminoides

GINKGO
Ginkgo biloba

CHINESE WITCH HAZEL
Hamamelis mollis

GINKGO

G. biloba (ginkgo, maidenhair tree)

The Japanese have a special affection for the ginkgo tree, a plant that is a holdover from the days when dinosaurs roamed the earth. Its survival to modern times is largely due to Buddhist monks, who saved it from extinction by planting it in their temple gardens; it no longer exists in the wild. Ginkgoes probably arrived in Japan from mainland China along with Buddhism, around 800 A.D., and have been a feature of Japanese gardens ever since. They are admired for their resilience and for the fan-shaped foliage that turns a beautiful golden color in the fall. Ginkgoes are used as specimen trees, as windbreaks and are sometimes pruned in the manner of bonsai.

There is only one species of ginkgo and it grows 80 to 100 feet tall. But it grows slowly: an 8- to 10-foot sapling takes 10 to 12 years to become 20 feet tall, and it may be 20 years before the tree's long, asymmetrical branches fill out to produce the rounded shape typical of the ginkgo's maturity. Its fan-shaped leaves, 4 inches across, resemble those of the maidenhair fern, hence the tree's common name. They offer little shade when the tree is young. In the spring, the ginkgo bears inconspicuous male and female flowers on separate trees. Female trees are seldom planted, however, because in late fall they bear foul-smelling yellow fruit.

Once recommended for urban plantings because it tolerated fumes and dust, the ginkgo has been discovered to be among the first trees damaged by noxious air pollutants. But it does withstand high winds and in Japan, where much of the housing is wood, it is also appreciated for its ability to resist fire.

HOW TO GROW. The ginkgo is hardy in Zones 5-9. It does well in full sun and almost any moist, well-drained soil. Plant in fall or spring. Prune young trees to shape them in early spring; because of their height, mature trees are seldom pruned. Propagate male ginkgoes from cuttings of new wood. Seedlings do not produce their first flowers for 20 years or more.

GOLD BAND LILY See *Lilium*
GOLDEN BAMBOO See *Phyllostachys*
GOLDEN BELL See *Forsythia*
GRASS, EULALIA See *Miscanthus*
GRASS, MONDO See *Ophiopogon*

H

HAMAMELIS

H. japonica (Japanese witch hazel); *H. mollis* (Chinese witch hazel)

In Japan, as in America, the witch hazel is grown primarily for its yellow midwinter flowers, whose unexpected color animates the monochromatic landscape. The two species of this plant used in Japanese gardens are intensely decorative, with twisted, crimped flowers that look like unravelled balls of string. Both plants, one Chinese, the other Japanese, are large shrubs whose erect branches are sometimes pruned into the shape of small trees.

The Japanese witch hazel grows 8 to 10 feet high and equally wide. Its dangling yellow flower petals are ¾ to 1 inch long, tinged with purple at the base, and bloom in small clusters along the bare branches in February. The glossy oval leaves, which come later, are 2 to 3½ inches long. In the fall they turn yellow and red. The Chinese witch hazel grows 10 to 15 feet tall and equally wide. It blooms even earlier, in January, and its flowers are fragrant and more profuse, clustering thickly along the branches; the petals are

1 to 1¼ inches long, golden yellow with red bases. The oval leaves are downy, 3 to 5 inches long, and turn yellow in the fall. Both species come in varieties whose flower colors and configurations may be different.

HOW TO GROW. Both Japanese and Chinese witch hazel are hardy in Zones 3-8, and are tolerant of industrial pollution but not of high winds, which in winter may damage their blooms. They thrive in full sun or partial shade and do best in a moist, well-drained acid soil, pH 5.5 to 6.5, supplemented with peat moss. Plant witch hazels in the spring or fall. Prune them in the spring, after flowering. Propagate from cuttings of new wood taken in the spring.

HAWTHORN, YEDDO See *Raphiolepis*
HEAVENLY BAMBOO See *Nandina*

HEMEROCALLIS

H. aurantiaca (orange day lily); *H. flava* (lemon lily); *H. fulva* (tawny day lily)

Many of the day lilies grown in American gardens had their origins in Japan, where for centuries the day lily's fountain of leaves have been as important to the texture of the garden as its flowers have been to the garden's color. Day lilies are all perennials and, in the warmer parts of Japan, their foliage sometimes remains green all winter. Although each trumpet-shaped flower lasts only a day, the many buds on each flower stalk open successively, so that cumulatively the plant has a long season of bloom. Day lilies have been hybridized extensively, and most species now have many flower colors and forms. They range from pale yellow to deep brick red, and may be single or double flowered. The three species listed here are all typically Japanese, though the original provenance of some may be China.

Orange day lily has flower stalks 2 to 3 feet tall and 2-foot-long leaves. It blooms from early to midsummer and has 4-inch orange flowers tinged with purple. Lemon lily has 2-foot-long leaves and arching flower stalks 3½ feet long. Its lemon-yellow flowers, 3½ inches wide, bloom from early to midsummer and are fragrant. Tawny day lily, a much hybridized species, has 3-foot-long leaves with wavy edges, and 4-foot flower stalks. Its flowers shade from orange to brick red and each petal has a pale orange stripe down its center. In its standard form the flowers are 4½ inches wide, but one variety, *H. fulva* Flore-Pleno has 5- to 6-inch flowers, while on another, Kwanso, these wider blooms are double flowered. This species blooms all summer long.

HOW TO GROW. Orange day lily is hardy in Zones 6-9, lemon lily in Zones 3-9 and tawny day lily in Zones 2-9. They do well in sun or partial shade and in any good garden soil but may take as long as three years to become established. Plant in spring or fall, spacing root clumps 2 to 3 feet apart. Propagate by dividing root clumps in spring or fall.

HIBISCUS

H. mutabilis (cotton rose); *H. syriacus* (rose-of-Sharon, shrub althea)

Large flowers generally do not fit Japanese ideas of garden scale, but the hibiscus is an exception. Single hibiscus plants are placed close to the house, where their blooms can be seen close up, or in a far corner, where distance enhances the value of the flower size. In severe winters, cotton rose may die back to the ground but usually returns the following spring; rose-of-Sharon is hardier. Their flowers appear in late summer and last into the fall, providing autumn color.

Cotton rose, a native of China, usually grows to a height of 6 feet but may reach 15 feet; it spreads to about 6 feet. The

TAWNY DAY LILY
Hemerocallis fulva 'Flore-Pleno'

ROSE-OF-SHARON
Hibiscus syriacus

For climate zones, see map, page 151.

119

flowers are 3 to 4 inches across, opening in the morning as white or pink and darkening to deep red by nightfall; they last only one day. The leaves are downy, about 4 inches across, with three to five lobes. Rose-of-Sharon, a somewhat smaller species, grows 6 to 12 feet high, with a spread of 4 to 6 feet. The flowers are 2½ to 4 inches across, and come in colors ranging from white through pink to purple, the petals shading from pale at the edge to darker in the center. The gray-green leaves, 2 to 3 inches across, may be either oval or indented and usually are divided into three lobes.

HOW TO GROW. Cotton rose is hardy in Zones 8 and 9; rose-of-Sharon in Zones 5-9. Both grow best in a sunny location in moist, well-drained soil. In warm climates, plant any time from fall to spring; the hardier rose-of-Sharon may be planted in either spring or fall in areas subject to frost. Regular pruning is not required, but either shrub may be pruned into the shape of a small tree, if desired, or may be clipped into a more compact form. This pruning should be done in the early spring before growth begins, since flowers are produced on the current season's growth. Propagate hibiscus from seeds, from cuttings of the current year's growth taken in the early summer or from cuttings of mature wood taken in early spring. Seeds germinate readily but flowers may not duplicate those of the parent plant.

HINOKI FALSE CYPRESS See *Chamaecyparis*
HOLLY See *Ilex*
HOLLY FERN, JAPANESE See *Cyrtomium*
HORSETAIL See *Equisetum*

HOSTA (FUNKIA)

H. fortunei (Fortune's plantain lily); *H. glauca,* also called *H. sieboldiana* (Siebold's plantain lily); *H. plantaginea* (fragrant plantain lily, August lily)

Most of the hostas familiar to American shade gardeners are indigenous to Japan; in fact, Japanese horticulturists are largely responsible for the many cultivated varieties available. Few gardens of any size in Japan are without a clump or two of these decorative plants.

All hostas are known for their foliage, which varies in size, shape and coloration but is almost always large-scaled, and for their sprays of trumpet-shaped, summer-blooming flowers, which contain 15 to 30 blooms that open in succession over a period of two weeks. Fortune's plantain lily has shiny pale green leaves, 5 inches long and 3 to 6 inches wide; its flowers are pale lavender, 1½ inches long, and rise above the foliage on 2- to 3-foot-tall stalks. Siebold's plantain lily has blue-tinged leaves 10 to 15 inches long and 6 to 10 inches wide; its flower stalks are shorter than the leaves, so that its sprays of lilac-colored flowers, each 1½ inches long, seem to nestle in the foliage. The fragrant plantain lily has heart-shaped leaves, 6 to 10 inches long. It blooms toward the end of summer, its pure white, waxy flowers tilting upward on flower stalks 1½ to 2½ feet tall. This species of hosta is one of the few whose flowers are fragrant. Royal Standard is a very fragrant hybrid.

HOW TO GROW. Hostas are hardy in Zones 3-9 and are very easy to grow. They thrive in almost any moist, well-drained soil, but do best in one that is enriched with peat moss. Light shade is necessary for the best leaf color. Set out plants in the fall or spring, spacing Fortune's plantain lily and fragrant plantain lily 18 inches apart, Siebold's plantain lily 24 inches apart. Hostas seed themselves; therefore, flowers should be removed before seeds form in order to prevent clumps from becoming overcrowded. Propagate by dividing clumps in the early spring.

FRAGRANT PLANTAIN LILY
Hosta plantaginea 'Royal Standard'

HYPERICUM
H. chinensis (willow-leaf St.-John's-wort); *H. patulum* (goldencup St.-John's-wort)

These two low-growing semievergreen shrubs, both Chinese in origin, are particularly popular for shady spots in Japanese gardens. They are used under trees, between rocks and along the banks of ponds, where their golden yellow flowers show to best advantage. Although they normally become 2 to 3 feet tall and spread as much as 3 feet wide, they can be cut back by a third, if desired, and can even be clipped and shaped into a matlike ground cover. Willow-leaf St.-John's-wort has narrow leaves 1 to 3 inches long; the leaves of goldencup St.-John's-wort are the same length but wider. The flowers of both species, 1½ to 2 inches across, are borne singly or in sprays at the ends of slightly drooping branches from midsummer to fall; those of goldencup St.-John's-wort tend to be more profuse, especially in named varieties. One of the most popular of these cultivated strains is Hidcote, a dwarf form with large flowers whose named varieties include Sungold.

HOW TO GROW. St.-John's-worts are hardy in Zones 6-9. They thrive in any well-drained soil in full sun or partial shade except in hot areas, where some shade is essential. Set out plants in the early spring, spacing them about 18 inches apart. In Zone 6, cover plants in winter with evergreen boughs or salt hay, or provide a permanent mulch of wood chips, pine needles or chunky peat moss, 2 to 4 inches deep. If winters are excessively cold, St.-John's-worts may lose their leaves but will generally produce new growth if cut back to ground level in early spring. This is also the season when they should be pruned. Propagate new plants from stem cuttings of new growth taken in late summer, by dividing plants in early spring or fall or by sowing seeds as they ripen or in early spring.

I

ILEX
I. crenata (Japanese holly); *I. rotunda* (Kurogane holly); *I. serrata* (Japanese winterberry)

In Japan, hollies are used extensively as accent plants and hedges near rocks and ponds. They are valued for their dense dark green foliage and long-lasting berries and are often pruned into ornamental rounded shapes. Japanese holly in its standard form is a bushy evergreen shrub that reaches an ultimate height of 15 to 20 feet. It has stiff, finely toothed leaves, up to 1¼ inches long, and black ¼-inch berries. But in its many varieties, both size and foliage may differ. The Japanese holly in all its forms grows well in polluted urban settings.

Kurogane holly, a fast-growing evergreen tree, may grow up to 60 feet tall in its native Japan, but in North America it seldom becomes more than 8 to 20 feet tall. It bears spineless oval leaves 1½ to 3½ inches long on purple stems and has ¼-inch oval red berries. Japanese winterberry, a deciduous shrub, grows 4 to 10 feet tall. Its dark green finely toothed leaves, 1½ to 3 inches long, drop in winter, exposing tiny berries that may remain on the branches until spring. On the standard form the berries are red, but one variety has white berries and another yellow berries. On all hollies, berries are borne only on female plants, and only when a male plant is grown nearby.

HOW TO GROW. Japanese holly is hardy in Zones 6-10, Kurogane holly in Zones 7-10 and Japanese winterberry in Zones 5-10. All thrive in full sun or partial shade, but in shade, plants bear fewer berries. They do best in a well-drained acid soil, pH 5.5 to 6.5. Set out plants in early

SUNGOLD ST.-JOHN'S-WORT
Hypericum patulum 'Sungold'

JAPANESE HOLLY
Ilex crenata

For climate zones, see map, page 151.

121

KIRILOW INDIGO
Indigofera kirilowii

JAPANESE IRIS
Iris kaempferi 'Peacock Strut'

spring, placing female plants within 100 feet of a male. Provide a permanent 2- to 4-inch mulch of pine needles, wood chips or ground bark to keep the roots moist and cool. Feed in early spring by scattering cottonseed meal or rhododendron-azalea-camellia fertilizer beneath the plants. Water plants in summer but allow them to become somewhat dry in fall, to resist winter cold better. Prune in late winter or early spring. Japanese holly can also be shaped by bending and weighting its branches. Propagate from cuttings taken from deciduous plants in midsummer and from evergreens in late summer. Or start from seeds ripened over winter and sown in the spring.

INDIGO See *Indigofera*
INDIGO, CHINESE See *Indigofera*
INDIGO, KIRILOW See *Indigofera*

INDIGOFERA

I. incarnata (Chinese indigo); *I. kirilowii* (Kirilow indigo)

These indigos, native to China but long cultivated in Japan, are tender deciduous shrubs with delicate flower spikes and fernlike foliage. In a Japanese garden they are often placed between rocks or stones or at the edge of a pond. Their compound leaves are composed of 7 to 13 oval leaflets arranged alternately along the leaf stems, and their flower spikes, which resemble those of the pea, are made up of 20 to 40 tubular blooms. Chinese indigo grows 1 to 1½ feet high. Its downy leaflets are 1 to 1½ inches long, and the individual flowers on the 6- to 8-inch flower spikes are ¾ inch long. The flowers, which bloom in midsummer, are white with a crimson base. The variety *I. incarnata alba*, white Chinese indigo, bears pure white flowers. Kirilow indigo, a taller plant, grows 3 to 4 feet high, but has finer leaves; the individual leaflets are only ½ to 1¼ inches long. Its rose-pink flowers, spotted with darker rose at the base, are ¾ inch long and form spikes 4 to 6 inches high. They bloom from early summer to midsummer. Both of these indigos may die to the ground in severe winters; however, they readily sprout new growth the following spring. Their dense root structure makes them excellent for locations where soil erosion is a problem.

HOW TO GROW. Chinese indigo is hardy in Zones 6-8, Kirilow indigo in Zones 4-8. They do best in a sunny location and a moist, well-drained soil. Plant them in fall or early spring. Indigos may be pruned to accentuate their shape, but maintenance pruning is seldom required. Some gardeners, however, cut this shrub back to the ground in the fall or spring to encourage new and bushier growth. Propagate from stem cuttings taken in the spring, from seeds or by division in early spring before new growth starts.

IRIS

I. ensata (sword-leaved iris); *I. kaempferi* (Japanese iris); *I. laevigata* (rabbit-ear iris); *I. sanguinea* (avame iris)

The bright, fleeting colors of irises in bloom provide a counterpoint to the subdued greens and browns that dominate the Japanese garden. A classic plant for hundreds of years, the iris is most often planted in masses. Set at the edge of a pond, irises are made doubly beautiful by their reflections in the water. They are also planted among garden stones. The beardless flowers of sword-leaved iris, Japanese iris, rabbit-ear iris and avame iris are composed of three erect petals called standards and three outer petal-like sepals called falls. All bloom in early to midsummer. These four Asiatic natives have erect sword-shaped foliage that dies to the ground in winter. The flowers of the sword-leaved iris vary in color from white to purple and have purple veins; the standards are often darker than the falls. The 1½-foot foliage is slightly taller than the flower stalks. The 3-foot-tall Peacock Strut is a hybrid Japanese iris with flowers that are 8 inches across. The white falls are tinged with lavender-blue, and the standards are a deeper shade of the same blue. Rabbit-ear iris, which flourishes in boggy areas, has 4- to 6-inch-wide reddish-purple flowers marked with yellow. Its foliage is 2 feet high. The avame iris has violet-blue falls and standards with yellow markings. Its ½-inch-wide leaves are 1½ feet tall.

HOW TO GROW. These four irises are hardy in Zones 4-9. They all grow best in full sun and an acid soil. Rabbit-ear iris should be planted in shallow water, while a moist location is suitable for the other species. Plant in spring, setting the roots of sword-leaved iris, Japanese iris and avame iris 2 to 3 inches below soil level and the roots of rabbit-ear iris 2 to 3 inches below water level. Divide plants to propagate and, at three- or four-year intervals, to prevent crowding.

IVY, BOSTON See *Parthenocissus*
IVY, JAPANESE See *Parthenocissus*

J

JASMINE See *Jasminum*
JASMINE, CAPE See *Gardenia*

JASMINUM

J. nudiflorum (winter jasmine)

This rambling deciduous plant, half shrub and half vine, is usually set among stones in the Japanese garden or, with a support, is used as a screen. In the American South it may reach a height of 15 feet and begin blooming as early as November, the green branches becoming lined with 1-inch bright yellow flowers. Farther north, winter jasmine may grow no more than 8 feet tall and flower in early spring. The shiny green leaves, which appear after the flowers, are composed of three slender leaflets each. Though it withstands pruning well, winter jasmine should not be planted in a cramped space. The tips of its arching branches root readily if they touch the ground.

HOW TO GROW. Winter jasmine is hardy in Zones 6-9. It can also be grown in the warmest part of Zone 5 if planted in a warm, protected spot—for example, near the south wall of a building. Cold winter winds may damage the flower buds. Plant winter jasmine in full sun and in a well-drained soil. Prune after flowering, since flower buds are formed on the previous season's growth. If old stems are no longer flowering well, cut them back to the ground to encourage new growth. Propagate from rooted branches or from cuttings.

JETBEAD See *Rhodotypos*
JUDAS TREE, CHINESE See *Cercis*
JUNIPER See *Juniperus*

JUNIPERUS

J. chinensis (Chinese juniper)

Their handsome shapes and foliage make these junipers favorite evergreen shrubs for a Japanese garden. Native from Japan to the Himalayas, they are long-lived and tolerate many adverse conditions—drought, wind, salt spray, smog and virtually any soil. The foliage is of two kinds: sharp-pointed young needles and scalelike mature needles that cling tightly to the twigs. In fall female plants produce gray-blue berries that often cling for more than one season. These slow-growing shrubs respond well to pruning and can

WINTER JASMINE
Jasminum nudiflorum

GOLD COAST JUNIPER
Juniperus chinensis aurea 'Gold Coast'

For climate zones, see map, page 151.

be kept at a constant size without difficulty. They are often trained as bonsai.

One variety of Chinese juniper, Kaizuka, called Hollywood juniper in the United States, forms a broad cone 15 feet tall in 25 years. Its twisting branches are densely covered with gray-green needles. Older plants tend to lean toward one side and may be pruned to accentuate this shape. Hollywood juniper is used as a windbreak in Japanese gardens and is also planted alone where its picturesque form is conspicuous. Another variety, *Aurea*, the Gold Coast juniper, is a compact, spreading shrub whose gold-suffused needles darken in winter. A mature plant can be kept 12 to 18 inches tall and 4 to 5 feet wide indefinitely with light pruning. It is attractive next to a stone path, in front of rocks, or as an edging for groupings of taller plants.

HOW TO GROW. Chinese junipers are hardy in Zones 6-9 in full sun. They do best in well-drained soil, either alkaline or acid, but tolerate dry, rocky or sandy soil. Normally they do not need to be fertilized, but weak plants may be strengthened by scattering cottonseed meal beneath them in spring. Prune in early spring before growth starts. To control size, also prune in summer and again in fall if necessary. Do not plant within several hundred feet of apple trees, hawthorns or cotoneasters because junipers are susceptible to cedar-apple rust, which causes galls.

K

KATSURA TREE See *Cercidiphyllum*

KERRIA
K. japonica (Kerria)

Kerria is a deciduous flowering shrub native to Japan and China that can be used in many places in a Japanese garden. Although usually planted by itself, often at the side of a pool, beneath tall trees or on a hillside slope, it may also be used in a shrub border. The five-petaled yellow-orange flowers bloom for only a week or so in spring, but a scattering of flowers may appear in summer and fall. This shrub provides interest all year long: its bright green 4-inch-long wedge-shaped leaves turn yellow in the fall and new branches remain green all winter. Kerria grows to a height and spread of 3 to 5 feet and has a dense, rounded form. The variety *K. japonica pleniflora*, called globeflower kerria, grows from 5 to 7 feet tall. Its flowers, which have overlapping petals, bloom over a two- or three-week period. Kerrias may be pruned to maintain a regular form.

HOW TO GROW. Kerrias are hardy in Zones 5-9. They grow best in a moist, well-drained soil supplemented with peat moss or compost. Plant shrubs in fall or spring. They grow best in partial shade, though they tolerate full sun. In cold regions the ends of twigs may be killed by frost. These dead tips should be removed in early spring. Globeflower kerria is less likely to suffer such damage. Since flowers are formed on the previous season's growth, major pruning should be done immediately after flowering. Old main stems that no longer flower profusely should be cut back to the ground to encourage new growth. Propagate by cuttings of new growth taken in early spring, by cuttings taken in fall or winter or by rooting branches by layering.

KERRIA, WHITE See *Rhodotypos*
KUROGANE HOLLY See *Ilex*

L

LACE SHRUB See *Stephanandra*
LADY PALM See *Rhapis*

GLOBEFLOWER KERRIA
Kerria japonica pleniflora

LAGERSTROEMIA
L. indica (crape myrtle)

Crape myrtle, a large deciduous shrub or small tree that is attractive the year around, is admired by the Japanese for its late summer flowers. Ranging in color from white to red or lavender, depending on the variety, the small crinkled flowers appear in clusters up to 12 inches long. A fast-growing plant native to China, crape myrtle may reach a height of 20 feet or more. Its trunks and branches are covered with smooth gray-brown bark that flakes off to reveal pinkish new bark beneath. In winter, its orderly, sculptural form is striking against a background of evergreens. Side branches may be removed to emphasize the upward thrust of the trunks. The leaves, 1 to 2½ inches long, are bronze when they unfold, becoming deep green as they mature. They turn yellow-orange in autumn before falling. Crape myrtle is usually planted singly.

HOW TO GROW. Crape myrtle is hardy in Zones 7-10. It requires full sun and a moist, well-drained soil that is supplemented with peat moss or compost. Pruning should be done in late winter. Any shoots killed by frost should be cut back. The new growth will produce flowers in the current season. Plant only container-grown or balled-and-burlaped plants; bare-rooted plants are difficult to establish. New plants can be easily propagated from cuttings taken in late fall, late spring or early summer.

LAUREL, JAPANESE See *Aucuba*

LESPEDEZA
L. bicolor (shrub bush clover); *L. japonica* (white bush clover); *L. thunbergii*, also called *L. sieboldii, L. formosa, L. penduliflora* or *Desmodium penduliflora* (purple bush clover)

In Japan, bush clover is traditionally known as one of the seven flowers of autumn because its late blooms herald the arrival of that season. Poems and paintings have been addressed to the grace and beauty of these deciduous shrubs, and gardeners appreciate them for their versatility. They may be allowed to grow naturally into tall shrubs 6 to 10 feet high, clipped into hedges, or trained over arching supports.

All three of these species, native to Japan, have similar leaves and flowers. Each leaf is composed of three downy leaflets, 1 to 2 inches long, and the flowers, borne in 2- to 6-inch sprays, have butterfly petals like those of the pea. They differ mostly in flower color and period of bloom. Shrub bush clover has rose-purple petals, sometimes edged in white, and blooms in late summer. White bush clover, true to its name, has white flowers and blooms in midfall. Purple bush clover blooms in late summer and early fall and has rose-purple flowers. In very cold winters, purple bush clover may die back to the ground, but this does not affect the following year's flowers, for all bush clovers bloom on new growth. The flowers are followed by inconspicuous pods.

HOW TO GROW. Shrub bush clover is hardy in Zones 4-8; white and purple bush clovers in Zones 5-8. They need full sun and do best in a sandy, well-drained soil. Plant them in spring, setting hedge plants 1½ to 2½ feet apart. Prune them in spring, severely if necessary, as new growth sprouts quickly. Propagate from cuttings of new wood taken in the spring or by seed.

LIGUSTRUM
L. japonicum (Japanese privet); *L. ovalifolium* (California privet)

Privets are among Japan's classic hedge plants, clipped severely to form screens and windbreaks. However, the Jap-

CRAPE MYRTLE
Lagerstroemia indica

SHRUB BUSH CLOVER
Lespedeza bicolor

For climate zones, see map, page 151.

125

SUWANNEE RIVER PRIVET
Ligustrum japonicum 'Suwannee River'

SHOWY JAPANESE LILY
Lilium speciosum

anese also use them as broad-leaved evergreen shrubs under the shade of trees. California privet grows rapidly, reaching heights of 9 to 15 feet in five or six years. Both are tolerant of such difficult conditions as city smog, drought and salt air, but Japanese privet is hardier. It has glossy dark green oval leaves, 2 to 4 inches long, that end in points. In summer, clusters of fragrant white flowers, 3 to 4 inches long, appear at the tips of branches. One variety, Suwannee River, grows up to 6 feet tall in six to eight years, but it bears few flowers and no fruit. California privet, despite its name, is of Japanese origin. Its shiny oval leaves are 2 to 2½ inches long, and its clusters of pungent summer-blooming white flowers, similar in size to those of the Japanese privet, are followed by black berries. One variety, *L. ovalifolium aureum,* has leaves with wide yellow borders and grows 6 to 8 feet high; another, *L. ovalifolium variegatum,* has leaves with edges of creamy white. The variegated privets tend to lose their dual coloration if they are grown in the shade.

HOW TO GROW. Japanese privet is hardy in Zones 7-10, California privet in Zones 6-9. Both grow well in sun or partial shade and in any soil. Set out plants in spring or fall, spacing them 1½ to 3 feet apart for hedges. Fertilize them only if growth seems exceptionally slow, scattering cotton-seed meal beneath them in spring. Privets grown as shrubs can be pruned once a year to control their size and shape; in frost zones this should be done in the spring, but in mild climates it can be done at any time. For hedges and formal shapes, privets can be sheared up to three times a year: in early spring as new growth starts; in summer whenever new branches are 3 to 4 inches long; and in fall to maintain a neat shape through the winter.

LILIUM

L. auratum (gold band lily); *L. lancifolium* (tiger lily); *L. speciosum* (showy Japanese lily)

Many of the familiar hybrid lilies of American gardens are descendants of these tall, stately Japanese summer-flowering bulbs. Too large to use in massed plantings in the average Japanese garden, they can nevertheless be found in small clumps, growing between dwarf evergreen shrubs or in the open shade of tall trees. All three species bear their flowers along the tops of erect stems lined alternately with slender, lance-shaped leaves 7 to 9 inches long.

The gold band lily, a native of Japan, grows 5 to 8 feet tall and produces immense fragrant white flowers, 10 to 12 inches across, with yellow stripes and speckled with red-brown spots. The tiger lily, native to the Chinese mainland as well as Japan, is 3 to 6 feet tall. It has red-orange flowers, 3 to 5 inches across, marked with black spots. The tiger lily's petals curve backward in an arc to meet the stem. The Japanese lily bears fragrant 4- to 6-inch-wide flowers on 4- to 6-foot stems; the blooms are white, usually with purple spots, although sometimes the spots are rose or crimson.

HOW TO GROW. Gold band, tiger and showy Japanese lilies are hardy in Zones 4-8. They need a moist, slightly acid soil, pH 6.0 to 6.5, enriched with leaf mold or peat moss, but good drainage is essential. Otherwise the bulbs will rot. They do well in either sun or partial shade, but in sun their roots should be kept cool in summer with a mulch. Plant bulbs 12 inches deep in the fall, any time before frost sets in, spacing them 8 to 10 inches apart. Fertilize in early spring, and again just before the flowers bloom. Propagate from the small bulbils found in the axils of the leaves, where they join the stem, or by removing large scales from the outsides of the bulbs; new bulbs will form at the bases of the scales when they are planted.

126

LILY See *Lilium*
LILY, DAY See *Hemerocallis*
LILY, PLANTAIN See *Hosta*
LILY-TURF, DWARF See *Ophiopogon*
LOTUS See *Nelumbo*
LOTUS, EAST INDIAN See *Nelumbo*
LOTUS, , SACRED See *Nelumbo*

LYGODIUM
L. japonicum, (Japanese climbing fern)

The long twining stems and feathery foliage of Japanese climbing fern make it equally suited to carpeting the ground or coiling around tree trunks, bridge railings or trellises. Its stems grow 8 to 10 feet long and bear triangular fronds 4 to 8 inches long and equally wide. Each frond is made up of many pale green papery leaflets; the fertile fronds, which produce spores, have more leaflets than the sterile fronds. Although the fronds are deciduous, dying back to the stem in winter, new ones appear the following spring. Despite their common name, these fast-growing plants are native to all of temperate-zone eastern Asia. Nurseries frequently list the species incorrectly as *L. scandens,* a less hardy, tropical vine.

HOW TO GROW. The Japanese climbing fern is hardy in Zones 7-10. It grows best in partial shade but will tolerate dappled sunlight. Plant it in a moist, well-drained acid soil, pH 5.5 to 6.5, composed of 1 part garden loam, 1 part builder's sand and 2 parts peat moss or leaf mold. Set out plants in the spring or fall, placing them at the depth they were previously growing. During the growing season, keep the soil constantly moist but never soggy. Normally ferns do not need to be fed, but if leaves turn yellow, scatter fish-meal fertilizer around the plants in spring or midsummer. In spring, cut off dead fronds before new leaves develop. Propagate additional plants by dividing plants in spring before new growth begins or by sowing spores that develop on the back of fertile fronds.

M
MACLEAYA
M. cordata (plume poppy, tree celandine)

The plume poppy, a native of Japan and China, is a large, handsome perennial that grows 8 feet tall in a single summer, then dies back to the ground in the winter. Its size, in addition to its branching habit and coarse-textured foliage, makes it a bold accent plant. In Japanese gardens it is frequently placed on the far side of a pond or in the background of a garden that is designed to resemble a wilderness with rampant, unplanned growth. Its placement is also dictated by its vigorous roots, which send up suckers around the plant and can become invasive.

The plume poppy's leaves are gray-green, 8 inches across, and deeply lobed, somewhat like the leaves of a fig tree. The flowers, blooming in late summer, are tiny cream-colored blooms that rise above the foliage in graceful plumelike clusters about a foot long. In autumn, seed pods follow the flowers, also in plumelike clusters. Like other members of the poppy family, the plume poppy has stems that are hollow and filled with sap.

HOW TO GROW. The plume poppy is hardy in Zones 3-8. It does well in either sun or partial shade and adapts to any soil, although a soil rich in peat moss or leaf mold suits it best. Set out plants in the spring, giving the roots 3 or 4 feet in which to grow. Divide roots every three or four years to prevent overcrowding. Propagate from suckers or by dividing root clumps.

JAPANESE CLIMBING FERN
Lygodium japonicum

PLUME POPPY
Macleaya cordata

For climate zones, see map, page 151.

STAR MAGNOLIA
Magnolia stellata

JAPANESE CRAB APPLE
Malus floribunda

MAGNOLIA

M. obovata (silver magnolia, whiteleaf Japanese magnolia); *M. stellata* (star magnolia)

Deciduous magnolia trees are of ornamental value in a Japanese garden for their showy fragrant flowers and their rich foliage. Silver magnolia is most effective when planted singly, with ample room to develop its tall, natural form. The smaller star magnolia is a better choice for a garden of modest size. Both species have smooth gray bark and large oval leaves with smooth edges. In late summer and fall, oval brown cones reveal bright red or orange seeds. Magnolias tolerate city pollution but are damaged by winter winds.

The silver magnolia is a large open-branched tree of conical shape. A native of China and Japan, it grows from 50 to 100 feet tall. Cup-shaped flowers, which appear in the spring after the leaves have unfolded, are up to 8 inches across. White when first open, they fade to a peach color. The anthers are bright crimson. Fuzzy and blue-white on the undersides, the leathery leaves are 8 to 10 inches long.

The hardiest and earliest to flower of these magnolias is the star magnolia, a small, shrubby tree that may have more than one trunk. A 4-foot tree becomes 6 to 10 feet tall in five or six years. At maturity the slow-growing star magnolia is 15 to 25 feet tall with a dense, rounded shape. The narrow petals of the white flowers appear before the leaves in spring. The star-shaped flowers, 3 to 4 inches across, become tinged with rose as they begin to fade. The dark green leaves are 4 to 5 inches long, with paler undersides. In the fall, they turn bronze or yellow, brightest when the tree is in full sun.

HOW TO GROW. The silver magnolia and star magnolia both grow in Zones 5-9. Plant in full sun or partial shade. They grow best in fertile, moist, well-drained soil that is very acid, pH 5.5 to 6.5, and enriched with organic matter such as peat moss or compost. Mulch young trees with organic matter to keep the soil cool, moist and weed free. Do not transplant established trees. Fertilize in the spring with a balanced plant food such as 10-10-10. Young growth responds well to pruning, which should be done in the summer. Large cuts do not heal well and should be made only when absolutely necessary. Train plants to the desired shape when they are young. Magnolias are usually propagated from cuttings of new growth taken in the summer. Seeds should be sown in the autumn as soon as they ripen. Plant balled-and-burlaped or container-grown plants in the early spring before new growth starts.

MAIDENHAIR TREE See *Ginkgo*

MALUS

M. floribunda (Japanese crab apple, showy crab apple); *M. halliana* (flowering crab apple)

Classic Japanese literature includes many references to the crab apple in its springtime bloom. The clusters of five-petaled 1- to 1½-inch flowers do not open simultaneously, and the different colors of buds and blossoms create a subtly shaded show before the leaves unfold. In the garden these small deciduous trees are best displayed singly or in small groupings with evergreen trees in the background.

Growing up to 25 feet with a spread of 15 feet or more, the Japanese crab apple dependably blossoms and fruits with great abundance every year. It is rounded in form and densely branched. The flower buds are a deep red but when fully open the fragrant flowers are rose-colored fading to pale pink. The yellow-and-red fruit, ⅜ inch across, ripens from late summer through fall. The pointed oval leaves are 2 to 3 inches long and have sharply toothed edges. Young branches are fuzzy and reddish brown. Blooming while young, this Japanese native vigorously grows in city, seashore or container plantings.

A smaller species is the flowering crab apple, which grows to 18 feet in height and has a naturally open branching pattern. Young twigs are purple and the pointed oval leaves have purple midribs. The rose-colored flowers develop into purple fruit ⅜ inch in diameter. This crab apple is a native of China and Japan.

HOW TO GROW. The Japanese crab apple grows in Zones 4-9 and the flowering crab apple in Zones 5-9. A location with full sun is best. Plant in moist but well-drained slightly acid soil enriched with organic matter such as peat moss, compost or leaf mold. Plant in spring or fall. Feed in the spring with a balanced fertilizer such as 10-10-10. Mulch young plants with compost, wood chips or other organic mulch to keep soil cool, moist and weed free. Prune young trees to develop more open branching. Older trees that have become dense should have some of the branches removed for better appearance and to improve air circulation and light penetration. Prune after flowering. Propagate from cuttings.

MAPLE See *Acer*
MIMOSA See *Albizia*

MISCANTHUS
M. sinensis (eulalia grass)

In Japan, the blooming of eulalia grass marks the arrival of autumn. Although it grows wild on mountains and in fields, this tall ornamental grass is often planted in a Japanese garden at water's edge or on the slope of a hill, where its arching leaves sway gently in the wind. A perennial native to Japan, China and Taiwan, eulalia grass grows in leafy clumps 8 to 10 feet high that slowly increase in width each year. A single clump will become 4 feet wide in 20 years, but some clumps eventually reach 10 feet. The plant's blue-green leaves are barely an inch across. A prominent white stripe bisects each leaf. The leaves persist in winter, turning light brown. *M. sinensis variegatus*, striped eulalia grass, reaches a height of 4 to 6 feet and has lengthwise yellow stripes; *M. sinensis zebrinus*, zebra grass, has yellow horizontal bands and grows 6 to 8 feet tall.

In early fall, eulalia grass bears 8-inch-long feathery spikes made of small greenish-white flowers. According to an ancient Japanese custom, the flower spikes are cut to decorate homes at the time of the midautumn full moon. Fan-shaped seed stalks, up to one foot long, follow the flowers. Eulalia grass is sometimes incorrectly called pampas grass.

HOW TO GROW. Eulalia grass grows in Zones 4-10. Striped eulalia grass and zebra grass are hardy in Zones 6-10. Eulalia grass and its varieties require full sun but can be planted in any moist-to-damp soil. In late winter cut any dead stems back to the ground. Propagate from seed or by dividing clumps in early spring.

MOMI FIR See *Abies*
MONDO GRASS See *Ophiopogon*

MOSS

The ideal ground cover for a Japanese garden is moss. Growing on rocks, between paving stones, over logs and around stone wash basins, these tiny plants create the feeling of age and permanence that the Japanese admire. Their rich colors and velvety textures have made them a favorite of Japanese landscape designers, who have collected and cultivated them for centuries, drawing upon some 20,000 differ-

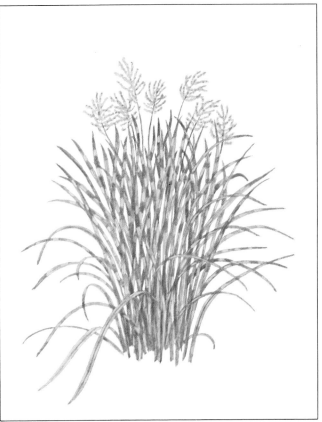

EULALIA GRASS
Miscanthus sinensis

For climate zones, see map, page 151.

ent kinds. There is a moss for almost any moist location. As a group, they withstand heat and cold, grow very slowly and live a long time; some moss gardens in Japan are hundreds of years old.

True mosses grow $1/16$ to 24 inches tall. They have many tiny flat leaves and stems that are often too closely packed to distinguish. The leaves expand when wet and close up when dry. Thousands of plants bunch together to make a patch of moss. Like ferns, mosses grow from spores. The spores develop green threadlike branches called protonema, which push into the ground and eventually develop leaves. The plants do not have true roots but attach themselves by tiny rootlets to the material on which they grow. By absorbing water, mosses allow moisture to soak into the ground gradually and help enrich the soil when they decay.

HOW TO GROW. Mosses grow throughout the United States. Most do best in open shade, where there is some sun in the morning and late afternoon, but a few kinds tolerate deep shade. All thrive in very moist, fertile soil. The easiest way to acquire moss for the garden is to transplant a strip from your own or a neighbor's woods; few nurseries carry mosses. If possible, lift the moss attached to part of the material on which it is already growing; otherwise gently remove moss with a wide knife, tearing as few of the threadlike protonema as possible. Press the strip into muddy soil on rocks or at the base of trees. Keep moist but not soggy; too much moisture without sun will cause the plants to develop mold. If the leaves dry out, plants are revived by soaking with water.

MOSS SAWARA FALSE CYPRESS See *Chamaecyparis*
MOUNTAIN ASH See *Sorbus*
MYRTLE, CRAPE See *Lagerstroemia*
MYRTLE, CREEPING See *Vinca*
MYRTLE, TRAILING See *Vinca*

N

NANDINA

N. domestica (nandina, heavenly bamboo, sacred bamboo)

Not truly a bamboo but similar in its foliage, this evergreen shrub is one of the classical plants of Japanese gardens. It is grown for its splendid red berries, which remain on the plant through most of the winter, and for its dainty foliage. Typically the Japanese prune some of the stems of nandina back to the ground, so the character of the foliage is accentuated. It is most often grown as a single accent plant—under trees, beside rocks, beside a stone water basin. Sometimes it is used as a hedge plant, and also as a subject for bonsai.

Nandina grows slowly, usually to a height of 4 to 8 feet. Its slender stems bear compound leaves, each made up of three to five loosely spaced leaflets, 1 to 3 inches long. The leaves are flushed with bronze in early spring, turn deep green in summer and become bright red in fall. Small white flowers bloom in clusters nearly a foot long in early spring. They are followed by equally large clusters of $1/2$-inch red berries. One variety, *N. domestica alba*, bears white berries.

HOW TO GROW. Nandina grows well in Zones 7-10. North of Zone 7, winter may kill the top of the plant but the roots will usually survive if well mulched. Nandina does best in full sun but also grows in partial shade. It thrives in a moist, well-drained soil enriched with peat moss; the plant should always be watered well. Plant nandina in the spring or fall, setting hedge plants 2 feet apart. Feed annually in the spring by scattering cottonseed meal around the plants. Prune in early spring, cutting some stems back to the ground in the Japanese manner. Propagate from seeds, which germinate in several months, or from stem cuttings.

NANDINA
Nandina domestica

NARCISSUS

N. tazetta (polyanthus narcissus)

One variety of the widely distributed polyanthus narcissus is native to China and is a popular springtime flower in Japanese gardens. It is often planted in small clumps against rocks, emerging from a bed of moss that hides the withered foliage during dormancy. This Chinese variety, *N. tazetta orientalis,* sometimes called the Chinese sacred lily or the joss flower, is very similar in appearance to the hybridized polyanthus narcissuses grown by American gardeners but is less hardy. For Western gardens based on Japanese designs, the more familiar forms are acceptable substitutes.

Polyanthus narcissuses produce fragrant flowers in clusters of four to eight blooms on 12-inch stalks. Each flower has six pure white petals and a shallow lemon-yellow crown, although hybridized forms such as Cragford may have cups of orange or red, sometimes edged with a deeper-colored band. The leaves are flat and grasslike, about ¾ inch wide, and are the same length as the flower stalk. None of the polyanthus narcissuses is particularly hardy, but in cold climates they are often forced indoors.

HOW TO GROW. Polyanthus narcissuses can be grown outdoors only in Zones 8-10. They do well in either full sun or partial shade in a light well-drained soil enriched with bone meal. Plant bulbs in fall, setting them 3 to 6 inches deep and 6 to 8 inches apart. Fertilize annually in the early spring by scattering additional bone meal around the plants before or just as the foliage appears. When bulbs become crowded, every three or four years, lift them and separate them. Propagate from offsets, the small bulbs that form at the base of the original bulb.

NELUMBO

N. nucifera (sacred lotus, East Indian lotus)

Cherished for centuries as a Buddhist symbol of life, the sacred lotus was once grown only in the large water gardens of temples and palaces; however, the introduction of dwarf varieties has broadened its usefulness to include pools of lesser size. In Japan, its exquisite flowers fill the air in summer with fragrance, and it is considered the official flower of the month of August.

Both the flowers and leaves of this exotic water plant are borne well above the water's surface and are mirrored in it. The flowers open from delicately pointed buds and last only three days, closing each night; fully open, they resemble roses in full bloom. When the petals fall, a large flat-topped fruit appears; it is perforated with holes that release seeds as a pepper shaker does. Soft and yellow when first ripe, the fruit turns woody as it dries and is used in ornamental winter arrangements.

The standard sacred lotus grows 3 to 6 feet tall and has giant parasol-shaped leaves 1 to 3 feet wide; the flowers range from creamy white through pink to deep rose, depending on the variety, and are 12 inches across. Dwarf versions like Momo Botan, which the Japanese call the rice-bowl lotus, become 10 to 12 inches tall, with leaves 6 inches across and 2- to 3-inch flowers. All forms of the sacred lily grow from brittle tubers that resemble sweet potatoes; they send out spreading runners and in small pools are best grown in containers that somewhat restrict their size.

HOW TO GROW. Sacred lotuses do well in Zones 4-10, but in areas where roots might freeze they should be protected or moved indoors during the winter. For the best flowers, they need full sun and a water temperature between 60° and 70°. In large ponds, tubers can be planted directly in soil under 1 to 3 feet of water, or seeds can be rolled into clay pellets

POLYANTHUS NARCISSUS
Narcissus tazetta 'Cragford'

SACRED LOTUS
Nelumbo nucifera

For climate zones, see map, page 151.

MONO BOTAN SACRED LOTUS
Nelumbo nucifera 'Momo Botan'

PYGMY WATERLILY
Nymphaea tetragona 'Georgi'

and dropped in the water. For container-grown lotuses, use baskets, boxes or tubs filled with heavy garden soil containing 1 part clay for every 3 parts of garden soil.

Place the tuber in a moist depression in the soil, taking care not to touch the growing tips, which break off easily. Cover with an additional inch of soil, leaving the growing tips exposed; lotuses will not grow if the tips are covered. Add an additional ½ inch of sand to keep soil from muddying the water. Place large lotuses in containers under 8 to 10 inches of water, dwarf varieties under 6 to 8 inches of water. As growth begins, lower large varieties to a maximum depth of 12 inches, smaller varieties to 8 to 10 inches. Each month during the growing season, feed lotuses with two tablets of aquatic-plant fertilizer.

In severe-weather areas, protect lotuses in the winter by digging up the tubers, removing foliage and storing tubers indoors in soil or sand at temperatures between 35° and 45°. Keep the soil or sand constantly moist. Remove container-grown plants from their soil every two years in the spring; cut away old growth and replant the younger sections with several growing points attached. Propagate additional plants by dividing tubers in the spring.

NIKKO FIR See *Abies*
NIPPON DAISY See *Chrysanthemum*

NYMPHAEA
N. tetragona (pygmy waterlily)

The cultivation of waterlilies is frequently assigned to special pools in Japanese gardens. If the garden is small, the pygmy waterlily is a logical choice; its dainty flowers are 1½ to 2½ inches in diameter. The many varieties differ mostly in such subtle distinctions as, for instance, the comparative sizes of inner petals and outer petals, or of outer petals and sepals. In Japan, one popular variety is *angusta,* which is native to that country and to China. However, gardeners in North America substitute a Siberian variety, *Tetragona* Georgi.

All pygmy waterlilies have white flowers that bloom on successive afternoons for three to five days. Their leaves are dark green mottled with reddish-brown, 3 to 4 inches across, and they grow from a tuber that is 3 to 6 inches long. Each plant spreads to fill less than one square foot of the surface of the water.

HOW TO GROW. Pygmy waterlilies grow in Zones 4-10, but where winter weather is severe, roots should be protected or the plants moved indoors. They grow best in full sunlight; five to eight hours of daily sun ensures good flowers. Plant pygmy waterlily tubers upright in 6-inch containers filled with garden soil, free of leaf material, silt or rotted wood. Place the container in water 2 to 4 inches deeper than the exposed crown—where leaves start. Feed every two or three weeks during the growing season with slow-release aquatic fertilizer tablets labeled 4-8-5 or 5-10-5. Every two years, repot plants, removing older growth and replacing old soil with new.

The roots of pygmy waterlilies survive freezing temperatures, but in water it is preferable either to cover pools with wood and a layer of burlap or to move plants indoors. Store in a cool basement, covering the plants with moist burlap. Store them in well-ventilated rodent-proof containers such as wire baskets. Propagate pygmy waterlilies from seeds collected from seed pods just before they burst in midsummer. Plant in shallow pans, covered with 2 inches of water. As soon as floating leaves appear, transplant to larger pots and move to outdoor pools.

O

OLIVE, SWEET See *Osmanthus*

OPHIOPOGON

O. japonicus (dwarf lily-turf, Japanese snake's beard, mondo grass)

A dense, low-growing evergreen ground cover, dwarf lily-turf provides an important textural element in Japanese garden design. It is frequently grown in shady places as well as along the banks of pools or streams. Dwarf lily-turf forms grasslike 6- to 18-inch mounds consisting of a profusion of ½- to 1-foot arching dark green foliage from underground stems called rhizomes. In early summer the plants bear compact spikes of ¼-inch lilac flowers. Clusters of pea-shaped blue berries follow and ripen in the fall. The plants spread slowly when first planted. Established plants, however, become thick, broad masses.

HOW TO GROW. Dwarf lily-turf grows best in Zones 8-10. In colder areas, the plants are sometimes grown in pots, kept indoors in winter in a room where the minimum temperature does not fall below 40°, then set out when the weather is warm. The plants thrive in shade and require rich, moist soil; although they will grow in sun, they do not tolerate dryness. Little maintenance is necessary except keeping the plants from spreading beyond bounds and removing deteriorated sections. Propagate additional plants by division of clumps in early spring. Set segments 6 to 12 inches apart in soil enriched with leaf mold or compost.

ORIENTAL CLEMATIS See *Clematis*

OSMANTHUS

O. fragrans (sweet osmanthus, sweet olive); *O. fragrans aurantiacus* (Chinese sweet osmanthus)

Sweet osmanthuses are small evergreen trees with very fragrant flowers. A specimen is often allowed to grow unpruned to its full height to serve as the principal tree in a small Japanese garden; sweet osmanthuses also make excellent border plants and can be grouped as hedges and windscreens. Native to Japan and China, sweet osmanthuses grow to 10 feet or more in 8 to 10 years and may become 25 feet tall; they can easily be kept at a much lower height, for they withstand pruning well. They are also pruned to maintain a rounded form. Their shiny 2- to 4-inch leaves usually have smooth edges, though an occasional leaf has holly-like teeth. In late winter or early spring tiny clusters of ¼-inch flowers perfume the air; small, inconspicuous black berries develop afterward. Sweet osmanthus has greenish-white flowers. The Chinese sweet osmanthus has orange flowers.

HOW TO GROW. Sweet osmanthuses are hardy in Zones 8 and 9. They grow best in full sun and moist, well-drained soil supplemented with peat moss or leaf mold, but tolerate partial shade and dry soil. Plant at any time of the year. Normally plants do not need fertilizer, but weak plants may be strengthened by scattering cottonseed meal beneath them in the spring. Prune at any time using hand clippers rather than shears to prevent damage to the foliage. Propagate additional plants from cuttings in late summer.

P

PACHYSANDRA

P. terminalis (Japanese pachysandra, Japanese spurge)

Japanese pachysandra, one of the most popular ground covers in the United States, is indeed a native of Japan; the mat-forming evergreen is widely used in Japanese gardens as a green border, in shady spots, on slopes or banks, or as a

DWARF LILY-TURF
Ophiopogon japonicus

SWEET OSMANTHUS
Osmanthus fragrans

For climate zones, see map, page 151.

JAPANESE PACHYSANDRA
Pachysandra terminalis

TREE PEONY
Paeonia suffruticosa

textural contrast to more delicate grasses and mosses. A hardy perennial, Japanese pachysandra becomes 8 to 12 inches tall. Glossy dark green foliage grows on fleshy stems in clusters of saw-toothed 1- to 3-inch-long oval leaves that contain the extra chlorophyll that allows survival in deep shade. In spring, 2- to 3-inch spikes of greenish-white flowers appear above the leaves. Once it is established, pachysandra spreads rapidly by means of creeping, underground stems to form a rich, tapestry-like covering.

HOW TO GROW. Japanese pachysandra grows in Zones 5-9. Partial shade is preferable, but the plants will thrive even in deep shade. Although they withstand competition from tree roots well, plants in such locations may require fertilizer periodically. Fertile, acid, damp soil is best, and Japanese pachysandra benefits from a mulch of oak leaves, wood chips or ground bark to conserve moisture. Very little care is necessary except to keep the plants from spreading beyond bounds. Propagate by dividing clumps in spring or by taking cuttings in summer. Plant Japanese pachysandra 6 to 12 inches apart in spring or early summer in soil enriched with peat moss or leaf mold.

PAEONIA

P. lactiflora (Chinese peony); *P. suffruticosa* (tree peony)

Peonies have had a place of honor in Japanese gardens for hundreds of years. Their spectacular, fragrant spring flowers have inspired festivals and are a recurrent motif in Japanese art. The 3- to 4-inch-wide flowers of the perennial Chinese peony have satiny white petals that are arranged in a single row around yellow stamens. The dark green foliage forms a rounded mass about 2 feet high; both the stems and the veins of the leaves are suffused with a reddish tone. The foliage dies back to the ground in winter, emerging again in early spring as red shoots. A very long-lived plant, the Chinese peony may still flourish at 50 years of age or more. It is usually planted in masses in a sunny spot in the garden.

The tree peony, brought to Japan from China by Buddhist monks in the 17th Century, is a 3- to 6-foot-tall deciduous shrub with a naturally dense, rounded shape that is often emphasized by pruning. It bears 6-inch-wide white or pink flowers with ruffled petals among pale green deeply lobed leaves. A fence makes an attractive backdrop for the profuse flowers and also helps protect this slow-growing shrub from wind. The tree peony is often grown in a container. There are many varieties of both species, extending the color range through red and purple. These varieties may have single or double flowers up to 12 inches across.

HOW TO GROW. The Chinese peony is hardy in Zones 3-8 and in the West Coast section of Zone 9, the tree peony in Zones 5-8. Although they grow best in full sun, both species tolerate partial shade; in fact, the tree peony needs to be shielded from the midday sun. A slightly acid well-drained soil supplemented with peat moss or leaf mold is best for both. Good drainage is essential, since the roots may otherwise rot. Plant Chinese peonies in early fall, taking care that the red crown buds are no more than 2 inches below soil level. Deeper planting prevents flowering. Plant balled-and-burlaped or container-grown tree peonies at any time; bare-rooted plants should be set out only in fall. Provide both species with a heavy mulch during the first winter after planting. Thereafter, little care is required. Propagate the Chinese peony by division in fall. Prune the tree peony in spring after it flowers.

PAGODA TREE, JAPANESE See *Sophora*
PAINTED FERN, JAPANESE See *Athyrium*

PALM, LADY See *Rhapis*
PARASOL TREE, CHINESE See *Firmiana*

PARTHENOCISSUS
P. tricuspidata (Boston ivy, Japanese ivy)

Boston ivy, a native of Japan despite its most familiar name, is a deciduous vine that attaches itself to stonework and other surfaces with sticky, sucker-like holdfasts. It is planted where it can climb walls, fences, arbors, over rocks or up trees with rough bark. It may also be used as a ground cover, grown in containers, or even trained as a bonsai. It is appreciated by the Japanese for its bold, beautifully colored foliage. The young leaves are red, turning to a glossy green as they mature. In the fall, they become red, yellow, or orange before falling. Up to 8 inches across, the leaves vary in shape. They may be wide ovals with coarse teeth, two or three deep lobes, or three separate leaflets. The thin stems may become 60 feet long. On vertical surfaces they form patterns that are attractive in winter. In the summer, 1- to 2-inch clusters of small yellow-green flowers are produced. These are followed in the fall by round ¼-inch blue-black fruit with a silver cast. The fruits are eaten by birds.

If grown as a ground cover, Boston ivy will form a carpet 12 inches deep. It is tolerant of city and seashore conditions. Because it grows so fast, Boston ivy can withstand heavy pruning to keep it within bounds. It should not be allowed to grow between roof shingles or in rain gutters or to climb a house that has wood siding, since its tenacious holdfasts may cause damage.

HOW TO GROW. Boston ivy grows in Zones 5-10 in full sun or partial shade. It does best in deep, moist, well-drained soil enriched with organic matter such as compost, peat moss or leaf mold. Plant in spring or autumn, using container-grown stock. Set 3 to 4 inches apart at the base of the support. Once established, it will withstand drier conditions. Fertilize in the spring, working a balanced fertilizer such as 10-10-10 into the soil. Prune in early spring to limit or shape growth. The growing tips can be pinched out to promote branching. Newly planted Boston ivy will need tying or staking until it attaches itself to supports. Propagate from stem cuttings taken in the spring or from seeds sown in the fall.

PEONY See *Paeonia*
PERIWINKLE, COMMON See *Vinca*
PHOENIX TREE See *Firmiana*

PHOTINIA
P. glabra (Japanese photinia); *P. villosa* (Oriental photinia)

Japanese photinia and Oriental photinia can be small trees or large shrubs and are used in Japanese gardens as hedges, planted as specimens or massed in front of larger trees. Often the branches of a shrubby young plant are selectively pruned so it will take on a more treelike form. Both photinias bear clusters of tiny white flowers in the spring, followed in the fall by bright red berries. Fast growing, they will increase by 1 to 2 feet a year when young. The evergreen Japanese photinia may reach a height of 20 feet but can be kept smaller with pruning. Its leaves are red when young, changing to green with age. Small teeth line the edges of the shiny leaves. The flower clusters are 4 inches across and the red fruits gradually turn black during the winter.

Oriental photinia, found not only in Japan but also in Korea and China, is 10 to 15 feet tall at maturity. A deciduous species, it has leaves that are slightly smaller and more leathery than those of Japanese photinia. When young, they are slightly fuzzy, but they become smooth later. Dark green

BOSTON IVY
Parthenocissus tricuspidata

ORIENTAL PHOTINIA
Photinia villosa

For climate zones, see map, page 151.

BLACK BAMBOO
Phyllostachys nigra

JAPANESE ANDROMEDA
Pieris japonica

during the summer, in the fall they turn a reddish-bronze. The flat flower clusters are only 2 inches across, but the berries are larger than those of the Japanese photinia.

HOW TO GROW. Japanese photinia grows well in full sun or partial shade in Zones 8-10. The Oriental photinia is hardy in Zones 5-10 and requires full sun. Plant either species in spring in a moist, well-drained soil enriched with peat moss, compost or leaf mold. Allow the soil to dry slightly in the fall to allow the foliage of the Japanese photinia to mature before cool temperatures arrive. If its leaves are yellowish, fertilize in the spring with cottonseed meal. Photinias may be pruned during the summer to limit their size or change the shape. Pinching off the tips of new growth will force branching and, with the Japanese photinia, increases the amount of new red growth. Propagate from cuttings taken in late spring or summer.

PHYLLOSTACHYS

P. bambusoides aurea, also called *P. aurea* (golden bamboo, fishpole bamboo); *P. nigra* (black bamboo)

It is impossible to imagine Japan without bamboo. Although these tall grasses are native to China, they have been naturalized in Japan for centuries and grow wild in dense groves on the hillsides. Small clumps of bamboo customarily punctuate the doorway to a house and their shadows pattern the translucent shoji screens that separate house from garden. The plants are usually pruned so that only two or three stems rise from each root, and the stems are often defoliated at the bases, intensifying their airy appearance.

Bamboos have hollow, jointed stems that rise from creeping underground stems; they may shoot up 15 feet or more in only three months, depending on the species. Their long evergreen leaves dangle from short leafstalks that emerge at the stem joints. In some bamboos, inconspicuous flowers, like those of grass, sometimes appear in the summer. Bamboos spread so rapidly they need an underground barrier to prevent them from invading the rest of the garden.

Golden bamboo grows 10 to 15 feet tall or taller and has golden yellow stems, up to 1½ inches thick, with very prominent joints near the bases. Its dark green leaves, 2 to 4½ inches long, are serrated on one side. Black bamboo usually grows 8 to 12 feet tall but may reach 25 feet. Its striking 1¼-inch-thick stems are green with black spots when young, maturing to solid black with dramatic white bands. It produces many narrow blue-green leaves, 2 to 5 inches long.

HOW TO GROW. Both bamboos are hardy in Zones 8-10. They do best in full sun in moist, well-drained soil, but will tolerate partial shade and somewhat poorer soil. Choose a location protected from strong winds. Set out nursery plants at any time, spacing them 2 to 3 feet apart. To prevent bamboo from spreading, place metal barriers underground, 2 to 3 feet deep, around the growing area. Keep soil constantly moist, watering plants profusely in spring when new growth starts and during hot, dry weather. In severe winters, if temperatures drop below 10° protect roots with a winter mulch of leaves. From spring to fall, feed once a month with lawn fertilizer. To control size and maintain vertical lines, break off young shoots as they appear in spring (in Japan these shoots are eaten). To thin, cut mature stems down to the ground. Propagate by dividing plants in early spring.

PIERIS

P. japonica (Japanese andromeda)

Native to central and southern Japan where it has traditionally been a favorite for tea gardens and temple gardens, Japanese andromeda is a broad-leaved evergreen shrub with handsome foliage and graceful flowers. Japanese gardeners often plant it in groups, either under large trees or beside rocks. Andromedas become 4 to 6 feet tall with an equal spread and have pleasantly curving branches. The shiny oblong leaves, 1½ to 3 inches long, are bronze colored when young, but then turn green in the summer. In spring, the branch tips bear drooping clusters of white flowers, 3 to 6 inches long. After the blooms fade, new pink-green buds form and remain on the bushes until the following spring, giving the plants the appearance of being in bloom throughout most of the year. Japanese andromedas grow slowly, reaching their maximum height in five to eight years. If sheltered, they tolerate cold relatively well, and they thrive in the salty, breezy air of the seashore, provided the climate is not excessively hot.

HOW TO GROW. Japanese andromedas grow in Zones 5-8 in the East and in Zones 8 and 9 in coastal areas of the Pacific Northwest. They thrive in light shade and will grow in full sun if kept moist at all times. Japanese andromedas require a moist, well-drained soil enriched with 1 part peat moss or leaf mold to 2 parts soil. Plant andromedas in spring or early fall, spacing them 3 to 4 feet apart if grouped. In colder areas, give them a location sheltered from strong wind. Fertilize in early spring with a light scattering of cottonseed meal or rhododendron-azalea-camellia fertilizer. Mulch permanently with pine needles, wood chips or chunky peat moss to prevent roots from drying. Japanese andromedas are by nature shapely plants, so little pruning is required. Propagate from stem cuttings taken in late summer or from seed.

PINE See *Pinus*
PINE, COW'S-TAIL See *Cephalotaxus*
PINE, UMBRELLA See *Sciadopitys*

PINUS

P. densiflora (Japanese red pine); *P. thunbergiana* (Japanese black pine)

The Japanese red and black pines, indispensable in the Japanese landscape, are used pruned or unpruned as hedges, windbreaks, background plantings or as single design elements. The Japanese consider the black pine to be a masculine tree, the red pine a feminine tree. Both are pyramid-shaped when young but become more rounded with age. They have long, thin needles and woody cones, which take several years to develop but then remain on the tree for several more years. The Japanese black pine is very tolerant of salt air and both trees are tolerant of wind and dry soil but are sensitive to pollution. They grow rapidly when young, becoming 10 feet tall in 10 years, and are long-lived.

The Japanese red pine grows 90 to 120 feet tall, with horizontal branches that tend to twist and knot, forming an open, irregular shape. It has flexible blue-green needles, 3 to 5 inches long, and produces many cones 2 inches long. Young growth may be green, yellow or purple; older wood on trunks and limbs is reddish-orange and roughly textured.

The Japanese black pine grows 100 to 130 feet tall. A rugged and picturesque tree, it has dense, wide-spreading branches. Its 3- to 5-inch-long dark green needles are stiff, thick and sharp. The bark is dark gray or black; the cones are 2½ inches long.

HOW TO GROW. The Japanese red and black pines are hardy in Zones 5-10 and should have full sun. They do best in a well-drained acid soil, pH 5.0 to 6.5, but if given extra care when young, they will tolerate dry, rocky or sandy soil once established. In poor sandy soil they will be dense and slower growing. Plant pines in the spring or early fall, choos-

JAPANESE BLACK PINE
Pinus thunbergiana

For climate zones, see map, page 151.

JAPANESE PITTOSPORUM
Pittosporum tobira

MARIE'S BALLOONFLOWER
Platycodon grandiflorus 'Mariesii'

ing plants less than 4 feet tall unless they have been special-
ly grown in a nursery. They may be left totally unpruned,
but usually at least the lower branches are removed from
young trees to allow a clear length of trunk to show. Pruning
is generally done in the summer, fall or winter. When trained
as a hedge, however, pines should be pruned in late spring
or early summer, when the young shoots are half grown.
Propagate from seed.

PITTOSPORUM
P. tobira (Japanese pittosporum)

Japanese pittosporum, a broad-leaved evergreen shrub, is
native to the central and southern parts of Japan. Surprisingly, it is not used much in private gardens although it is
frequently seen in public gardens and along Japanese streets
and roadways. It is a sturdy plant, resistant to salt air and
smog, and it has a naturally rounded shape that adapts well
to various kinds of formal pruning, as a hedge of windbreak
or as a single decorative specimen plant. Its average height is
6 to 10 feet, and after a decade or so it becomes equally
wide, forming a symmetrical mound. The leaves are leathery
dark green ovals, 1½ inches wide and 2 to 4 inches long. In
spring, the plant bears 2- to 3-inch clusters of small creamy
white blossoms that have a delicate orange or lemon scent.
These are followed in the fall by brown egg-shaped berries,
½ inch long. One variety, *P. tobira variegata,* has leaves
edged in white and grows only 4 to 6 feet tall.

HOW TO GROW. Japanese pittosporums grow best in the
warmth of Zones 7-10. The plants flourish in both full sun
and light shade, and although a well-drained, sandy soil is
preferred, pittosporums will tolerate nearly any soil. Plant in
spring, setting hedge plants 2 to 3 feet apart. If plants appear
weak or spindly, sprinkle a small amount of 5-10-5 fertilizer
on the ground around the bushes, dusting it out to the perim-
eter of the branches. Shapely plants by nature, Japanese
pittosporums require little maintenance pruning but may
be clipped into ornamental shapes, if desired, in spring and
early summer. Propagate Japanese pittosporums from stem
cuttings of new growth taken in midsummer. Start the cuttings in a cold frame, then plant them in pots kept in a frost-
free location until planting time the following spring.

PLATYCODON
P. grandiflorus (balloonflower, Chinese bellflower)

For centuries the balloonflower has been a popular Japanese garden perennial. It forms a neat clump that spreads
very little, flowers continuously from midsummer to fall and
decorates the foot of a tree as handily as it softens the base of
a sunny rock. The plants reach their full height in one season
of growth, dying back to the ground each winter, and will last
with little or no attention for more than 20 years. The
flowers in the traditional Japanese varieties are usually blue-
purple, although some varieties have white blooms. The
buds are balloon shaped, accounting for their common name,
but the opened flowers are saucer shaped, 2 inches wide.
The leaves are 2 to 3 inches long, oval and slightly toothed.
Normally the balloonflower is 2 to 3 feet tall, but a dwarf
variety, Mariesii, grows only 18 inches high.

HOW TO GROW. Chinese balloonflowers are hardy in Zones
3-10 and will grow in almost any kind of soil; however, they
prefer a soil that is rich, moist and well drained. They do
well in either full sun or partial shade. Plant in either spring
or fall, spacing root clumps 12 inches apart. Balloonflowers
should not be transplanted, once they are established, and
are best propagated from seed sown in the spring or by
setting out young container-grown plants.

PLUM YEW See *Cephalotaxus*
PLUME POPPY See *Macleaya*

PODOCARPUS
P. macrophyllus (yew podocarpus)

This tall, shrubby evergreen tree satisfies many of the ideals of Japanese landscape design. It is naturally picturesque, with irregular horizontal branches, slightly drooping at the tips, and a broadly columnar shape. In large gardens it may be left unpruned, but yew podocarpus also responds well to pruning. In coastal areas, yew podocarpus is frequently used as a hedge or windbreak because its foliage withstands salt air.

In most gardens, yew podocarpus grows slowly, 8 inches or less a year, to about 30 feet tall, but after many years it may reach 60 feet. It has flat supple needles, 3 to 4 inches long and ½ inch wide; when young the needles are uniformly pale green, but with age the top surfaces darken.

The yew podocarpus is native to the mountains of Japan, but one frequently used variety, Maki, grows wild in China. Sometimes called shrubby yew podocarpus, it has branches that are more erect than those of the species and more densely covered with needles. Although yew podocarpus survives salt air, it is damaged by air pollution.

HOW TO GROW. Yew podocarpus is a tender evergreen, growing only in Zones 8-10. It grows in full sun or, where summers are hot, in light shade. Ideally it should have a moist, well-drained acid sandy soil, pH 5.5 to 6.5, enriched with peat moss or leaf mold. Set out balled-and-burlaped or container-grown trees any time from spring through fall. If foliage becomes pale, fertilize in the spring with cottonseed meal. Prune the trees when they are actively growing, to maintain shape or limit size. Propagate from seeds sown as soon as they are ripe or from cuttings of new growth taken in the summer.

POPPY, PLUME See *Macleaya*
POTOMAC CHERRY See *Prunus*
PRIVET See *Ligustrum*

PRUNUS
P. glandulosa (flowering almond); *P. serrulata* (Oriental cherry, Japanese flowering cherry); *P. subhirtella pendula* (weeping Higan cherry); *P. yedoensis* (Yoshino cherry, Japanese flowering cherry, Potomac cherry)

For centuries, ornamental cherries have been used in Japanese landscaping, gracing small gardens as well as roadsides and large temple gardens. Gardeners become connoisseurs of the beautiful spring-blooming flowers and can draw upon many species and varieties. The ornamental cherries belong to the same genus as the almond, apricot, cherry, nectarine, peach and plum. They are deciduous shrubs or small trees, and their flowers—usually pink, rose or white—may be single or double and are usually borne in clusters. Single flowers have five rounded petals; double forms have up to 30 petals. Single-flowered types produce red to black fruit during the summer, but it is often inconspicuous. The pointed, oval leaves are medium green with finely toothed edges, and each has two small red bumps, called glands, at the base. The bark is sometimes a shiny red and may have interesting cracks and striations. Ornamental cherries grow relatively fast and are short-lived shallow-rooted plants with brittle wood, readily broken. They are sensitive to pollution and endangered by rodents, which may chew the bark.

The flowering almond is native to China and Japan. It is a bushy shrub, 3 to 5 feet tall and equally wide. In the

SHRUBBY YEW PODOCARPUS
Podocarpus macrophyllus 'Maki'

SHIROTAE ORIENTAL CHERRY
Prunus serrulata 'Shirotae'

For climate zones, see map, page 151.

DOUBLE-FLOWERED WEEPING HIGAN CHERRY
Prunus subhirtella 'Yae-shidare-higan'

YOSHINO CHERRY
Prunus yedoensis

spring, its branches are covered with ½-inch-wide flowers, which may be pink or white, single or double, depending on the variety. The dark red fruit, ⅜ to ½ inch long, ripens during the summer. The leaves are pointed and smooth, 1½ to 4 inches long.

The Oriental cherry grows wild in Japan and becomes a 60-foot tree. But in gardens it rarely exceeds 20 to 25 feet. There are many varieties, some of them differing very little from one another, and names are often confused. Depending on the variety, the flowers may be single or double, white or pink, ½ to 2½ inches across and appear before or with the leaves. Often fragrant, the flowers are usually borne in clusters of three to five. The fruit is black and the size of a pea. The leaves are long and narrow, smooth and shiny, and blue-white on the undersides; on many varieties the young leaves are bronze, turning green as they mature. Shirotae, also called Mt. Fuji, is a broad, spreading tree that has slightly drooping branches and long, drooping flower clusters. Semidouble to double, the fragrant flowers are 2 inches wide, with ruffled white petals.

The weeping Higan cherry is native to Japan and grows 12 feet tall and equally wide. Its long, drooping branches sweep to the ground and bear clusters of two to five light-pink flowers, 1½ inches across, with notched petals. The tree's small leaves, 1 to 3 inches long, give it a fine-textured appearance. One variety, Yae-shi-dare Higan, grows 25 to 30 feet tall and has dark pink double flowers. The Higan cherry is more tolerant of seashore and city conditions than other ornamental cherries.

The Yoshino cherry, also a native of Japan, forms a broad, graceful tree with arching branches; believed to be a hybrid of *P. subhirtella pendula* and *P. serrulata*, it needs room to develop its form. This is the cherry planted in great numbers around the Tidal Basin in Washington, D.C. It blooms in very early spring, producing fragrant single pale pink flowers, 1 to 1½ inches across, that fade to white with age. One variety, Akebono, also called Daybreak, has darker pink flowers. The Yoshino cherry's black fruit ripens in early summer. Its foliage is dense and the bark is gray-black. It does not tolerate pruning well.

HOW TO GROW. The flowering almond is hardy in Zones 4-10; the Oriental, weeping and Yoshino cherries, in Zones 6-10. All produce the best flowers in full sun, and should have a moist, well-drained, fertile, slightly acid soil, pH 6.0 to 7.0. Plant ornamental cherries in early fall or spring. Mulch them in the summer to keep the soil cool and moist, and wrap the bark in the fall to prevent winter sunscald and rodent damage. When young, feed annually in the spring, using a balanced fertilizer such as 10-10-10. Very little pruning and training is necessary, and too much can be detrimental, as wounds do not heal readily. However, an annual pruning of young plants helps to develop well-spaced uncrowded branching patterns. The best time for pruning is late fall or early spring. Propagate from cuttings taken in late summer and wintered over in cold frames.

Q

QUINCE, FLOWERING See *Chaenomeles*
QUINCE, JAPANESE See *Chaenomeles*

R

RAPHIOLEPIS
R. umbellata (Yeddo hawthorn)

A broad-leaved evergreen shrub with a naturally rounded form, the Yeddo hawthorn is a favorite with Japanese gardeners. It is prized for its sturdiness and slow growth as well as for its handsome appearance, and is often placed under trees, beside rocks or at the water's edge. The Yeddo hawthorn becomes 9 to 12 feet tall with an 8- to 10-foot spread. The dark leathery leaves are 2 to 3 inches long, and are oval, tapering to points. In summer, the plants produce fragrant clusters of ¾-inch pure white flowers on stiff flower stalks; these give way in the fall to clusters of pear-shaped blue-black berries. Yeddo hawthorns tolerate salt air and city pollution.

HOW TO GROW. Yeddo hawthorn grows best in Zones 8-10 but will withstand occasional light frost if grown in a protected location. The plants are best suited to California, Florida and the Gulf Coast. They thrive in full sun or partial shade and will tolerate a wide variety of soil conditions, including dryness during periods of drought. Plant Yeddo hawthorns in early spring or fall, and keep young plants watered well. Prune the naturally compact bushes only to remove straggling shoots that mar the plant's shape. Propagate from seed or from stem cuttings of new growth, including a piece of the main stem, taken in late summer or early fall.

RED PINE, JAPANESE See *Pinus*
REDBUD See *Cercis*

RHAPIS
R. excelsa (lady palm)

The lady palm probably originated in China but was imported into Japan centuries ago, where it was cultivated by designers of the great classical gardens for its exotic subtropical appearance—though in fact it survives winter cold of 20°. In mild areas it is planted directly in the garden; elsewhere it is usually grown in a container and kept indoors in winter. Like bamboo, which it resembles, it is often placed in front of a fence or outside the translucent wall screens of a Japanese house, where its leaves and stems create interesting patterns. This small palm grows 5 to 10 feet tall and has stiff stems sheathed near the base with coarse, dark brown fiber. The fan-shaped leaves, 1 to 2 feet wide, are deeply notched in typical palm-tree fashion, drooping gracefully at the ends of curving stalks. Flowers and fruit seldom develop outside the tropics.

HOW TO GROW. The lady palm grows outdoors only in Zones 9 and 10. The plant requires light shade and does best in a moist, well-drained soil enriched with peat moss or leaf mold. Water well during the growing season to ensure good growth, and feed annually by sprinkling a commercial fertilizer, such as one recommended for African violets, around the plant's roots. Propagate from young shoots or suckers that spring up around the main plant.

RHODODENDRON
R. keiskei (Keisk rhododendron); *R. metternichii* (leatherleaf rhododendron); *R. indicum* (indica azalea); *R. kuisianum* (Kyushu azalea); *R. linearifolium* (spider azalea); *R. mucronatum* (snow azalea)

Although most of the rhododendrons grown in Japanese gardens came originally from China, they have been an integral part of Japanese landscape design for many centuries, prized for their lovely trumpet-shaped spring flowers. One of the great classical gardens, built for the imperial villa at Shugakuin in the 17th Century, contains a remarkable two-tiered clipped tapestry hedge composed partly of rhododendrons of many colors planted in a band 30 feet wide across a hillside. The Japanese still like to plant rhododendrons massed on sloping sites, but they also use them as single specimens along the edges of pools and streams, under trees

YEDDO HAWTHORN
Raphiolepis umbellata

LADY PALM
Rhapis excelsa

For climate zones, see map, page 151.

KEISK RHODODENDRON
Rhododendron keiskei

SPIDER AZALEA
Rhododendron linearifolium polypetalum

or against rocks. Several of the small-leaved species are pruned into rounded bushes or low cushion shapes. Rhododendrons commonly used in Japan are the Keisk and leatherleaf species; all the other popular species are actually azaleas of the *Rhododendron* genus—and many of them are evergreen rather than deciduous shrubs. (Azalea flowers have five pollen-bearing stamens, while rhododendrons have 10 or more.) Not surprisingly, the Japanese have a long history of azalea breeding, and some of the hybridized azaleas most familiar to Western gardeners, such as the Kurume azaleas, are Japanese in origin.

RHODODENDRONS: Keisk rhododendron grows no higher than 2½ feet tall and has yellow flowers 2 inches across. Its oval, pointed evergreen leaves, about 2 inches long, are olive green on top, rusty brown on the undersides; in autumn, they turn bronze red. Leatherleaf rhododendron grows 8 feet tall and has oval evergreen leathery leaves, 6 inches long, glossy on top, downy and rusty brown on the undersides. The flowers are rose pink.

AZALEAS: The indica azalea is one of the oldest Japanese azaleas, bred since ancient times, and it is the type most commonly used for ornamental pruning. It is a slow-growing evergreen shrub that eventually becomes 3 to 6 feet tall. Its 1½-inch-long oval leaves grow on finely twigged branches. In the species, the flowers are red tinged with purple, about 2 to 3 inches wide, but it has been bred in many other colors. Kyushu azalea is a semievergreen spreading shrub, growing 3 feet tall, but up to 5 feet wide. Its leaves are bright green, about 1 inch long. The plant is covered in late spring with a solid mass of purple 1-inch-wide flowers.

The spider azalea is an unusual species. It is a 4-foot-tall shrub with narrow, ribbon-like evergreen leaves, 3 inches long and ½ inch wide, and rose-pink flowers with deeply divided petals. In one variety, *R. linearifolium macrosepalum,* the plant is somewhat smaller, 3 feet tall, and the leaves are deciduous and 3 inches long. But the flowers are even more curiously shaped than those of the species; they have 1¼-inch-long sepals that overshadow the petals. The flowers of this variety are fragrant and have been bred in several colors; in one, Polypetalum, flower petals and leaves are so similar in size that the plant seems to have pink and green leaves. The snow azalea, another type commonly used for ornamental pruning, grows 6 feet high and 4 to 6 feet wide. Its many branches are densely covered with oval evergreen leaves, 1½ to 2½ inches long, matted with hairs. Its fragrant white flowers, 1 to 3 inches wide, often bloom in pairs and may be stained with green, lilac or pink at the base, depending on the variety.

HOW TO GROW. Keisk rhododendron is hardy in Zones 5-9. Leatherleaf rhododendron is less cold resistant and grows best in Zones 6-10. The remaining azaleas do well in Zones 5-10. Rhododendrons grow best in partial shade, since full sunlight tends to bleach the flowers. They need an acid soil with a pH of 5.0 to 6.0, well mulched with organic material. Mix garden loam with equal parts of coarse sand and ground bark or oak leaves before planting. Soil around the rhododendrons' shallow roots must be kept cool and moist but well drained. All except leatherleaf rhododendron transplant well in the spring, or in the fall if mild winter weather does not damage the shallow-rooted plants. Fertilize once a year after the plant blooms with a mixture of 5-10-5 and cottonseed meal. Prune rhododendrons after the flowers have faded to induce new growth. Most evergreen rhododendrons are propagated from cuttings rooted in sand or a mixture of sand and peat. Deciduous rhododendrons are propagated by seed, grafting or cutting.

RHODOTYPOS

R. scandens (jetbead, white kerria)

Jetbead, a deciduous shrub, provides interest in a Japanese garden during every season. The 2-inch white flowers, reminiscent of wild roses, first open in late spring and continue to appear off and on until midsummer, an unusually long flowering season. The 2- to 3-inch leaves, which have toothed edges, cling to the shrub until quite late in the fall. Clusters of small shiny black fruits that follow the flowers persist through the winter. Native to China and Korea as well as Japan, jetbead grows 3 to 6 feet high and about the same width. The branches are greenish-brown and arching, the lower ones often reaching the ground. It may be pruned to accentuate its naturally rounded contours. Jetbead is usually combined with other plants in a shrub border and can also be used beneath large trees that cast light shade.

HOW TO GROW. Hardy in Zones 5-8, jetbead is easily grown in almost any kind of soil, but it does best in one supplemented with leaf mold or peat moss. Plant in partial shade or full sun. Prune in spring. Propagate from seed or cuttings taken at any time from late spring through winter.

ROSE, COTTON See *Hibiscus*
ROSE-OF-SHARON See *Hibiscus*

S

SACRED BAMBOO See *Nandina*
SACRED LOTUS See *Nelumbo*
ST.-JOHN'S-WORT, WILLOW-LEAF See *Hypericum*

SALIX

S. babylonica (Babylon weeping willow)

A broadly spreading deciduous tree with long, slender, drooping branches, the Babylon weeping willow symbolizes feminine grace and beauty to the Japanese. Used in private gardens as well as in parks surrounding temples and palaces, this weeping willow, a native of China, seems most in harmony with the landscape when planted beside a pond or stream. It needs ample room to develop its natural form.

Besides its graceful shape, the Babylon weeping willow is treasured for its fine-textured foliage, which rustles with the slightest breeze. The narrow pale green leaves are 1 inch across and 6 inches long and have gray-green undersides and toothed edges. The variety *S. babylonica crispa* has leaves curled in a spiral around the branches.

The Babylon weeping willow attains its mature height of 25 to 30 feet quickly, growing at a rate of 5 or 6 feet a year when it is young. Its width is about 25 feet. The tree is not long-lived, however, and the limbs of mature trees frequently break in windstorms. The extensive root system prevents erosion of pond and stream banks but can clog a drainage or septic system.

HOW TO GROW. The Babylon weeping willow is hardy in Zones 5-10. It requires full sun and grows best in moist soil. The roots are not harmed if they are submerged by periodic flooding. If plants are not growing well, feed them in spring with a balanced fertilizer such as 10-10-10. Young Babylon weeping willows should be pruned each year in late winter or early spring to maintain a single trunk, to remove lower branches, and to develop a pleasing shape. Stem cuttings, taken in fall or winter, are easily rooted. Plant new trees in spring. If a row is being set out, space the plants 10 to 12 feet apart to prevent the mature trees from being crowded.

SASANQUA CAMELLIA See *Camellia*
SCHOLAR TREE, CHINESE See *Sophora*

For climate zones, see map, page 151.

JETBEAD
Rhodotypos scandens

BABYLON WEEPING WILLOW
Salix babylonica

UMBRELLA PINE
Sciadopitys verticillata

JAPANESE PAGODA TREE
Sophora japonica

SCIADOPITYS
S. verticillata (umbrella pine)

Not every garden can accommodate a 120-foot-tall umbrella pine, but it is a familiar feature of the Japanese landscape nonetheless. This native evergreen, which grows wild in the mountainous regions of Japan, is valued for its dense, dark green, narrowly cone-shaped effect and for its decorative needles and bark. And although it ultimately becomes very large, it grows so slowly—6 inches or less a year—that it is often used as a specimen tree in gardens of modest size.

Unlike many pine trees, the umbrella pine keeps its lower branches, right down to ground level. It has flat needles, up to 6 inches long that are dark green above, light-green on the underside, and marked with two pale stripes. The needles are arranged in whorls around the branches, much like the spokes of an umbrella. The cones are 5 inches long, and 2 inches wide; they are borne in erect clusters and take two years to reach maturity. Umbrella pines are susceptible to damage by air pollution, salt air and wind.

HOW TO GROW. Umbrella pines are hardy in Zones 6-9, except in Florida and along the Gulf Coast. They do not grow well in hot, dry areas and should be protected from strong winter winds. In cool areas they tolerate full sun but in areas with hot summers they need partial shade. Set out plants no taller than 1½ feet in spring or fall, in deep, moist, well-drained neutral-to-acid soil, pH 6.0 to 7.0, enriched with peat moss or leaf mold. If foliage becomes yellow, feed in spring with cottonseed meal. Umbrella pines are naturally symmetrical and very rarely need pruning to maintain their shape; however, they should be trained to one strong central stem. Propagate additional plants from seeds, sown in spring or fall or from cuttings of mature wood, taken in winter or early spring.

SCOURING RUSH, COMMON See *Equisetum*
SCOURING RUSH, DWARF See *Equisetum*
SHOWY CRAB APPLE See *Malus*
SHOWY JAPANESE LILY See *Lilium*
SHRUB ALTHEA See *Hibiscus*
SILK TREE See *Albizia*
SILVER SHEAF See *Astilbe*
SNAKE'S BEARD, JAPANESE See *Ophiopogon*
SNOWBELL, FRAGRANT See *Styrax*
SNOWBELL, JAPANESE See *Styrax*

SOPHORA
S. japonica (Japanese pagoda tree, Chinese scholar tree)

The Japanese pagoda tree, also called the scholar tree, is well named. Some of its best features require a scholar's patience to be appreciated. The tree's creamy white flowers, shaped like those of the pea, do not begin to appear in appreciable numbers until the tree is 20 to 30 years old, and its interesting corrugated bark and knobby roots only develop with age. In Japan, this broad, handsome deciduous tree grows 80 feet tall, and its spreading branches form a rounded canopy covering an area equal to the height. Its soft compound leaves, 9 to 12 inches long, are composed of from three to eight pairs of 2-inch leaflets, bright glossy green above, gray-green beneath. The flowers appear in spikes 10 to 15 inches long in late summer or fall, lasting at least a month. If the summer has been sunny, the flowers will be followed in the fall by seed pods 3 to 4 inches long, which turn brown and cling to the tree well into the winter months. Also of landscape interest is the smooth green bark that becomes deeply cut with age.

Pagoda trees are slow-growing, taking eight to 10 years to

become 20 feet tall. They withstand city conditions, strong winds, drought and hot weather. One variant, *S. japonica pendula,* the weeping pagoda tree, has slender, drooping branches that trail on the ground; this is usually a grafted plant, with the shoots of the weeping form grafted onto *S. japonica* stock. This variety seldom flowers.

HOW TO GROW. Pagoda trees are hardy in Zones 5-8 and do well in full sun or very light shade. They thrive in a deep, moist, well-drained sandy soil. Plant in the spring. The trees need very little care, once established. Feed in the spring only if the foliage appears yellow. To allow for walking and sitting beneath the tree, remove the lower, drooping branches in the spring. Otherwise, pruning is usually unnecessary; the rounded crown develops naturally. Propagate by seed or from cuttings of new growth taken in summer.

SORBUS

S. alnifolia (Korean mountain ash); *S. commixta* (Japanese mountain ash)

The mountain ashes of the Orient, like those of North America, add color and design to the garden throughout most of the year. In spring, they bear clouds of delicate white blossoms; in autumn, their branches are heavy with orange berries that attract birds; and in winter, their exquisite silky gray bark, especially that of the Korean mountain ash, accents the winter landscape.

The Korean mountain ash is considered by many gardeners to be the most attractive of all the ashes. It grows 40 to 50 feet high, is pyramidal or oval in outline, and has 4-inch oval leaves that are borne singly instead of in fern-shaped clusters, as on other mountain ashes. The leaves change to scarlet and orange in autumn. The white flowers of this species are nearly an inch in diameter and very prolific; they form clusters 2 to 3 inches across. In the fall, the scarlet ½-inch fruits appear in large flat clusters.

The Japanese mountain ash is a much smaller tree, 20 to 30 feet high, and is more columnar in shape; when young it resembles a Lombardy poplar. Its compound leaves, 1½ to 3 inches in length, are made up of 11 to 15 leaflets that turn yellow in the fall. In the spring, clusters of tiny white blossoms, 3 to 5 inches across, bloom at the tips of purple-red branches; the flowers ripen in the autumn into bright red berries ⅓ inch across.

HOW TO GROW. The Korean and Japanese mountain ashes are hardy in Zones 6-8. They thrive in full sun in any well-drained soil. Plant them in spring or fall. Prune young trees in late winter or early spring to encourage higher branching. The mountain ashes are propagated from seed and occasionally from cuttings.

SPIKE WINTER HAZEL See *Corylopsis*
SPIREA, FALSE See *Astilbe*
SPIREA, FLORIST'S See *Astilbe*
SPURGE, JAPANESE See *Pachysandra*

STEPHANANDRA

S. incisa, also called *S. flexuosa* (cut-leaf stephanandra, lace shrub)

The cut-leaf stephanandra familiar to many North American gardeners is a native Japanese shrub whose graceful form and finely cut foliage have earned it a prominent place in Japanese landscape design. Planted on the gentle slope of an artificial hill, the stephanandra echoes the hillside's curve with its arching branches, and its tolerance of shade puts it high on the list of shrubs for growing under trees. Sometimes it is used as an informal hedge. In its standard form this

KOREAN MOUNTAIN ASH
Sorbus alnifolia

DWARF CUT-LEAF STEPHANANDRA
Stephanandra incisa crispa

For climate zones, see map, page 151.

JAPANESE STEWARTIA
Stewartia pseudocamellia

JAPANESE SNOWBELL
Styrax japonica

deciduous plant grows 4 to 8 feet high and spreads 3 to 5 feet wide, but there is a dwarf version, *S. incisa crispa,* that is much more compact, only 2 to 3 feet high. Both plants have sweeping branches and tiny zigzag stems whose cinnamon-brown color is attractive in winter when the plant is bare. In summer these branches are densely covered with feathery green leaves, 1 to 3 inches long, that have jagged, deeply indented edges. The leaves are tinged red all through the growing season and in the fall turn purple or reddish-orange. By comparison, the flowers are relatively insignificant. They bloom in early summer in clusters 1 to 3 inches long, made up of many tiny greenish-white flowers.

HOW TO GROW. Cut-leaf stephanandra is hardy in Zones 5-8. It does best in sun but tolerates shade, and thrives in almost any moist, well-drained soil. For best results add peat moss or leaf mold. Plant stephanandra in spring. Prune it, if desired, to encourage bushier growth, although this may spoil its naturally graceful growth habit. In the spring cut back old and weak stems to the ground. Cut-leaf stephanandra's branches root where they touch the ground, and these new shoots can be cut off and transplanted. Plants can also be started from stem cuttings taken in early summer.

STEWARTIA

S. pseudocamellia (Japanese stewartia)

The native Japanese stewartia, called pseudocamellia for its cup-shaped white flower, is a tall, shapely deciduous tree that grows up to 50 feet high. It is always used as a specimen tree, even in temple gardens, because of its size and because it is too decorative for a mass planting. The tree has an almost perfect pyramidal shape, with a straight trunk and horizontal branches. The oval leaves are 3 inches long, tapering to points, and in autumn they turn deep purple. The camellia-like flowers, which bloom in midsummer, are 2½ inches across, with velvety petals and orange-tipped stamens; in the autumn the flowers are followed by glossy red berries. Even the bark of the Japanese stewartia is decorative: it is reddish-brown and in the winter it peels off in large flakes.

HOW TO GROW. Japanese stewartia is hardy in Zones 7 and 8. It grows best in a sunny location and a moist, well-drained soil. Plant in the early spring in the tree's permanent location; stewartia is not easily transplanted. Pruning is seldom required; the tree has a natural orderly shape. Propagate additional plants from seed or from stem cuttings of new growth taken in midsummer.

STRAWBERRY TREE, JAPANESE See *Cornus*

STYRAX

S. japonica (Japanese snowbell); *S. obassia* (fragrant snowbell)

These two Oriental species of snowbell are small shrublike deciduous trees with the horizontal branching that the Japanese favor in their landscape design. They reach heights of 15 to 30 feet and in summer bear dangling clusters of pure white bell-shaped flowers, ¾ inch long, with prominent yellow stamens. The Japanese snowbell grows slowly, a 5- to 6-foot tree taking seven to 10 years to reach 15 feet, with an ultimate height of 30 feet. The branch spread equals the height. The leaves are oval, 1½ to 3 inches long, with pointed tips; in the fall the foliage turns red and yellow. The flower clusters are 3 inches long and in fall are followed by gray fruit, ½ inch long. The fragrant snowbell grows somewhat more rapidly, reaching its mature size of 20 to 30 feet in 15 years. Its leaves are almost round, 4 to 8 inches long and wide, and they too turn red and yellow in the fall. Its flowers, as its name implies, are fragrant and bloom in clusters that hang down 6 to 8 inches. The oval fruits, which develop in the fall, have a velvety surface.

HOW TO GROW. Japanese and fragrant snowbells are hardy in Zones 5-9, the fragrant snowbell being particularly resistant to cold. They do best in full sun but will tolerate light shade, and in Japan they are often used as under-story trees beneath larger trees. They prefer a light, well-drained soil and are best planted in early spring. The snowbells are seldom pruned; their shapes are naturally attractive. Propagate from seed; cuttings do not root easily. Except when young, snowbells are difficult to transplant.

SWEET OLIVE See *Osmanthus*

T

TAXUS

T. cuspidata (Japanese yew)

One of the standbys of Japanese landscape design is the native yew, a slow-growing evergreen that in the wild may become a tree 50 feet tall, but is more often found in gardens in its dwarf form, *T. cuspidata nana*. It is used as a single specimen plant, as a background for other plants, and it is often pruned into formal hedges or trained as bonsai. In both the tree and bush forms the Japanese yew has spreading branches and soft, dark green needles, ½ to 1 inch long, with two pale yellow bands on the underside. Male and female flowers are borne on separate plants, and the female flowers are followed by fleshy red fruit, ½ inch long. It is necessary to have at least one male plant near every six to eight female plants for these fruit to be produced. All parts of the plants are poisonous.

In its tree form the Japanese yew, when grown in gardens usually becomes only 25 feet tall and 20 feet wide, forming a broad, symmetrical pyramid. The dwarf Japanese yew, a dense, bushy plant with many stems, usually grows 3 to 6 feet tall and 6 to 12 feet wide. Yews live for hundreds of years and are tolerant of pollution and salt air.

HOW TO GROW. Japanese yews are hardy in Zones 5-9. They do well in full sun or deep shade and will tolerate almost any well-drained soil but thrive in a moist, slightly acid loam, pH 6.0 to 7.0. Plant in early fall or spring. To keep the soil cool and moist in summer, mulch with shredded bark or pine needles. Feed each spring with a light dusting of 5-10-5 or cottonseed meal. Yews can be pruned from spring to fall, readily forming new growth even if cut back to old wood. Spring is the best time for severe pruning; hedges may be pruned in spring and again in midsummer. Propagate from seed, as soon as the seed is ripe; from softwood cuttings taken in the summer; or from hardwood cuttings taken in early winter.

THREAD SAWARA FALSE CYPRESS See *Chamaecyparis*

THUJA

T. orientalis, also called *Platycladus orientalis* (Japanese or Chinese arborvitae)

Like its Western relatives, this Oriental evergreen comes in many forms, ranging from low, round bushes to tall, rather narrow trees. Their use in the Japanese garden depends on the variety. Some arborvitaes are used as single specimen plants or are grouped with other evergreens; the taller varieties are often used as hedges, separating the Japanese from their neighbors. All forms of the Japanese arborvitae have upright branches and flat fanlike leaves that grow at right

DWARF JAPANESE YEW
Taxus cuspidata nana

For climate zones, see map, page 151.

BERCKMAN'S GOLDEN ORIENTAL ARBORVITAE
Thuja orientalis aurea nana

CHINESE ELM
Ulmus parvifolia

angles to the branch. The leaves are actually composed of very small overlapping scalelike needles whose color varies from one variety to another. Egg-shaped cones are fleshy and blue-white when young, but become brown and woody with age; each cone is up to 1 inch long.

A typical example of Japanese arborvitae is the variety Aurea Nana, known commonly as Berckman's golden Oriental arborvitae, a compact rounded shrub that becomes up to 5 feet tall and 6 feet wide; its foliage is golden in spring, green in summer and bronze in the winter. Arborvitaes are tolerant of salt air, but they are sensitive to cold, dry wind and pollution. The upright-growing branches are easily broken off in high wind and by heavy snow and ice unless tied up loosely in winter with soft cord or plastic-coated wire.

HOW TO GROW. Japanese arborvitaes are hardy in Zones 6-9 but in warmer climates need a location with cool, moist air. They do best in full sun but will tolerate partial shade, although growth will be more open and foliage color less intense. They thrive in a moist, well-drained soil. Plant arborvitaes in early fall or spring, spacing plants 18 to 24 inches apart. If needles become pale, feed in spring with a light sprinkling of 5-10-5 or cottonseed meal. In summer, apply organic mulch around the base to keep the soil moist. Although no pruning is needed to develop shape, Japanese arborvitaes can be shortened by cutting back the top branches, made bushier by pinching out the growing tips or shorn lightly all over as new growth begins in spring. Propagate named varieties from cuttings and the species from seeds or cuttings.

TIGER LILY See *Lilium*
TONGUE FERN See *Cyclophorus*

U

ULMUS

U. davidiana japonica (Japanese elm); *U. parvifolia* (Chinese elm)

These two Oriental versions of the elm grace public parks and temple grounds in Japan, and can be found in private gardens large enough to accommodate their spreading habit of growth. Both are excellent shade trees.

The fast-growing Japanese elm may become 90 feet tall at maturity, with a spreading crown of 40 to 50 feet. Its branches are upright when young but gradually droop, creating a weeping effect. The leaves are oval, 3 to 5 inches long, and turn red in autumn. Inconspicuous flowers appear in early spring. The slow-growing Chinese elm reaches a height of 40 to 50 feet and has horizontal branches spreading up to 30 to 40 feet. With age, its gray bark peels in patches, creating a mottled effect. The Chinese elm's oval leaves, 1 to 3 inches long, are bright yellow in spring and red in autumn. Unlike most elms, it flowers in late summer, and in mild climates its leaves may stay green much of the winter.

HOW TO GROW. The Japanese and Chinese elms are hardy in Zones 6-9. Both need full sun and do best in a light, moist, well-drained soil that lets their shallow feeding roots expand horizontally. The Japanese elm will also tolerate a poor, dry soil. Both are pruned only to encourage their natural shape; pruning should be done in early spring. Oriental elms are propagated from seed; cuttings are difficult to root.

UMBRELLA PINE See *Sciadopitys*

V

VINCA

V. minor (common periwinkle, trailing myrtle, creeping myrtle)

Despite its non-Asiatic origin (it is a European plant), common periwinkle has been adopted by Japanese garden designers for its ability to grow in very deep shade. This trailing evergreen ground cover provides textural interest under dense evergreens, on the shady banks of ponds and along the edges of the *roji*, or narrow path, of a tea garden. This hardy plant becomes 2 to 6 inches tall and spreads to cover an area 3 feet wide. Its glossy tapered dark green leaves, up to 2 inches in length, are borne on slender, wiry stems. In very early spring, common periwinkle produces numerous 1-inch-wide, lavender-blue, star-shaped flowers; occasionally the flowers continue to appear through the summer into fall. Common periwinkle tolerates extreme cold but not intense heat. The plants spread quickly, taking root wherever nodes along their stems touch the ground.

HOW TO GROW. Common periwinkle is hardy in Zones 5-9; it does not do well in the hot, humid conditions of Florida and the Gulf Coast unless completely protected from direct sun. Elsewhere it does best in open shade but will tolerate deep shade as well. It will grow in nearly any moist, well-drained, slightly acid or neutral soil, preferably one that is enriched with compost, peat moss or leaf mold. Set the plants out in the early spring or fall, spacing them 12 to 18 inches apart. Once the plants are established, little maintenance is necessary except keeping them from spreading beyond the bounds dictated by the garden design. Propagate common periwinkle by dividing roots in early fall or spring, or from stem cuttings taken in late summer or fall.

WATERLILY See *Nymphaea*
WEEPING WILLOW, BABYLON See *Salix*
WINTERBERRY, JAPANESE See *Ilex*
WINTER HAZEL See *Corylopsis*

WISTERIA

W. floribunda (Japanese wisteria); *W. sinensis* (Chinese wisteria)

A deciduous twining vine grown for centuries in Japan, wisteria has a variety of landscape uses. It is one of the best ornamental vines for trellises, arbors and pergolas; it can also be trained to a small-tree form or used as bonsai. Pealike flowers are borne in large drooping clusters in the spring. Flowers will often not appear until the vines are 10 to 15 years old. Velvety green 6-inch seed pods, resembling beans, appear after flowering and last through the winter. Wisterias are very long-lived—their trunks may become several feet thick and their stems woody and gnarled with age. But the plants need protection from wind, and their flower buds are sometimes destroyed by late frosts. It is best to provide them with a southern or western exposure and to allow adequate space and sturdy support. Also, avoid planting wisteria near young trees as the vines may overgrow and strangle them.

Japanese wisteria shoots grow 25 to 35 feet long, their flowers blooming at the same time as the leaves appear in the spring. The flowers are violet, ¾ inch wide and sweetly fragrant, and the clusters are usually 8 to 20 inches long. The feathery compound leaves are composed of 13 to 19 leaflets, about 3 inches long.

Chinese wisteria grows to 50 feet or more and produces blue to violet flowers up to 1 inch long. These open all at once, before the leaves appear, in clusters 6 to 12 inches long. The leaves are composed of seven to 13 leaflets, each 3 inches long. The species Chinese wisteria is rarely fragrant.

HOW TO GROW. Wisterias are hardy in Zones 5-9 and need full sun. They do best in a moist, well-drained garden soil

COMMON PERIWINKLE
Vinca minor

CHINESE WISTERIA
Wisteria sinensis

For climate zones, see map, page 151.

enriched with peat moss or leaf mold. Plant them in spring, placing each one 10 to 12 inches from its support. Use container-grown vines, since field-grown plants often do not survive transplanting. Feed young plants each spring for several years with a general-purpose fertilizer such as 5-10-5 until they are well established; afterward, fertilize vines in spring with a complete fertilizer such as 10-10-10. Mulch in autumn in northern zones with pine boughs or leaves for winter protection. Young wisterias should be tied to supports until the branches are thick enough to support themselves. Established plants need regular pruning to contain growth and encourage flowering. In late summer, remove new growth to above the sixth or seventh leaf from the base of a branch.

Another way to encourage flowering is to prune the roots in early spring before new growth starts by digging a 20-inch-deep trench around the plant; space the trench 1 foot out from the trunk for each inch of trunk diameter. Wisteria can be trained to a tree form by staking and pruning severely for many years, until the trunk becomes thickened. Propagate by layering or from stem cuttings or seed.

WITCH HAZEL See *Hamamelis*

Y

YEDDO HAWTHORN See *Raphiolepis*
YEW, JAPANESE See *Taxus*
YEW, JAPANESE PLUM See *Cephalotaxus*

Z

ZOYSIA

Z. japonica (Japanese or Korean lawn grass); *Z. matrella* (Manila grass)

Lawns, in the Western sense, are seldom seen in Japanese gardens. In palace gardens, however, grassy areas were often set aside for games, and lawn grasses interspersed with graveled areas are sometimes used in sunny gardens where moss, the preferred ground cover, will not grow. Grasses are also used against rocks and water basins, or for carpeting the spaces between steppingstones. For such situations, the Japanese use zoysia grass, in either its native form or in the form of Manila grass, whose homeland is Southeast Asia. Both are creeping warm-climate ground covers that grow slowly but vigorously, spreading above and below ground.

Japanese lawn grass forms 5- to 9-inch clumps of coarse gray-green leaves; in spring or early summer, 1-inch purple flower clusters appear above the foliage. Manila grass has finer, shorter leaves, up to 4 inches tall, but taller flower clusters, 1½ inches long; the flowers are greenish-white. Manila grass tolerates shade and drought conditions. Both tolerate salt air and can be used in seaside gardens.

HOW TO GROW. Japanese lawn grass grows best in Zones 7-10, Manila grass in Zones 9 and 10. Both grasses turn brown when subjected to cool temperature and frosts. But they usually recover if not exposed to prolonged bouts of freezing and turn green again when night temperatures rise to 50°. Japanese lawn grass does best in full sun, Manila grass in either full sun or fairly dense shade. They do well in moderately acid or alkaline soil but prefer a sandy, moist soil in the range of pH 5.5 to 7.0. Plant zoysia in the form of plugs, small pieces of rootstock, in late spring or early summer when temperatures remain about 70°, setting them 6 inches apart. Feed in early spring and midsummer with a slow-release lawn fertilizer and keep the lawn watered well. Zoysia grass can be mowed to a height of 1¼ inches; to control its spread into unwanted areas, thin out the clumps. Propagate by planting small pieces of the rootstock.

MANILA GRASS
Zoysia matrella

American parallels with Japanese climate

To help you transplant Japanese garden artistry to an American setting, the listing of plants in the preceding chapter indicates the climate zones in which each plant grows best. This zone information is keyed to the map below, which divides the North American continent into 10 climate belts based on average minimum winter temperatures. Within each belt there are, of course, local variations. Temperatures in a garden at the bottom of a hill will be cooler than at the top. By contrast, a large body of water nearby can moderate fluctuations in air temperature. The microclimate of your area can be identified through experience or by checking with the county agricultural agent.

Although Japan, with its maritime climate, generally relies on plant materials that thrive in the relatively moderate winters of Zones 6 to 9, a surprising number of Japanese garden plants survive temperatures of −10°. This is partly due to the fact that many of the plants traditionally used in Japanese gardens are forest plants, native to the mountainous regions of the islands. On Japan's northwestern slopes, facing Russia, winter temperatures may fall far below zero. But the Japanese favor plants such as flowering quince and false cypress that flourish in a wide variety of climate conditions. Such plants are more dependable and therefore more likely to be long-lived—a quality that ranks high in Japanese garden design.

If winter temperatures in your area fall below those appropriate for a particular plant, substitute a related species that is more cold-resistant. Failing that, you could install a Japanese dry garden, using only rocks, raked gravel and Arctic lichen.

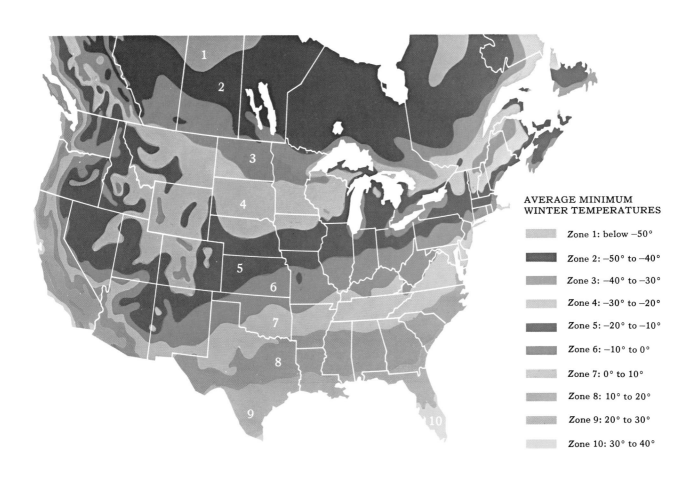

AVERAGE MINIMUM
WINTER TEMPERATURES

Zone 1: below −50°

Zone 2: −50° to −40°

Zone 3: −40° to −30°

Zone 4: −30° to −20°

Zone 5: −20° to −10°

Zone 6: −10° to 0°

Zone 7: 0° to 10°

Zone 8: 10° to 20°

Zone 9: 20° to 30°

Zone 10: 30° to 40°

Characteristics of 98 Japanese-garden plants

Listed below for quick reference are the species illustrated in Chapter 5.

	PLANT HEIGHT				LIGHT NEEDS			SHAPE			SPECIAL TRAITS								SOIL NEEDS					
	Under 1 foot	1 to 3 feet	3 to 6 feet	Over 6 feet	Deep shade	Partial shade	Full sun	Upright	Spreading	Trailing	Distinctive foliage	Evergreen	Distinctive branches or bark	Decorative fruit	Flowers	Fragrance	Slow growing	Decorative pruning	Acid	Neutral	Alkaline	Wet	Moist but well-drained	Dry
ABIES HOMOLEPIS (Nikko fir)			●		●	●	●	●	●	●								●	●				●	
ACER PALMATUM 'DISSECTUM' (threadleaf Japanese maple)			●		●		●	●						●	●			●	●				●	
ADONIS AMURENSIS (amur adonis)	●	●			●	●		●						●			●	●	●				●	
AKEBIA QUINATA (five-leaf akebia)			●		●	●	●	●		●	●			●	●	●			●				●	
ALBIZIA JULIBRISSIN ROSEA (pink silk tree)			●		●	●	●	●			●			●			●		●	●			●	
ANEMONE JAPONICA (Japanese anemone)		●			●		●				●			●				●	●	●			●	
ASTILBE ARENDSII 'ROSY VEIL' (astilbe)		●			●		●				●			●					●				●	
ATHYRIUM GOERINGIANUM PICTUM (Japanese painted fern)	●	●			●		●		●		●				●				●				●	
AUCUBA JAPONICA 'PICTURATA' (Japanese aucuba)			●	●	●		●	●	●		●	●		●				●	●	●			●	
BERBERIS THUNBERGII (Japanese barberry)		●	●		●	●		●		●	●	●	●		●	●		●	●	●			●	
BETULA PLATYPHYLLA JAPONICA (Japanese white birch)			●		●		●	●		●		●			●	●	●		●				●	
BUXUS MICROPHYLLA (littleleaf box)		●			●	●		●	●		●		●	●	●	●	●	●	●				●	
CAMELLIA JAPONICA (common camellia)			●		●		●	●		●	●			●			●	●	●				●	
CEPHALOTAXUS HARRINGTONIA (Japanese plum yew)			●		●	●	●	●		●	●	●		●	●		●	●	●				●	
CERCIDIPHYLLUM JAPONICUM (Katsura tree)			●		●		●	●	●		●								●	●	●		●	
CERCIS CHINENSIS (Chinese redbud)		●	●		●			●			●								●				●	
CHAENOMELES JAPONICA (Japanese quince)		●			●		●				●	●	●	●	●	●			●				●	
CHAMAECYPARIS PISIFERA FILIFERA (thread sawara false cypress)			●		●	●	●	●			●	●		●	●	●	●		●				●	
CHAMAECYPARIS PISIFERA SQUARROSA (moss sawara false cypress)			●		●	●	●	●			●	●		●	●	●	●		●				●	
CHRYSANTHEMUM MORIFOLIUM 'ALWAYS PINK' (decorative chrysanthemum)		●			●	●					●				●	●	●		●	●			●	
CHRYSANTHEMUM MORIFOLIUM 'YELLOW DIVINITY' (anemone chrysanthemum)		●			●	●					●				●	●	●		●				●	
CHRYSANTHEMUM MORIFOLIUM 'YELLOW NOB HILL' (large incurve chrysanthemum)		●			●	●					●				●	●	●		●				●	
CINNAMOMUM CAMPHORA (camphor tree)			●		●	●	●	●	●		●	●		●	●		●		●	●			●	
CLEMATIS ORIENTALIS (Oriental clematis)			●		●		●			●	●		●	●					●	●			●	
CORNUS KOUSA (Japanese dogwood)			●		●	●	●	●			●		●	●	●		●	●	●	●	●		●	
CORYLOPSIS SPICATA (spike winter hazel)		●			●	●	●	●			●			●	●				●				●	
CRYPTOMERIA JAPONICA (Japanese cedar)			●		●	●	●	●	●		●	●			●				●				●	
CUNNINGHAMIA LANCEOLATA (China fir)			●		●	●	●	●	●		●	●							●				●	
CYCLOPHORUS LINGUA (Japanese felt fern)		●			●		●				●								●				●	●
CYRTOMIUM FALCATUM (holly fern)		●			●		●	●			●	●							●				●	
DAPHNE ODORA (winter daphne)		●			●	●	●	●	●		●	●		●	●		●		●				●	
DEUTZIA SCABRA 'PRIDE OF ROCHESTER' (fuzzy deutzia)			●		●	●	●			●				●			●		●				●	
ENKIANTHUS PERULATUS (white enkianthus)		●			●	●	●	●		●				●				●	●				●	
EPIMEDIUM GRANDIFLORUM (bishop's hat)	●				●		●	●			●				●				●				●	
EQUISETUM SCIRPOIDES (dwarf scouring rush)	●				●		●				●	●	●						●		●		●	
FATSIA JAPONICA (Japanese aralia)			●		●	●	●	●			●	●		●	●			●	●				●	
FIRMIANA SIMPLEX (Chinese parasol tree)			●			●	●	●			●		●	●	●		●	●	●	●	●		●	
FORSYTHIA SUSPENSA (weeping forsythia)			●		●	●	●	●			●				●			●	●	●	●		●	
GARDENIA JASMINOIDES (gardenia)		●			●	●	●	●			●	●		●	●	●		●	●				●	
GINKGO BILOBA (ginkgo)			●		●		●	●			●				●	●	●	●	●	●	●		●	
HAMAMELIS MOLLIS (Chinese witch hazel)			●		●	●	●	●			●			●	●			●	●				●	
HEMEROCALLIS FULVA 'FLORE-PLENO' (tawny day lily)		●			●		●				●				●				●	●	●		●	
HIBISCUS SYRIACUS (rose-of-Sharon)			●			●	●	●							●			●	●				●	
HOSTA PLANTAGINEA 'ROYAL STANDARD' (fragrant plantain lily)	●	●			●		●		●						●	●			●	●	●		●	
HYPERICUM PATULUM 'SUNGOLD' (sungold St.-John's-wort)		●			●	●	●	●	●	●					●			●	●				●	
ILEX CRENATA (Japanese holly)			●		●	●	●	●	●		●				●	●			●				●	
INDIGOFERA KIRILOWII (kirilow indigo)		●				●	●							●			●		●				●	
IRIS KAEMPFERI 'PEACOCK STRUT' (Japanese iris)		●				●	●				●				●			●			●	●	●	
JASMINUM NUDIFLORUM (winter jasmine)			●			●	●	●							●				●				●	

	PLANT HEIGHT				LIGHT NEEDS			SHAPE			SPECIAL TRAITS								SOIL NEEDS					
	Under 1 foot	1 to 3 feet	3 to 6 feet	Over 6 feet	Deep shade	Partial shade	Full sun	Upright	Spreading	Trailing	Distinctive foliage	Evergreen	Distinctive branches or bark	Decorative fruit	Flowers	Fragrance	Slow growing	Decorative pruning	Acid	Neutral	Alkaline	Wet	Moist but well-drained	Dry
JUNIPERUS CHINENSIS AUREA 'GOLD COAST' (Gold Coast juniper)		•				•		•			•	•	•				•	•	•	•	•		•	•
KERRIA JAPONICA PLENIFLORA (globeflower kerria)			•	•		•	•	•			•		•				•	•	•	•	•		•	
LAGERSTROEMIA INDICA (crape myrtle)			•			•	•						•				•	•	•	•	•		•	
LESPEDEZA BICOLOR (shrub bush clover)			•			•	•						•		•		•	•	•	•			•	
LIGUSTRUM JAPONICUM 'SUWANNEE RIVER' (Suwannee River privet)		•				•	•	•			•	•			•	•	•	•	•	•	•		•	
LILIUM SPECIOSUM (showy Japanese lily)		•				•	•	•			•				•	•		•					•	
LYGODIUM JAPONICUM (Japanese climbing fern)			•			•		•	•	•	•							•					•	
MACLEAYA CORDATA (plume poppy)			•			•	•	•							•			•	•	•			•	
MAGNOLIA STELLATA (star magnolia)			•			•	•								•			•		•			•	
MALUS FLORIBUNDA (Japanese crab apple)			•			•	•							•	•	•	•	•		•			•	
MISCANTHUS SINENSIS (eulalia grass)			•			•	•				•	•				•							•	
NANDINA DOMESTICA (nandina)		•	•			•	•	•			•	•		•			•	•	•	•	•		•	
NARCISSUS TAZETTA 'CRAGFORD' (polyanthus narcissus)		•				•	•								•								•	
NELUMBO NUCIFERA (sacred lotus)		•				•	•	•			•			•	•	•						•		
NELUMBO NUCIFERA 'MOMO BOTAN' (Momo Botan sacred lotus)	•					•	•	•			•			•	•	•						•		
NYMPHAEA TETRAGONA 'GEORGI' (pygmy waterlily)	•					•	•	•			•											•		
OPHIOPOGON JAPONICUS (dwarf lily-turf)	•	•			•	•	•				•	•					•	•	•	•	•		•	
OSMANTHUS FRAGRANS (sweet osmanthus)			•			•	•				•	•				•		•	•	•	•		•	
PACHYSANDRA TERMINALIS (Japanese pachysandra)	•					•				•	•	•						•					•	
PAEONIA SUFFRUTICOSA (tree peony)		•				•	•	•			•		•		•	•	•	•	•				•	
PARTHENOCISSUS TRICUSPIDATA (Boston ivy)	•	•	•	•		•	•	•	•	•	•		•	•			•	•	•	•	•		•	
PHOTINIA VILLOSA (Oriental photinia)			•			•	•				•		•	•			•	•	•	•	•		•	
PHYLLOSTACHYS NIGRA (black bamboo)			•			•	•	•			•	•	•				•	•	•	•	•		•	
PIERIS JAPONICA (Japanese andromeda)		•			•		•	•			•	•			•	•		•					•	
PINUS THUNBERGIANA (Japanese black pine)			•			•	•	•	•		•	•	•				•	•	•	•			•	•
PITTOSPORUM TOBIRA (Japanese pittosporum)			•			•	•				•	•			•	•	•	•	•	•	•		•	
PLATYCODON GRANDIFLORUS 'MARIESII' (Marie's balloonflower)		•				•	•	•							•			•	•	•	•		•	
PODOCARPUS MACROPHYLLUS 'MAKI' (shrubby yew podocarpus)			•		•	•	•				•	•				•	•	•	•				•	
PRUNUS SERRULATA 'SHIROTAE' (Shirotae Oriental cherry)			•			•	•						•	•	•	•		•					•	
PRUNUS SUBHIRTELLA 'YAE-SHIDARE-HIGAN' (double-flowered weeping Higan cherry)			•			•	•						•	•	•	•		•					•	
PRUNUS YEDOENSIS (Yoshino cherry)			•			•	•						•	•	•	•		•					•	
RAPHIOLEPIS UMBELLATA (Yeddo hawthorn)			•			•	•				•	•		•	•			•	•	•	•		•	•
RHAPIS EXCELSA (lady palm)		•	•			•	•				•	•						•					•	
RHODODENDRON KEISKEI (Keisk rhododendron)		•				•		•	•		•	•			•			•					•	
RHODODENDRON LINEARIFOLIUM 'POLYPETALUM' (spider azalea)			•			•	•	•			•				•			•	•	•			•	
RHODOTYPOS SCANDENS (jetbead)			•			•	•	•			•		•	•	•		•	•	•	•	•	•	•	
SALIX BABYLONICA (Babylon weeping willow)			•			•	•				•		•										•	
SCIADOPITYS VERTICILLATA (umbrella pine)			•			•	•	•				•	•				•		•	•			•	
SOPHORA JAPONICA (Japanese pagoda tree)			•			•	•				•		•	•	•		•						•	
SORBUS ALNIFOLIA (Korean mountain ash)			•			•	•				•			•	•				•	•	•		•	
STEPHANANDRA INCISA CRISPA (dwarf cut-leaf stephanandra)		•				•	•				•				•				•	•	•		•	
STEWARTIA PSEUDOCAMELLIA (Japanese stewartia)			•			•	•				•		•	•	•								•	
STYRAX JAPONICA (Japanese snowball)			•			•	•				•				•	•							•	
TAXUS CUSPIDATA NANA (dwarf Japanese yew)		•			•	•	•	•	•		•			•			•	•	•	•	•		•	
THUJA ORIENTALIS AUREA NANA (Berckman's golden Oriental arborvitae)		•				•	•	•	•		•	•											•	
ULMUS PARVIFOLIA (Chinese elm)			•			•	•				•		•		•		•						•	
VINCA MINOR (common periwinkle)	•				•	•				•		•			•				•	•	•		•	
WISTERIA SINENSIS (Chinese wisteria)			•			•	•						•	•	•		•						•	
ZOYSIA MATRELLA (Manila grass)	•				•	•	•	•	•		•				•				•	•	•		•	

Acknowledgments

The index for this book was prepared by Anita R. Beckerman. For their help in the preparation of this book, the editors wish to thank the following: Charles E. Allen, Landscape Architect, Fort Lauderdale, Fla.; Martin Amt, Special Assistant to the Director of Japanese Art, Freer Gallery of Art, Washington, D.C.; William H. Baker, A.S.L.A., Wallis-Baker & Associates, P.A., Winter Park, Fla.; Mr. and Mrs. Woody Bates, Atlanta, Ga.; Edmund J. Bennett, Bethesda, Md.; Mrs. Manuel Bloom, Houston, Tex.; Dr. and Mrs. Theodore Bradley, Carmel, Calif.; Mr. and Mrs. William G. Brakefield, Arlington, Va.; Joseph R. Cipolari, Alexandria, Va.; Mrs. James R. Cody, Houston, Tex.; Dr. John L. Creech, Director, National Arboretum, Washington, D.C.; Sue Davis, Houston, Tex.; Ted Deglin, New York, N.Y.; Capt. and Mrs. Ward W. deGroot III U.S.N. (Ret.), Arlington, Va.; Dr. Paul Donoghue, Stamford, Conn.; Polly Fairman, Poly-en Gardens, Princeton, N.J.; Enid Farmer, Lexington, Mass.; Mr. and Mrs. Lincoln Foster, Falls Village, Conn.; Ron Foster, Ron Foster Landscape Contracting Co., Orlando, Fla.; Betty Freudenheim, Chicago, Ill.; Mr. and Mrs. Peter Gallagher, Atherton, Calif.; The Gambrill Family, Alexandria, Va.; Robert M. Goka, Frank's Nursery and Flowers, Northridge, Calif.; Harold Greer, Greer Gardens, Eugene, Ore.; Mr. and Mrs. F. Otto Haas, Ambler, Pa.; Sandra Hinson, Orlando, Fla.; Jane Hoffstetter, Boca Raton, Fla.; Yoshitoshi Itahashi, Carmel, Calif.; Mrs. Albert Kraft Jr., Vice President, Kraft Landscape Nursery, Deerfield Beach, Fla.; Patricia Kroh, Long Boat Key, Fla.; Hoichi John Kurisu, Portland, Ore.; Mr. and Mrs. Richard Lea, Seattle, Wash.; Toshiyuki J. Maeda, Registered Landscape Architect, Chevy Chase, Md.; Patricia McElfresh, Scottsdale, Ariz.; Dr. and Mrs. Arthur J. Mourot, Alexandria, Va.; Eijiro and Eiichi Nunokawa, Monterey Park, Calif.; Tsutomu Okabayashi, Houston, Tex.; Frank M. Okamura, Brooklyn, N.Y.; Mr. and Mrs. K. Patrick Okura, Bethesda, Md.; Mr. and Mrs. John A. Planting, Menlo Park, Calif.; Edward C. Plyler, Alexandria, Va.; William Jay Rathbun, Curator of Japanese Art, Seattle Art Museum, Wash.; Col. Carn R. Reid, Landscape Architect, Boynton Beach, Fla.; Toshio Saburomaru, E. Palo Alto, Calif.; G. E. Sayre, Alexandria, Va.; James R. Sharp, Arlington, Va.; Yoshiaki Shimizu, Curator, Japanese Art, Freer Gallery of Art, Washington, D.C.; Dorothy Slater, Denver, Colo.; Perry D. and Peter D. Slocum, Slocum Water Gardens, Winter Haven, Fla.; Priscilla Smith, Librarian, Freer Gallery of Art, Washington, D.C.; Col. and Mrs. Wilfred Smith, Alexandria, Va.; David Snyder, New Orleans, La.; Thomas Soderstrom, Curator, Department of Botany, Smithsonian Institution, Washington, D.C.; Rick Stoff, Fenton, Mo.; Mr. and Mrs. Philip A. Straus, Mamaroneck, N.Y.; Dr. Haruo Tsuchiya, Yamagata City, Japan; University of California, Los Angeles, Calif.; Thomas H. Wallis, A.S.L.A., Wallis-Baker & Associates, P.A., Winter Park, Fla.; Krent Wieland, Landscape Designer, Plantation, Fla.; Nobe Yamakoshi, Park Ridge, Ill.; Yoder Brothers, Inc., Barberton, Ohio; the Rev. Susumu Yoshida, Honolulu, Hawaii; John Zemanek, Associate Professor of Architecture, University of Houston, Tex.; Janet Zich, Half Moon Bay, Calif.

Picture credits

Bibliography

Allen, Mea, *Plants That Changed Our Gardens*. London: David & Charles, 1974.

Bland, John H., *Forests of Lilliput: The Realm of Mosses and Lichens*. Prentice-Hall, 1971.

Bloom, Adrian, *Conifers for Your Garden*. Charles Scribner's Sons, 1972.

Boger, H. Batterson, *The Traditional Arts of Japan*. London: W. H. Allen & Co., 1964.

Bowers, Clement Gray, *Rhododendrons and Azaleas*. The Macmillan Company, 1960.

Bush-Brown, James and Louise, *America's Garden Book*. Charles Scribner's Sons, 1958.

Chittenden, Fred J., ed., *The Royal Horticultural Society Dictionary of Gardening*, 2nd ed. Clarendon Press, 1974.

Condor, Josiah, *Landscape Gardening in Japan*. Dover Publications, 1964.

Conrad, Henry S., *How to Know the Mosses and Liverworts*. William C. Brown Co., 1956.

Eliovson, Sima, *Gardening the Japanese Way*. Howard Timmins, 1970.

Engel, David H., *Japanese Gardens for Today*. Charles E. Tuttle Company, 1959.

Fukuda, Kazuhiko, *Japanese Stone Gardens*. Chartes E. Tuttle Company, 1960.

Garden Life, *Wagaya No Niwa No Sekkeizu*. Tokyo: Seibundo Shinkosha, 1978.

Greer Gardens Catalogue. Greer Gardens, 1979.

Harada, Jiro, *The Gardens of Japan*. London: The Studio Limited, 1928.

Harada, Jiro, *Japanese Gardens*. Charles T. Branford Co., 1956.

Harrison, Charles R., *Ornamental Conifers*. Hafner Press, 1975.

Hayakawa, Masao, *The Garden Art of Japan*. Transl. by Richard L. Gage. Weatherhill, 1977.

Healey, B. J., *The Plant Hunters*. Charles Scribner's Sons, 1975.

Holborn, Mark, *The Ocean in the Sand: Japan From Landscape to Garden*. Shambhala, 1978.

Hume, H. Harold, *Azaleas-Camellias*. The Macmillan Company, 1963.

Hume, H. Harold, *Azaleas: Kinds and Culture*. The Macmillan Company, 1948.

Hyams, Edward, *A History of Gardens & Gardening*. Praeger Publishers, 1971.

Ishida, Shozo, *Niwa Tsukuri Nyumon*. Tokyo: Nosangyoson Cultural Society, 1967.

Ishimoto, Tatsuo, *The Art of the Japanese Garden*. Crown Publishers, 1958.

Ishimoto, Tatsuo, and Kiyoko Ishimoto, *The Japanese House*. Crown Publishers, 1963.

Ito, Teiji, *The Japanese Garden*. Tokyo: Zokeisha Publications, 1972.

Japanese Gardens and Miniature Landscapes. Brooklyn Botanic Garden, 1975.

Keene, Donald, *Landscapes and Portraits*. Kodansha International, 1971.

Kitamura, Fumio, and Yurio Ishizu, *Garden Plants in Japan*. Tokyo: Kokusai Bunka Shinkokai (The Society for International Cultural Relations), 1963.

Kodansha, *Sakutei No Jiten*. Tokyo: Kodansha, 1978.

Kokusai Bunka Shinkokai, *Traditions of the Japanese Garden*. East-West Center Press, 1962.

Kramer, Jack, *Gardening with Stone and Sand*. Charles Scribner's Sons, 1972.

Kuck, Loraine, *The World of the Japanese Garden*. Walker/Weatherhill, 1968.

Lawson, Alexander High, *Bamboos: A Gardener's Guide to Their Cultivation in Temperate Climates*. Taplinger Publishing Co., 1968.

Loewer, H. Peter, *Growing and Decorating with Grasses*. Walker and Company, 1977.

Marshall, Nina L., *Mosses and Lichens*. Doubleday & Company, 1908.

Masters, Charles O., *Encyclopedia of the Water-Lily*. T.F.H. Publications, 1974.

Mori, Osamu, *Nihon No Teien*. Tokyo: Yoshikawa Kobunkan, 1964.

Mori, Osamu, *Typical Japanese Gardens*. Transl. by Atsuo Tsuruoka. Japan Publications, 1963.

Murasaki, Lady, *The Tale of Genji*. Transl. by Arthur Waley. Random House, 1960.

My Home Series, *Niwazukuri*. Tokyo: Shufu To Seikatsusha, 1972.

Naito, Akira, *Katsura: A Princely Retreat*. Transl. by Charles S. Terry. Kodansha International, 1977.

Nakane, Kinsaku, *Kyoto Gardens*. Transl. by M. L. Hickman & Kaichi Minobe. Osaka, Japan: Hoikusha Publishing Co., 1977.

Newsom, Samuel, *A Japanese Garden Manual for Westerners*. Tokyo News Service, 1968.

Noko To Engei, *Niwaki To Zoengijutsu*. Tokyo: Seibundo Shinkosha, 1977.

Reader's Digest Encyclopaedia of Garden Plants and Flowers. London: Reader's Digest Association, 1971.

Reader's Digest Illustrated Guide to Gardening. Reader's Digest Association, 1978.

Ross, Nancy Wilson, *Three Ways of Asian Wisdom: Hinduism, Buddhism, Zen*. Simon & Schuster, 1978.

Saito, Katsuo, *Japanese Gardening Hints*. Tokyo: Japan Publications, Inc., 1969.

Saito, K., and S. Wada, *Magic of Trees & Stones: Secrets of Japanese Gardening*. Transl. by Richard L. Gage. Japan Publications Trading Co., 1964.

Shigemori, Kanto, *Nihonteien No Shuho*, Vols. 1-5. Tokyo: Mainichi Shinbunsha, 1976.

Shimonaka, Kunihiko, ed., *Kokumin Hyakka Jiten*. Tokyo: Heibonsha, 1961.

Staff of the L. H. Bailey Hortorium, Cornell University, *Hortus Third: A Dictionary of Plants Cultivated in the United States and Canada*. Macmillan Publishing Co., 1976.

Sunset Editors, *Sunset Ideas for Japanese Gardens*. Lane Book Publishing Co., 1968.

Taylor, N., ed., *Taylor's Encyclopedia of Gardening*, 4th ed. Houghton Mifflin Company, 1961.

Thomas, Dr. G. L., Jr., *Goldfish Pools, Water-lilies and Tropical Fishes*. T.F.H. Publications, 1965.

Tyler-Whittle, Michael, *The Plant Hunters*. Chilton Book Company, 1970.

Vertrees, J. D., *Japanese Maples: Momiji and Kaede*. Timber Press, 1978.

Wada, Kunihei, *Katsura: Imperial Villa*. Transl. by Don Kenny. Osaka, Japan: Hoikusha Publishing Co., 1978.

Welch, H. J., *Dwarf Conifers*. London: Faber & Faber, 1966.

Wilson, Ernest H., *Aristocrats of the Trees*. The Stratford Co., 1930.

Wyman, Donald, *Shrubs and Vines for American Gardens*. The Macmillan Company, 1969.

Wyman, Donald, *Trees for American Gardens*. The Macmillan Company, 1965.

Wyman, Donald, *Wyman's Gardening Encyclopedia*. Macmillan Publishing Co., 1977.

Index

Numerals in italics indicate an illustration of the subject mentioned.

a *bies, 98, chart* 152
*Acer, 98-*99*, chart* 152; *palmatum dissectum atropurpureum,* 57. See *also* Maple, Japanese
Adonis, 99, chart 152
*Akebia, 99-*100*, chart* 152; Japanese, 62
Albizia, 100, chart 152. See *also* Mimosa
Almond, flowering. See *Prunus*
Althea, shrub. See *Hibiscus*
Amur adonis. See *Adonis*
Andromeda, 12, 58. See *also Pieris*
*Anemone, 100-*101*, chart* 152
Apricot, 68
Apricot, Japanese flowering, 9, 12; misnamed plum, 9
Aralia japonica. See *Fatsia*
Arbor, 62, 85
Arborvitae. See *Thuja*
Ardisia, 58
Asarum, 60
Ash, Japanese, 57. See *also Sorbus*
Ashikaga Yoshimitsu, Shogun, patron of arts, 14
Aspidistra, 60; used for *ikebana* arrangements, 60
Astilbe, 101, chart 152
Asymmetry, 9, 34, 35; in plan of *tsukiyama,* or hill garden, *10*
*Athyrium, 101-*102*, chart* 152. See *also* Painted fern, Japanese
Aucuba, 58, *102, chart* 152; Japanese, 66, *67*
August lily. See *Hosta*
Azalea, *50,* 53, 64, 66; bloom floating in rock-studded stream, *32;* clipped, *26-27;* making evenly rounded mound, *54;* pruning, 63; rock, 13; rounded, to suggest hills, *10.* See *also Rhododendron*
Azalea, Kurume, *66*

b abylon weeping willow. See Weeping willow
Baby's tears, *50,* 90
Balloonflower. See *Platycodon*
Bamboo, 34, *59-*60, 64, *96;* barricading horizontally spreading stems, 60; black, thinned and stripped of lower foliage, *72-73;* dwarf, for ground cover, 60; edible shoots of, 60; full-grown cane for fences and household goods, 60; linear grace of, 8; pruning of, 70; vigorous plants, spreading horizontally and vertically, 60. See *also Nandina; Phyllostachys*
Bamboo, fishpole. See *Phyllostachys*
Bamboo, golden. See *Phyllostachys*
Bamboo family crest, *13*
Bamboo fence. See *Fence*
Bamboo grass, *28*
Barberry, 58. See *also Berberis*
Basin, water. See Water basin, stone
Bellflower, Chinese, 12, 60. See *also Platycodon*

Bench *(koshikake),* 29
Berberis, 103, chart 152. See *also* Barberry
*Betula, 103-*104*, chart* 152
Birch, white. See *Betula*
Bishop's hat. See *Epimedium*
Bittersweet, Japanese, 62
Black bamboo, *72-73.* See *also Phyllostachys*
Black pine. See Pine, black
Blue flags, 60
Bonsai, 14
Borrowed scenery *(shakkei),* a garden technique, 17
Boston ivy. See *Parthenocissus*
Boxwood, Japanese, 58; rounded, to suggest hills, *10.* See *also Buxus*
Branch bending techniques, 61
Bridge, 75, *78-79, 94-95;* arched, 14; arched stone, *30-31;* arching, of weathered redwood, *94;* built at angle to major view, 79; course of, 34; earth *(dobashi),* 79; eight-plank bridge *(yatsuhashi),* 94; elimination of, in Zen gardens, 15; hand-carved granite, *95;* imitation stone, made of concrete, 79; location of, 78; made of unpainted natural materials, 78; of peeled or unpeeled logs, how to make, 79; of single massive slab of stone, 79; small, to imply water, 33; in strolling garden, 17; wooden, how to make, 79
Buddhism, influence on early garden-making, 11
Bush clover. See *Lespedeza*
Buttercup winter hazel. See Winter hazel
Buxus, 104, chart 152. See *also* Boxwood

c amellia, 64, *65, 104-*105*, chart* 152; symbol of, in ancient Japan, 65
Camphor tree. See *Cinnamomum*
Cape Jasmine. See *Gardenia*
Cedar, Japanese, *28,* 55; grove of, 9; pruned into rounded, decorative shapes, 55. See *also Cryptomeria*
Celandine, tree. See *Macleaya*
Cephalotaxus, 105, chart 152
*Cercidiphyllum, 105-*106*, chart* 152. See *also* Katsura tree
Cercis, 106, chart 152
*Chaenomeles, 106-*107*, chart* 152. See *also* Quince, flowering; Quince, Japanese
Chamaecyparis, 107, chart 152. See *also* Cypress, false
Cherry, 12; placement of, in Japanese garden, 68
Cherry, Japanese flowering, 20, 58. See *also Prunus*
Cherry, Kwanzan, 58. See *also Prunus*
Cherry, weeping Higan, 58, *69.* See *also Prunus*
Cherry, Yoshino, 58. See *also Prunus*
China fir. See *Cunninghamia*
Chinese indigo. See *Indigofera*
Chinese Judas tree. See *Cercis*
Chinese juniper. See *Juniperus*
Chinese parasol tree. See *Firmiana*
Chinese redbud. See *Cercis*
Chinese sweet osmanthus. See *Osmanthus*

Chrysanthemum, 13, 66, *108-*109*, chart* 152; edible petals of, 16; symbolism of, 16
Chrysanthemum family crest, *13*
Cinnamomum, 109, chart 152
Cinquefoil, 13
*Clematis, 109-*110*, chart* 152; Japanese, 62
Climate zone map, for Japanese-style gardens, *151*
Climbing fern, Japanese. See *Lygodium*
Clover, bush. See *Lespedeza*
Cobbles, 38; suggesting course of winding dry stream bed, 38; used in decorative bands under eaves of gutterless roof, 38
Concealment, partial: of paths, streams and waterfalls, 9, 34
Cornel, Japanese. See *Cornus*
Cornelian cherry. See *Cornus*
Cornus, 110, chart 152. See *also* Dogwood
Corylopsis, 110-111, chart 152
Cotton rose. See *Hibiscus*
Cow's-tail pine. See *Cephalotaxus*
Crab apple. See *Malus*
Crape myrtle, 66. See *also Lagerstroemia*
Creeping gardenia. See *Gardenia*
Creeping myrtle. See *Vinca*
Cryptomeria, 55; low-growing, 58
Cunninghamia, 111-112, chart 152
Cyclophorus, 112, chart 152. See *also* Felt fern
Cydonia japonica. See *Chaenomeles*
Cypress, false, 55; dwarf Hinoki, 55; low-growing, 58. See *also Chamaecyparis*
Cyrtomium, 112-113, chart 152

d aisy, Nippon. See *Chrysanthemum*
Daphne, 113, chart 152
Day lily. See *Hemerocallis*
Deciduous shrubs for Japanese gardens, 58-59; forsythia, 58; hawthorn, 58; Japanese tree peony, 58; kerria, 58; viburnum, 58; winter hazel, 58; witch hazel, 58
Deciduous trees for Japanese gardens, 55, *57-*58, *68-69;* flowering quinces, 58; ginkgo, 57; Japanese ash, 57; Japanese cherries, 20, 58; Japanese maples, 34, 57; Katsura tree, 57; Kousa dogwood, 57; red lace leaf maple, 57; star magnolia, 58; threadleaf maples, 57; weeping willow, 12, 58
Design, principles of, in gardens, 33-35
Desmodium penduliflora. See *Lespedeza*
Deutzia, 13, *113-*114*, chart* 153
Dobashi (earth bridge), 79
Dogwood, pruning, 63. See *also Cornus*
Dry-landscape gardens: at Daisenin temple, 27; filler around large rocks, 38; of Myoshinji temple in Kyoto, *15;* at Ryoanji temple in Kyoto, 15-16, *24-25, 42-43;* seascape at Daichi temple, *26-27;* at Shinnyoin temple, *26;* at Tofukuji monastery, 26. See *also* Sand gardens
Dwarf Japanese cedar. See *Cryptomeria*
Dwarfing trees and shrubs, 14

elm, Chinese and Japanese. *See Ulmus*
Enkianthus, 114, chart 152
Epimedium, 114-115, chart 152
Equisetum, 115, chart 152. *See also*
  Scouring rush
Erosion: prevention of, in hill garden,
  10
Eulalia grass. *See Miscanthus*
Evergreen, 64, 66, *67, 70-73, chart*
  152-153; different colors of, 54; false
  cypresses, 55; Japanese black pine,
  46, 54-55, 64, 70; Japanese cedars or
  cryptomerias, 55; Japanese red pine,
  55; in Japanese-style gardens, *67,*
  70-73; junipers, 55; ornamental
  pruning of, 70; podocarpus, 55;
  pruning, *59;* slow-growing, 9, 33, 55

false cypress. *See Cypress, false*
False spirea. *See Astilbe*
Family crest, Japanese, *13. See also*
  Mon
Fatsia, 58, 115-*116, chart* 152
Felt fern, *96. See also Cyclophorus*
Fence, 75, 80-83; bamboo, how to make,
  80, *82-83;* basic framework, 80;
  corrugated, *81;* frame, how to make,
  82; how to lengthen horizontal
  bamboo poles, *82;* lashing bamboo
  poles together for, 82, 83; materials
  for, 80; open mesh, *81;* of ready-made
  bamboo shades, *81;* sleeve
  (sodegaki), 81, 82-83; solid, *81;*
  where to obtain bamboo for, 83
Fern, 16
Fern, felt, *96. See also Cyclophorus*
Fern, holly. *See Cyrtomium*
Fern, Japanese climbing. *See Lygodium*
Fern, Japanese painted. *See* Painted
  fern, Japanese
Fern, tongue. *See Cyclophorus*
Fir. *See Abies*
Fir, China. *See Cunninghamia*
Firmiana, 116, *chart* 152
Fishpole bamboo. *See Phyllostachys*
Florist's chrysanthemum. *See*
  Chrysanthemum
Florist's spirea. *See Astilbe*
Flower arranging *(ikebana),* 14
Flowering cherry trees, 20, 58
Flowering crab apple. *See Malus*
Flowering fruit trees, 64
Flowering plants, *chart* 152-153
Flowering quince. *See Quince, flowering*
Foliage of plants, *chart* 152-153
Forsythia, 58, 116-*117, chart* 152;
  pruning, 63
Fragrant plants, *chart* 152-153
Fruit tree, flowering, 64
Full-moon maple. *See Acer*
Funkia. *See Hosta*

gardenia, 58, *117, chart* 152; sheared
  into soft mounds, 58
Gateway, 83
Genji, Prince, 13
Ginger, wild, 60
Ginkgo, 118, chart 152
Gneiss, 37
Gold band lily. *See Lilium*
Gold-dust tree. *See Aucuba*
Golden bamboo. *See Phyllostachys*

Golden bell. *See Forsythia*
Golden Pavilion, *6,* 14, 22-23
Granite, 37
Grass, bamboo, *28*
Grass, eulalia. *See Miscanthus*
Grass, Manila. *See Zoysia*
Grass, mondo. *See Ophiopogon*
Gravel, *10;* colors of, 39; how to make
  rake for patterns in, *40;* patterns in,
  40, *42-43;* simulation of water with,
  10; used for sand garden, *39. See also*
  Sand garden; Water, simulation of,
  with gravel and rocks
Ground cover, *10;* asarum, 60;
  aspidistra, 60; bellflowers, 60; blue
  flags, 60; dwarf bamboos, 60;
  flowering moss, 61; Irish moss, 61;
  Japanese spurge, 60; moss, 60-62;
  moss sandwort, 61; nandina, 60;
  pachysandra, 60; wild ginger,
  60
Grouping principles in garden, 34, *35*

hamamelis, 118-119, *chart* 152. *See*
  also Witch hazel
Hawthorn, 58. *See also Raphiolepis*
Hazel, winter. *See Winter hazel*
Hazel, witch. *See Witch hazel*
Heian garden design, 11-14; arched
  bridge in, 14; introduction of
  flowering plants in, 12; *ishitate-so*
  (stone arranging priests), 14; islands in
  ponds of, 12; *Sakuteiki* (treatise on
  Japanese gardens), 12-13; samurai
  influence on, 14; streams in, 12, 13;
  Tale of the Genji, The, 13, 30; various
  kinds of waterfalls in, 12. *See also*
  Japanese gardens; Japanese gardens,
  history and development; Kyoto
Hemerocallis, 119, chart 152
Hemlock, Japanese, *89*
*Hibiscus, 119-*120, *chart* 152
Higan cherry, weeping, 58, *69;* trained
  to arching trellis, 69
Hill garden *(tsukiyama),* 10, 40;
  avoiding erosion in, *10;* edging for,
  10; modest, in corner of yard, *10;* plan
  and creation of, *10,* 40-41; pond for,
  40-41; in tiny space, *10*
Hinoki false cypress, 55. *See also*
  Chamaecyparis
Holly, 58. *See also Ilex*
Holly, Japanese. *See Ilex*
Holly fern. *See Cyrtomium*
Honeysuckle, Japanese, 62
Horsetail. *See Equisetum*
Hosta, 64, 97, *120-121, chart* 152
Hydrangea, Japanese, 64
Hypericum, 121, chart 152

ikebana (flower arranging), 14;
  aspidistra used in, 60
*Ilex, 121-*122, *chart* 152
Indica azalea. *See Rhododendron*
Indigo. *See Indigofera*
Indigofera, 122, chart 152
Indoor-outdoor living concept, 8;
  bringing out essential nature of
  materials, 8; and design of traditional
  house, 8. *See also* Japanese house,
  traditional
Iris, 12, *122-*123, *chart* 152; *laviegata,*

62, 122. *See also* Iris, Japanese
Iris, Japanese, 62, *96. See also Iris*
Iris family crest, *13*
Irish moss, 61
Ise Shrine, Japanese garden at, 9
Ishitate-so, 14
Islands: elimination of, in Zen gardens,
  15; in ponds, 11, 12; in stroll gardens,
  17
Ivy, *89*
Ivy, Boston. *See Parthenocissus*
Ivy, Japanese. *See Parthenocissus*

japanese aralia. *See Fatsia*
Japanese ash, 57
Japanese aucuba. *See Aucuba*
Japanese bamboo. *See Bamboo*
Japanese black pine. *See Pine, black*
Japanese boxwood, 58
Japanese cedar, 55; grove of, 9; pruned
  into rounded, decorative shapes, 55
Japanese cedar, dwarf. *See Cryptomeria*
Japanese climbing fern. *See Lygodium*
Japanese cornel. *See Cornus*
Japanese cornelian cherry. *See Cornus*
Japanese evergreens. *See Evergreen*
Japanese fir. *See Abies*
Japanese flowering apricot, 9, 12;
  misnamed plum, 9
Japanese flowering cherries, 20, 58;
  Kwanzan, 58; weeping Higan cherry,
  58; Yoshino, 58
Japanese garden(s): asymmetry in, 9,
  10; and belief in indoor-outdoor
  living, 8; designer's contribution to
  scene of, 7; history and development
  of, 9-17; ideas and concepts from
  ancient myths and beliefs
  incorporated in, 7-8; importance of
  constancy in, 9; mystery in, 9, 34;
  niwa (garden) at Ise Shrine, 9;
  ornaments in, 83; rock-and-sand
  gardens, 10, 15, 18, *24-27,* 38-39; *roji*
  (dewy path) in, 16; *shibui* (quiet
  beauty) in, 9; stroll gardens, 10, 17,
  18, *30-31,* 40; tea gardens, 10, 16, 18,
  19; tsukiyama (hill garden), *10,* 40;
  value of privacy and serenity in, 9; *vs.*
  English-style rock gardens, 37; what
  it is not, 7; Zen gardens, 14-16, *24-27*
Japanese garden(s), finishing touches to,
  74-95; bridges, 75, 78-79, *94-95;*
  fences, 75, 80, *81-83;* gateway, 83;
  nobedan (broad) paths, 75, 78, 90, *91;*
  paths, 76, *77,* 78, 86, *90-91; shika*
  odoshi (deer scare), *78;* simple
  shelters, 75, 85; steppingstone
  (tobi-ishi) paths, 75-76, *77, 90-91;*
  stone lanterns, *31,* 34, 75, 85, *88-89;*
  stone pagoda, *74;* water basin, *29,* 34,
  75, 83, *87. See also* Bridge(s);
  Fence(s); Lanterns, stone or concrete;
  Path(s)
Japanese garden(s), history and
  development of, 9-17; additions of
  ponds, 11; effect of Buddhism on, 11;
  Emperor's imperial gardens, 9, 11;
  Empress Suiko's garden, 11; 14th
  Century, *6;* Golden Pavilion, 14, 18;
  at Heiankyo, 11-14; introduction of
  trees, rocks and flowers, 11;
  ishitate-so (stone-arranging priests),
  14; islands in ponds, 11, 12;

kare-sansui (dry-landscape gardens), 15-16, *24-27;* at Myoshinji, *15;* in Nara region, 11; *Sakuteiki* (treatise on Japanese gardens), 12-13; stroll gardens *(kaiyushiki),* 10, 17, *30-31;* tea gardens, 10, 16, 18, *19, 28-29;* waterfalls, 12; Zen gardens, 14-16, *24-27. See also* Heian garden design; Japanese garden(s); Waterfalls

Japanese garden design, basic maxims of, 34, *35*

Japanese garden masterpieces, 18, *19-31;* cones of sand at Daitokuji, *27;* Golden Pavilion, 14, 18; at Saihoji in Kyoto, 18, *20-21;* seascape at Daichi temple, *26-27;* at Shinnyoin temple, *26;* stroll garden at Katsura Detached Palace in Kyoto, 18, *30-31;* at three-tiered pavilion over lake, *22-23;* Tofukuji monastery garden, *26*

Japanese hemlock, *89*

Japanese holly. *See Ilex*

Japanese holly fern. *See Cyrtomium*

Japanese hosta, 64

Japanese house, traditional: airy interior spaces, 8; gardens enclosed by fennes and wall, 8; shelteed vrandas, 8; sliding screens, 8

Japanese hydrangea, 64

Japanese iris. *See* Iris, Japanese

Japanese ivy. *See Parthenocissus*

Japanese laurel. *See Aucuba*

Japanese lily, 64

Japanese maple, 34, *49,* 57. *See also Acer*

Japanese painted fern. *See* Painted fern, Japanese

Japanese photinia, pruning, *59*

Japanese pittosporum. *See Pittosporum*

Japanese quince. *See* Quince, Japanese

Japanese red pine, 55; Tanyosho pine, 55

Japanese snake's beard. *See Ophiopogon*

Japanese snowbell. *See Styrax*

Japanese spurge. *See* Spurge, Japanese

Japanese stewartia. *See Stewartia*

Japanese strawberry tree. *See Cornus*

Japanese-style garden: advantages of, 8-9; choosing plants for, 64, *65-73;* minimal maintenance and care of, 8, 44, 62; seasonal accents in, *66-67, 68-69. See also* Plants for Japanese-style gardens

Japanese-style garden, creation of, 33-51; arrangement of rocks, 38; basic maxims of Japanese garden design, 34; building a pond, 40-41; criteria for selection of rocks, 37-38; drawing plans on paper, 36; experimenting in small areas, 33; hill garden, *10,* 40-41; making waterproof stream bed, 42; preparing holes for rocks, 38; principles of grouping according to number of elements, 34, *35;* sand garden, *39,* 40, 42, *43;* securely anchoring rocks, *37,* 38; setting the largest rock, 38; sources of rocks, 37; space between groups of plants, 53; using cobbles under eaves of gutterless roof, 38; various kinds of stones for waterfalls, 12, 41-42. *See also* Plants for Japanese-style

gardens; Rocks; Sand gardens

Japanese-style garden, elements for, 33-34; enclosures, 34; evergreens, 54; paths, 34; plants, 33-34; small garden shelter, *29,* 34; stone, 33; stone lantern, 34; water, real or implied, 33; water basins, *29,* 34. *See also* main entries for above-mentioned items

Japanese tree peony, 58

Japanese water landscapes, Western interpretations of. *See* Water landscapes, Western interpretation of

Japanese white birch. *See Betula*

Japanese winterberry. *See Ilex*

Japanese yew. *See Taxus*

Japanese zelkova, 57

Jasmine, Cape. *See Gardenia*

Jasmine, Japanese, 62. *See also Jasminum*

Jasminum, 123, *chart* 152. *See also* Jasmine, Japanese

Jetbead. *See Rhodotypos*

Judas tree, Chinese. *See Cercis*

Juniper, 55, *96;* gnarled branching of boughs, 8; low-growing, creeping varieties, 55, 58; pruned in *tamazukuri-style, 71. See also Juniperus*

Juniper, tamarix, *50*

Juniperus, 123-124, *chart* 153

k *aempferi* iris, *96*

Kaiyushiki (stroll garden), 10, 17, 18, *30-31,* 40; traditional design elements of, 17

Kamakura, samurai government in, 14

Kammu, Emperor, 11

Kare-sansui, 15-16. *See also* Dry-landscape garden

Katsura, tea garden at, *19*

Katsura tree, 57

Keisk rhododendron, *96. See also Rhododendron*

Kerria, 58, *124, chart* 153; white, *See Rhodotypos*

Korean artisan, 11

Korean mountain ash. *See Sorbus*

Koshikake (bench) roofed, *29*

Kurume azalea: pruned low, 66

Kyoto: Golden Pavilion, 14, 18; guidebook of, *Views of Celebrated Gardens of Kyoto,* 15; Heian gardens at, 11-14; Heiankyo, early name of Kyoto, 11; Myoshinji garden at, *15;* Ryoanji in, 15, *24-25, 42-43;* Saihoji garden at, 18, *20-21;* stroll gardens in, 18, *30-31;* Urasenke teahouse in, *28-29. See also* Heian garden design

Kyushu azalea. *See Rhododendron*

l ace shrub. *See Stephanandra*

Lady palm. *See Rhapis*

Lagerstroemia, 125, *chart* 153. *See also* Crape myrtle

Lanterns, concrete, *ishidoro* or stone, *31,* 34, 75, 85, *88-89;* effect of, 85; *kasuga, 88;* modern, *88;* placement of, 85; in strolling gardens, 17; in tea garden, 16; wired for electricity, *89; yukimi* (snow viewing), 85

Laurel, Japanese. *See Aucuba*

Lawn grass, Japanese or Korean. *See Zoysia*

Leather-leaf rhododendron. *See Rhododendron*

Lemon lily. *See Hemerocallis*

Lespedeza, 125, *chart* 153

Light requirements for plants, *chart* 152-153

Ligustrum, 125-126, *chart* 153. *See also* Privet

Lilium, 126, *chart* 153. *See also* Lily, Japanese

Lily, August. *See Hosta*

Lily, day. *See Hemerocallis*

Lily, gold band. *See Lilium*

Lily, Japanese, 64. *See also Lilium*

Lily, lemon. *See Hemerocallis*

Lily, plantain. *See Hosta*

Lily, tiger. *See Lilium*

Lily-turf, dwarf. *See Ophiopogon*

Limestone rocks, 37

Littleleaf box. *See Buxus*

Lotus, *52. See also Nelumbo*

Lotus, scared. *See Nelumbo*

Lygodium, 127, *chart* 153

m *acleaya,* 127, *chart* 153

Magnolia, 128, *chart* 153

Magnolia, star, 58. *See also Magnolia*

Maidenhair tree. *See Ginkgo*

Maintenance and care of Japanese gardens, 8, 44, 62

Makino forsythia. *See Forsythia*

Malus, 128-129, *chart* 153

Manila grass. *See Zoysia*

Maple: Japanese methods of enhancing color of foliage, 57; placement of, in garden, 57; pruning, 63

Maple, full-moon. *See Acer*

Maple, Japanese, 34, *49,* 57. *See also Acer*

Maple, red lace leaf, 57

Maple, threadleaf, 57, *96*

Metamorphic rocks, 37

Mimosa, *96. See also Albizia*

Mirror stone, 41

Miscanthus, 129, *chart* 153

Momi fir. *See Abies*

Mon (Japanese family crest), *13;* flower subjects for, *13*

Mondo grass. *See Ophiopogon*

Moss, 60-62, 129-130, *chart* 153; banks of pond layered with, *20-21;* care of, 60, 61, 62; checkerboard squares of stone and, *26;* in dry-landscape garden, 15; substitutes for, 61; in tea garden, 16; transplanting, 61; velvety softness of, 8

Moss, flowering, 61

Moss, Irish, 61

Moss sandwort, 61

Moss sawara false cypress. *See Chamaecyparis*

Mountain ash. *See Sorbus*

Mountains in stroll garden, 17

Murasaki, Lady, author of *The Tale of Genji,* 13

Myrtle, crape, 66. *See also Lagerstroemia*

Myrtle, creeping. *See Vinca*

n *andina,* 60, 66, *67, 130, chart* 153

Nara gardens, 11
Narcissus, 131, chart 153
Nelumbo, 131-132, chart 153. *See also* Lotus
Nikko fir. *See Abies*
Niphobolus lingua. See Cyclophorus
Nippon daisy. *See Chrysanthemum*
Niwa (garden), 9
Nobedan (stone pavement), 75, 78, 90, *91;* paths, 75, 78, 90, *91;* patterns of, 78; setting stones of, 78
Noblemen, garden designers, real and fictitious, 12-14
Nymphaea, 132, chart 153

Oak(s): column, *19;* giant, groves of, 9
Olive(s), *28*
Olive, sweet. *See Osmanthus*
Ophiopogon, 133, chart 153
Osmanthus, 133, chart 153

Pachysandra, 96, 133-134, chart 153. *See also* Spurge, Japanese
Paeonia, 134, chart 153. *See also* Peony, tree
Pagoda, stone, *74*
Pagoda tree, Japanese. *See Sophora*
Painted fern, Japanese, *96. See also Athyrium*
Palm, lady. *See Rhapis*
Paradisical gardens, 14; 17
Parasol tree, Chinese. *See Firmiana*
Parthenocissus, 135, chart 153
Path(s), 12, 16, 75-76, *77,* 78; course of, 34; materials for, 75; partial concealment of, 9, 34; patterns of, 34, 76; paved with rudimentary steppingstones, 16; plants along, 16; steppingstones *(tobi-ishi),* 75-76, *77, 86, 90-91, 92-93;* water-washed flagstones across pond, *90;* wider paths *(nobedan),* 75, 78, 90, *91. See also* Steppingstone paths
Pavilion(s), 85
Pebble(s), 15; bed of sea *(umi),* 29. *See also* Gravel
Peony, Chinese. *See Paeonia*
Peony, tree, 58, 64; double-flowered, *67. See also Paeonia*
Peony family crest *(mon),* 13
Pergolas, 62
Periwinkle. *See Vinca*
Phoenix tree. *See Firmiana*
Photinia, 135, chart 153; pruning, *59*
Phyllostachys, 136, chart 153
Pieris, 136-137, chart 153. *See also* Andromeda
Pine(s), 13, *28,* 53; asymmetrical shapes of, 56; pruned, *30;* pruning, *56;* pruning candles of new growth from, *56*
Pine, black, *46,* 54-55, 64, *74,* 96; pruning of, 63, 70; type of garden grown in, 55, 64. *See also Pinus*
Pine, cow's-tail. *See Cephalotaxus*
Pine, Japanese red, 55
Pine, Tanyosho, 55
Pine, umbrella. *See Sciadopitys*
Pine family crest *(mon),* 13
Pinus, 137, chart 153. *See also* Pine, black; Pine, Japanese red
Pittosporum, 138, chart 153

Planning Japanese garden on paper, 36
Plantain lily. *See Hosta*
Plants, Japanese: chosen for Japanese-style garden, 64, *65-73;* history of collectors of, 64; obstacles to collection of, 64
Plants for Japanese-style gardens, 53-63; bamboos, 59-60; blending into surroundings, 53; deciduous shrubs, 58-59; deciduous trees, 55, 57-58, *68-69;* evergreen, 54-55, *70-73;* evergreen shrubs, 58; flowering annuals and perennials, 62; ground covers, 60-62; by height, *chart* 152-153; by light needs, *chart* 152-153; pruning, 53, 54, 56, 59; by shape, *chart* 152-153; slow-growing, *chart* 152-153; soil needs, *chart* 152-153; species for accents, 53; species for major plantings, 53; vines, 62. *See also* Deciduous trees; Evergreen; Pruning
Platycladus orientalis. See Thuja
Platycodon, 138, chart 153. *See also* Bellflower, Chinese
Plum yew. *See Cephalotaxus*
Plume poppy. *See Macleaya*
Podocarpus, 55, *89,* 139, chart 153
Polyanthus narcissus. *See Narcissus*
Pond(s), 11, 12, 14, *30-31,* 48; arched bridge over, 14; banks of, layered with moss, *20-21;* construction of, 40-41; course of, 34; dragon-prowed boats on, 12; of flexible pool liner, 41; for hill garden, 40-41; islands in, 11, 12; recirculating pump for, 41; shape of, 40; shell of rigid plastic, 41; in strolling garden, 17; and weeping willows, 12. *See also* Pool(s)
Pond garden, 11-12, 55
Pool(s), *49. See also* Pond(s)
Privet: making evenly rounded mound from, *54. See also Ligustrum*
Pruning, 9, 53, *54, 56, 59,* 62-63, *66,* 70; azalea or privet, *54,* 63, *66;* bamboos, 70; black pine, 70; broad-leaved evergreens, 59; cedars, 55; dogwoods, 63; forsythia, 63; junipers, *71;* making evenly rounded mound, *54;* maples, 63; to open up tree or shrub so layers of space are visible between branches, 54; ornamental, plants for, *chart* 152-153; reasons for, 62; shapes, 70; *tamazukuri-*style, *54, 59,* 63, *71;* techniques, 62; weeping willows, 57-58; when to prune, 63
Prunus, 139-140, chart 153; *mume,* 9. *See also* Cherry
Pure Land Sect of Buddhism, influence in garden-making, 14
Pygmy waterlily. *See Nymphaea*
Pyrrosia lingua. See Cyclophorus
Pyrus japonica. See Chaenomeles
Pyxidanthera barbulata, 61

Quince, flowering, 58. *See also Chaenomeles*
Quince, Japanese, *50,* 66, *67. See also Chaenomeles*

Rabbit-ear iris. *See Iris*

Rakes for gravel patterns: how to make, *40;* how to use, *42. See also* Gravel
Raphiolepis, 140-141, chart 153. *See also* Hawthorn
Recirculating pump, 41
Red lace leaf maple, 57
Red pine. *See* Japanese red pine
Redbud, Chinese. *See Cercis*
Redvein enkianthus. *See Enkianthus*
Rhapis, 141, chart 153
Rhododendron, 141-142, chart 153; Keisk, *96;* slenderleaved, *89. See also* Azalea
Rhodotypos, 143, chart 153
Rock(s): arranged in overlapping fish-scale pattern, *26;* arrangements of, 35, 38; chafing gear used for hoisting, 38; constancy expressed in muted colors of, 9; criteria for selection of, 37-38; in dry-landscape garden, 15, *24-25, 26;* gneiss, 37; granite, 37; limestone, 37; metamorphic, 37; off-center placement of, 9; preparing holes for, 38; rugged strength of, 8; schist, 37; sedimentary, 37; selection of, in Japan, 37; simulation of water with gravel and, 10, *26, 27,* 33, *42, 45, 46, 47;* single, to suggest a hill, *10;* sources of, for Western gardeners, 37; spread line of, 37, 38; symbolism of, in dry garden of Myoshinji, *15;* that express definite terrain, 37-38; treated as symbolic elements, 37; volcanic, 37; where to set, 13. *See also* Stones
Rock azalea, 13
Rock gardens *vs.* Japanese gardens, 37
Rock nurseries, Japanese, 37
Rock-and-sand gardens, 10, 15, *24-27*
Roji (dewy path). *See* Tea garden(s)
Rose, cotton. *See Hibiscus*
Rose-of-Sharon. *See Hibiscus*
Rush, scouring, *96. See also Equisetum*
Ryoanji, garden at, 15-16, *24-25, 42-43;* arrangement of stones in, 15, *42-43;* raked pebbles in, 15, *42-43*

Sacred bamboo. *See Nandina*
Sacred lotus. *See Nelumbo*
St.-John's-wort, willow-leaf. *See Hypericum*
Sakuteiki (treatise on Japanese gardens), 12-13
Salix, 143, chart 153. *See also* Weeping willow
Samurai (warrior class), 14
Sand: cones of, at Daitokuji, *27;* constancy expressed in muted color of, 9; drainage for garden, 39; gardens of stone and, 10, 15, 18, *24-27,* 39; raked, in dry-landscape garden, 15
Sand garden, *39;* calculating amount of gravel to order for, 40; drainage for, *39;* how to make, *39;* how to use rake in, *43;* made mostly of gravel, 39; making rake for gravel patterns in, *40;* patterns suggesting water in, 40, *42, 45;* seascape in Philadelphia, *45;* styling the borders, *43*
Sandwort, moss, 61
Sasa pygmaea, 60
Sasanqua camellia. *See Camellia*

Sawara false cypress. *See Chamaecyparis*
Schist, 37
Scholar tree, Chinese. *See Sophora*
Sciadopitys, *144*, *chart* 153
Scouring rush, *96*. *See also Equisetum*
Screen(s): rice-paper, 8; sliding, 8
Sedimentary rocks, 37
Seen and hidden *(miegakure)*, a garden technique, 17
Sen Rikyu, 7, 16
Shelters, simple, 75, 85; functions of, 85; materials for, 85
Shibui (quiet beauty), 9
Shika odoshi (deer scare), 78
Shiki-ishi path, 90, *91*
Shima (island), in pond, 11
Shinto religion, 10
Shumisen, mountain in Buddhist cosmology, 11
Silk tree. *See Albizia*
Silver magnolia. *See Magnolia*
Silver sheaf. *See Astilbe*
Sleeve fence *(sodegaki)*, *81*, 82-83
Snake's beard, Japanese. *See Ophiopogon*
Snow azalea. *See Rhododendron*
Snowbell, fragrant. *See Styrax*
Snowbell, Japanese. *See Styrax*
Soil needs for plants, *chart* 152-153
Sole flower, 16
Sophora, *144*, *chart* 153
Sorbus, *145*, *chart* 153. *See also* Ash, Japanese
Spider azalea. *See Rhododendron*
Spike winter hazel. *See* Winter hazel
Spirea, 58
Spirea, false. *See Astilbe*
Spreading plants, *chart* 152-153
Spurge, Japanese, 60. *See also Pachysandra*
Star magnolia. *See* Magnolia, star
Stephanandra, *145*-146, *chart* 153
Steppingstone paths *(tobi-ishi)*, 75-76, 77, 86, *90-91*, *92-93;* bedding for, 78; in classic tea garden, 16; laying stones for, 76, 77, 78; origin of, 75; patterns of, 76, 77; in strolling garden, 17, *30-31*
Stewartia, *146*, *chart* 153
Stone(s): arrangement of, in garden at Ryoanji, 15, *24-25;* as basic material of garden, 33; checkerboard squares of moss and, *26;* cobbles, 38; crossing a stream on, 78; gardens of sand and, 10, 15, 18, *24-27;* given appearance of natural outcropping, *37*, 38; three basic shapes of, *36;* treated as symbolic elements, 37; for waterfalls, 41-42; where to set, 13. *See also* Rocks
Stone lanterns. *See* Lantern(s), stone or concrete
Stone pagoda, *74*
Strawberry tree. *See Cornus*
Stream(s), 41; in stroll garden, 17
Stream bed: crossed with steppingstones, 78; made waterproof, 42; partial concealment of, 34

Stroll garden(s) *(kaiyushiki)*, 10, 17, 18, *30-31*, 40; at Katsura Detached Palace in Kyoto, 18, *30-31; mie-gakure* (seen and hidden) technique in, 17; *shakkei* (borrowed scenery) technique in, 17; traditional design elements of, 17
Styrax, *146*-147, *chart* 153
Suiko, Empress, 11
Sword-leaved iris. *See Iris*

tachibana, Toshitsuna, author of *Treatise on Japanese Gardens*, 12
Tale of Genji, The, the garden in, 13
Tamarix juniper, *50*
Tamazukuri-style (rounded) pruning, 54, 59, 63, *71*
Tanyosho pine, 55
Taxus, *147*, *chart* 153
Tea ceremony, 16, 18, 28-29; water basin associated with, 83. *See also* Water basin, stone
Tea garden(s), 10, 16, 18, *19;* basin of water for ritual ablutions in, *29*, 83; plants along path of, 16; *roji* (dewy path) in, 16; roofed bench in, *29;* steppingstones in, 16, 75; at Urasenke teahouse in Kyoto, *28-29*
Teahouse(s), 16, 20, 29, *30-31*
Threadleaf maples, 57, *96*
Thuja, *147*-148, *chart* 153
Tiger lily. *See Lilium*
Tobi-ishi (steppingstones), wandering, 75. *See also* Path(s)
Tongue fern. *See Cyclophorus*
Tree(s): elimination of, in Zen gardens, 15; grouping, *35*
Tree peony. *See* Peony, tree
Trellis: arching weeping cherry trained to, 69
Tsukiyama. See Hill garden
Tsukubai (low water basin), 83-85; how to set up, 83-*84;* water piping system for, *84*, 85

ulmus, *148*, *chart* 153
Umbrella pine. *See Sciadopitys*
Ume (Japanese apricot), 9
Umi (sea), created with bed of pebbles, *29;* 84-85

viburnum, 58
Viewing garden, 15
Vinca, *148*-*149*, *chart* 153
Vine, Japanese, 62; akebia, 62; clematis, 62; honeysuckle, 62; jasmine, 62; wisteria, 62
Violet, mountain, 12
Volcanic rocks, 37

water: as basic material of garden, 33; elimination of, in Zen gardens, 15; lyricism of, 8; simulation of, with gravel and rocks, 10, *26*, *27*, 33, *42*, *45*, *46*, *47*

Water basin, stone, *29*, 34, 75, *87; chozubachi* (tall version), 83; placement of, 83; reproduction of, 83; *tsubakai* (low version), 83. *See also* Tea ceremony
Water landscapes (dry and wet), Western interpretations of, 44, 45-51; dry garden following path of former stream, *47;* dry seascape in Philadelphia, *45;* gravel garden in Seattle, *46;* man-made stream flowing between smooth rocks toward a pond, *50;* man-made watercourse with waterfall, rapids and two pools, *49;* natural streams supplying water for artificial pond carved from swamp, *51;* waterfall created on top of unused parking deck, 44, *48*
Waterfall(s), 12, 33, 41, *49;* created on top of unused parking deck, 44, *48; ito-ochi* (threadlike fall), 12; man-made, *66; nuno-ochi* (clothlike fall), 12; partial concealment of, 9; stones for, 41-42; *tsutai-ochi* (trickling fall), 12; various kinds of, 12, 41-42
Waterlily, pygmy. *See Nymphaea*
Weeping forsythia. *See Forsythia*
Weeping Higan cherry. *See* Higan cherry, weeping
Weeping willow, 12, 57, 58; pruned annually, 57. *See also Salix*
Whiteleaf Japanese magnolia. *See Magnolia*
Wild ginger, 60
Wildflowers, 12
Willow, weeping. *See* Weeping willow
Willow-leaf St.-John's-wort. *See Hypericum*
Winter daphne. *See Daphne*
Winter hazel, 58. *See also Corylopsis*
Winter jasmine. *See Jasminum*
Winterberry, Japanese. *See Ilex*
Wisteria, 12, 62, *149*-150, *chart* 153
Wisteria family crest *(mon)*, 13
Witch hazel, 58. *See also Hamamelis*

yew: low-growing, 58; slow-growing, 55
Yew, Japanese. *See Taxus*
Yew, Plum. *See Cephalotaxus*
Yew podocarpus. *See Podocarpus*

zelkova, Japanese, 57
Zen gardens, 14-15; cones of sand at Daitokuji, *27;* at Daisenin temple, *27;* elimination of trees, shrubs, bridges, islands and water in, 15, 24; *kare-sansui* (dry-landscape), 15-16; seascape at Daichi temple, *26-27;* at Shinnyoin temple, *26;* symbolism of material objects in, 15; at Tofukuji monastery, *26*
Zen sect of Buddhism, introduction into Japan, 14
Zones, climate: for Japanese-style gardens, 151
Zoysia, *150*, *chart* 153

PRINTED IN U.S.A.